D0051262

My Beautiful Mary
A Love Story

By Alex Gabbard

Author of the books: *Return to Thunder Road, Checkmate,*
Gaspee, I Am Gisele: Empress, Schwaigern,
Alec & Flora: The Story of a Family, and
Devil Bullet among the author's works on topics of historical
fiction, with 37 books published to date,
3 being recipients of
Book-of-the-Year awards in international competition
in their fields.

A True Story

Published by:

GPPress

1829 Grubb Rd.
Lenoir City, TN 37771

First Edition
Copyright © 2021 by Alex Gabbard

Book and cover design and layout by Alex Gabbard.

Contents

Before the Beginning

The big war had not begun when Garvey signed up for Coastal Artillery. For the eldest son to leave the farm in Wilkes County was a big step that took him through training followed by assignment to the huge guns around Seattle. During that time, he and his girl back home married, and Zell wanted to be with him. A train ride across America also took her to the west coast where she got a job in an aircraft factory, a true Rosie the Riveter. As a young married couple, Garvey and Zell lived the military life among other young husbands and wives in similar circumstances that had become the big one, another war that engulfed the world and mobilized the entire country toward combat. Everyone was worried about the future and wanted to do their part to end the sequence of events that seemed to be spiraling beyond control.

Morning sickness that began during November, 1943 led to a change of plan; Zell rode the rails back home to live with Garvey's parents. As the war raged on, threat of invasion declined such that Coastal Artillery was dissolved into regular U.S. Army that assigned Garvey to the 69th Infantry Division. After more training in heavy weapons, now a Corporal, he crossed the Atlantic with his 271st Infantry Regiment of the Division that was sent to fight in Europe.

On the 9th day of August, 1944, Zell brought their first child into the world. Named Mary Alice, family names, the baby was healthy and grew as did Sammy who was born about the same time to Robert and his wife, Nina. Like his older brother Garvey, Robert was called into the war that left two young mothers and their babies in the care of the homefolks on the farm, Cornelius and Mary.

Before Christmas that year, a letter for Garvey arrived with a photograph of Zell holding Mary Alice, the first time he held in his hand an image of his wife and baby daughter. On a Tuesday during summer of the following year, Zell was thinking of Garvey and sat down to write him another letter:

7

State Road, NC
July 17, 1945

Dearest Darling,

Just a few lines again tonight. Even though I havent no letter to ans. like I was to have.

Sure hope when this reaches my darling finds him in the best of health and enjoying his self if possible. As it has been several day sense I have heard from you which makes me awful uneasy about you. As for my self and the baby well as common.

We heard from Robert today he was well when he wrote the letter. I hope he is still ok.

Well they seems to be lots of the boys coming home from over seas. Some are getting discharged and others are just furlougs. Harvey Hanes has got home on a furlough. I heard he got 60 days at home.

Darling I want to see you just as bad as any body could, but I dont want you now and then have to see you leave again. I had rather they would keep you awhile longer over there if they have to. Darling I love you with all my heart and hope to see you real soon; and I hope to receive a long love letter tomorrow.

Your Aunt Rose has got her arm broken but is getting along alright I reckon. We didn't do anything about it until today and it has been broken over a week. I dont no why she didn't let us no. We were aiming to go over there, but it rained so we cant go until tomorrow.

Well honey I will close here from the one loves you always.
Your darling wife,
Zell Cheek
A Kiss +++

Several months after the war in Europe ended, he was released to return home. Arriving back home during late September, 1945, Mary Alice as a toddler was introduced to her father. With war's end, Robert returned home, too, and the Cheek families living across the gravel road from each other grew with new additions, boys and girls who grew up together with abundant work on their farms filling days, weeks, months, and years. As Mary Alice grew to school age, any fears she may have had going to and from school on the orange busses were softened by Sammy, Robert and Nina's first child, who was her companion during each of their twelve years in the public school system. During her first grade year, Mary Alice never missed a day of school or was tardy, her first academic achievement that was commemorated with a Perfect Attendance Certificate signed June 1, 1951 by C. B. Eller, Superintendant of Schools with additional signatures by the principle and her teacher. That first year of 39 A and B grades with only one C set her trend of welcoming school and wanting to excel, a life pattern that never changed.

During her 3rd Grade, Mary Alice earned 37 A grades with 17 B and 4 Cs for the school year. That trend continued, as in her 7th grade in which she earned 48 A grades, 51 B and no Cs. The next school year ended her schooling in the red brick school house at Pleasant Ridge when she graduated at the top of her 8th grade class and was assigned by the Wilkes County Board of Education to East Wilkes High School. By then, Mary Alice had accumulated report cards and school photos and similar documents that she kept, her growing number of personal treasures. As a "cotton top" first grader with fly-away hair, each successive year's photo shows her trend toward increasing beauty with gradually darkening hair into what she described as medium blond.

Through her teens, if Mary Alice had disappointments in the people she knew while growing up, she kept them largely to herself, a trend that she maintained throughout the reminder of her life. One disappointment did occur when nearing her sixteenth birthday that was to remain a memory. At a local auction attended with her father one day, a nicely made wind-up mantel clock caught her attention. Entering the bidding, her small amount of cash on hand came to the high bid. With her heart set on buying the clock as a gift intended for her father, her intentions made known, at the last moment, an uncle outbid her and took the clock to his home. Mary Alice was

9

heartbroken and never again had a favorable opinion of that uncle. That part of the auction was told around the community, and her grandmother bought another mantel clock for Mary Alice and gave it to her as a birthday gift. It sat on the mantel of the fireplace in the Cheek home for decades, always a reminder of how disappointed she had become of her uncle and how she so loved her grandmother for whom she was named.

While a girl, another favorite gift from her grandmother was a small and delicate bisque doll with working arms and eyelids. In a flowing gown and a blue bonnet, Mary Alice carefully kept this doll with heartfelt recollections of her grandmother, whose unexpected passing one day amid her flowers was the most crushing set back of Mary Alice's early life. Previous gifts from her grandmother included handmade doilies and intricately crocheted items that remained cherished memories, additions to her Hope Chest that were never used, just admired on occasion with their flood of memories bringing melancholy moments.

Her Hope Chest was to receive a slow trickle of items over the years, her scrapbook and school memorabilia in particular. Included were each of the annual black and white photos of her school years among a small collection of photos of her from birth onward. These photos remained sources of quiet reflection when Mary Alice entered upon nostalgic moments that gradually subsided as time went by, only to return with vigor when iphone technology enabled her to renew acquaintances with old friends during hours and hours of conversation that often recalled her early years.

Beginning high school during the fall of 1958 brought the end of eight years at Pleasant Ridge School. Into her little "School Memories" book of the 8th grade, Mary Alice collected photos and writings of her fellow students. She wrote that she was 13 and weighed 80 1/2 pounds. On the "Someone Special" page, she glued a photo and wrote the name "Bobby Joe Haynes". On the "My Pal" page, she glued a photo of Carolyn Lee Blackburn and wrote her name. Writing about herself, Mary Alice wrote, "Last year I was in the

10

8th grade, my teacher was Mr. Grady F. Miller. Last year we had 2 tests on one we were supposed to make 8.3 I made 9.0. On the next we were supposed to make 8.6 I made 9.3. I was Valedictorian. But I gave it to Bobby Joe Haynes. I also won the History Test and a spelling test, 'Pleasant Ridge School' ", then she wrote the names of teachers. Carolyn Blackburn remained a lifelong friend who wrote,

Dear Mary Alice, I have enjoyed being with you these past years. I wish you all the luck in all the world. And I hope the best is yet to come in your life. Love forever and always.

Years later, memories from that time were often conversations we had that helped me to learn who Mary Alice was as a child, that she retained entirely good memories of her life with high regard for many people that she came to know along the way. Through our years together, she occasionally looked through her year books for quiet reflection, always a pleasant walk down memory lane for her, that resulted in telling me of particular events and people, stories of her life that always told of being happy.

Four more years after Pleasant Ridge added high school memories that remained singularly filled with pleasant reflections of the most favored years of her life. So many friends, so many memories, once again a highlight of her days promoted further by attending reunions where recollections flowed freely, contact information collected and distributed, and closeness with longtime friends furthered.

Prolog

The hallways and classrooms of the new East Wilkes High School were filled with students who came each school day, most arriving and departing by orange buses driven by senior class boys. Each student presentably dressed conducted themselves with intentions to put forth their best, largely driven by emerging boy-girl aspirations that tended to develop into life-long relationships. With Sammy, Mary Alice was among the students arriving on those buses, then departing for homes after school on the same buses that ran regular routes each school day. Accustomed to excelling in her studies, she also developed lasting friendships from the beginning of those first eight years that went on to the new consolidated high school where more friends were made in the broader community.

The high school facilities were excellent and accommodated a full range of student activities from classrooms to athletics while teachers helped young minds grow with studies of broadening subjects. One encouragement in 4-H was to begin a long term project, a scrap book for what each student was interested in and wanted to do after graduation. Mary Alice began her scrapbook with picture post cards and similar items about destinations of interest, travels that she imagined to be in her future. In 9th grade science, one project was learning about photography and how images are developed from film. Results of her first developed film included small portraits of herself and friends in her class that went into her scrapbook.

Also along the way, Mary Alice was impressed with The Optimist's Creed and its *Promise Yourself* - admonishments that she came across in a magazine. Torn out and kept, it became another lifelong addition to her scrapbook. One of its admonishments, "to wear a cheerful countenance at all times and give every living creature you meet a smile;" was how she already lived with her friendly outlook toward other people.

12

Although encouraged at school, her travel interests were received rather differently at home; her father contributed little to ideas of traveling, having seen the horrors of the war in Europe. Although he brought home some mementoes that fascinated his daughter, her questions were rarely answered; bad memories for him. One of her interests included buying a slide projector and a set of slides that illustrated scenery from around the world in living color, a birthday purchase from school that remained with her thereafter. Another was her desire for a horse that would be pastured with the cows and stabled in the barn. Such a purchase and cost of ownership, needing a bridle and saddle along with care such as feeding and shoeing the horse was well beyond the family's means, resulting in Garvey giving Mary Alice a finely crafted plastic model of an Appaloosa and saddle that also remained with her thereafter.

The Cheek family was distant relatives of A.P and "Mother Maybelle" Carter who brought the two families together one weekend where talk and music remained a favorite among Mary Alice's memories. During talk, Sassa Carter, an attractive airlines stewardess at the time, encouraged her to consider air travel as a career after high school, but Garvey would have none of that. Protective of his family, especially his pretty daughter who had long been his tagalong around the farm, he had gradually settled from dark, disturbing, and haunting war memories into quiet home life with Zell and their growing family. The idea of Mary Alice in airplanes flying here and there was simply not acceptable.

One of her favorite stories of him was from that time. The Chatham Auditorium located on the grounds of the huge Chatham Blankets mill had long been the site of numerous events throughout each year that brought attendees to all sorts of entertaining venues. This memory was the time that the Blue Sky Boys brought their "bluegrass" style of country music to Elkin and the Auditorium. Just how her father was selected was not told, but he and his mandolin performed on stage with the "Boys" that night to become a favorite recollection that Mary Alice told with great satisfaction. His mandolin

13

survived and was given to a guitar playing grandson many years later who had it restored to playing beautifully.

Mary Alice grew up in the wholesome home that her father provided, although tempered with overtones of Primitive Baptist Church teachings that yielded little to the burgeoning youth culture that began with rock 'n' roll music of the 1950s. Song after song caught the attention of young radio listeners who were moved by the rock 'n' roll beat that encouraged dancing as regularly seen on TV's teen programming, *American Bandstand.* Almost everyone had a radio in their car or a "transistor radio", and talk of the latest tune on the Hit Parade were often topics of conversations. Black and white television sets in more and more homes broadcast a variety of shows of humor, singing, and dancing for light-hearted family entertainment. They showed girls the latest fashions, and Mary Alice noticed. Fashionable clothes remained a lifelong interest.

Soon there were High Fidelity, "Hi-Fi" record players in homes played by teenagers who accumulated growing numbers of 45 rpm records of favorite tunes often listened and danced to, radio tunes that were played over and over at home. She was among the first "baby boomers", the emerging generation that embraced the lively and exciting times. With friends who participated in school social functions, dances, attended ball games and similar activities, and who gathered for over-night pajama parties in one of their homes, Mary Alice was living the fun times. She saved her small earnings to buy her own portable "Hi-Fi", made record selections and enjoyed listening to favorite voices. A memento that she kept from that time in her life was an 8x10 black and white print of Fabian, a handsome teen idol of the Hit Parade and movies.

Her photography interests expanded with a new camera; she bought a Kodak Hawkeye that produced rather good photos, but the cost of film and its processing meant limited use. She did, however, capture moments of family travel, such as to Linville Caverns and Grandfather Mountain, along with her senior class trip to Washington DC, images that went into her photo album that she began in addition

14

to her scrapbook. A friend made sets of beautiful photos of her during her late teens that have survived, clearly showing Mary Alice to be a near flawlessly trim beauty.

Portrayals of the exciting teen life that swept through America with arrival of the "boomers" coming of driving age made it into theaters with films of beach parties, teen boys singing to teen girls, and girls singing to boys, fun, fun, fun, and Mary Alice noticed that, too, but her boy-girl relationships were kept distant.

During the summer of 1960, a knock at the front door of their Thurmond home brought sixteen year old Mary Alice. When she opened the door, a young man introduced himself as a college student working a summer job selling stainless steel cookware. He was soon to return to classes and had one set left that he offered to sell at a discount price. Being a Home Economics student in high school and well acquainted with cooking, Mary Alice was interested, but she did not have the money to buy it. The cookware appeared to be as high quality as the young man said, but it cost far more than pots and pans bought locally. The set would, however, make a desirable addition to her Hope Chest, a cedar chest that her father and mother gave her for her sixteenth birthday. Mary Alice was already looking ahead to her life to come. The time was also around her birthday, and discussion with her father led to Garvey agreeing to buy the set for her on her agreement to repay the purchase sometime later when she had the money, an uncomfortably high price for their limited funds on hand, but a stretch he was willing to make for her. That day, the conveniently packed box of assorted pieces of cookware was hers, and as proclaimed by the salesman, it did last a lifetime.

A recollection from that time occurred when she and her father were visiting a local preacher who dominated conversation by voicing strong opinions against the newly elected President John F. Kennedy. Mary described her increasing agitation that boiled over in disgust when she stood up and "told him off" in no uncertain terms, then left to sit in their car, thinking that her father would lambast her for being so outspoken. Instead, he complimented her saying that he did not have the guts to openly oppose the old preacher whom he did not agree with, either.

Meanwhile, her parents remained concerned with boy-girl relationships involving their daughter, keeping a skeptical eye on her that restricted dating. Boys at church functions were sort of okay, but no dates in cars at night were allowed. When attending high school functions such as ball games, she and girl friends traveled together, both a cost saving among them and another time to make long held memories that she later reminisced about as favorites, but boys were not included other than at a distance for fear of angering her father.

While a good student active in high school, athletics was not among them for Mary Alice; her physical constitution did not permit robust activities, a limitation that was not seen as a limitation, just the norm for her size five body of around one hundred pounds as she turned sixteen. Slow to mature, an attribute of her emerging and long lasting beauty was an engaging smile that remained an often noted quality of her bearing. Always a friendly, happy teen, out-going and personable, she liked to be around people, especially her many cousins that she grew up with as near neighbors. Wherever life took her later, to "go home" remained a singular desire that lasted beyond the demise of her parents, well into the lives of her own children. Along the way she met Ethyl Hutchens who remained a very special friend, but as the years went by, neither of them could remember when they first met. Ethyl was not a classmate, so how and when they met remained an unresolved topic of conversation in their lifelong friendship. Another lifelong friendship begun during her early years was with Irma Steele of Elkin. Irma and her sister were to become a big part of Mary Alice's future as witnesses to her wedding. As decades went by, reminisces with both Ethyl and Irma among many of her high school classmates brought recollections that produced plans to visit with friends from her teen years, desires that were to remain unfulfilled.

The 1959 - '60 school year included her second of four years of high school Home Economics that gave her well honed skills of

16

home life, such as making her own clothes. "Store bought" clothes were not common as she grew up, and hand-me-downs from family to family were the norm when usable clothes became outgrown. Good quality cloth also came as feed sack material that was washed and pinned to patterns, cut out, and stitched into new blouses, skirts, and dresses. Garvey supplied the empty sacks that Zell and Mary Alice washed, ironed, and used to make whatever they chose to stitch together, making a new wardrobe item that was a source of satisfaction.

Shoes, however, remained store bought items with saddle oxfords and penny loafers worn with bobbie socks the favorites among girls, but such purchases were usually made only when the first tobacco was sold during fall-of-the-year. A new sweater or jacket, even a new coat was a highlight of wintertime tobacco sales. Selecting a new dress for each Easter Sunday was a springtime gift from Garvey for both Zell and Mary Alice through her teens. With few clothes well cared for, life on their farm was much like most other families in the area. Households where one or both parents had incomes from jobs, such as with the huge Chatham Blankets mill complex in Elkin or one of the nearby furniture manufacturers, families adjusted to regular incomes that farmers did not have. The mill sold top quality fabrics with discount prices at its company store, and shopping with a Chatham employee enabled bringing selections home. With the foot powered treadle sewing machine in her home, Mary Alice made fashionable clothing using readily available paper patterns that were often swapped among her friends. By sixteen, her talent for designing and making fashions was well developed and remained so as she made many selections throughout her life, including making matching outfits for her young boys years later.

Volunteering to be a hostess for the Junior-Senior banquet and dance at the end of both her 9th and 10th school years was preparation for her own events when a Junior and a Senior. She prepared for her Junior Prom by making her own dress as did other classmates who could not afford to buy a gown at Spainhour's Department Store in

Elkin or from a store in Wilkesboro or Winston-Salem. With her selection of a light green taffeta fabric, she made a layered, floor length sleeveless gown that left shoulders bare, ideal for wearing a matching wrap and long white gloves. With a hoop skirt underneath, her ball gown was fitting for the Prom, but she had no date. The same dress with modest modifications was her gown for her Senior Prom the following year, May 13, 1962, where she wore a crown, the theme being Cinderella's Ball. Her friend Gail Martin was crowned the Prom's Cinderella with Johnnie Edwards as Prince Charming. Again that year, Mary Alice was without a date. Dating, even to attend her Junior and Senior Proms, was not part of her high school life.

Rapidly expanding television programming made radio and record voices real, and heart throbs were visually burned into the psyches of girls all across America. Like her friends, Mary Alice noticed Fabian, and Ricky Nelson (*Adventures of Ozzie and Harriet*), "Little Joe" Cartright (Michael Landon a star in *Bonanza*), and Pat Boone (*The Pat Boone Chevrolet Showroom*), just four among a host of television personalities who fed the temper of the times with good looks and lively music, when optimism and good times were expressions of programming, a time when clothes were worn with a flair for style, a time when Clairol advertising promoted "the natural look", exactly fitting her lifestyle because make-up was not allowed, only lipstick.

Elvis remained the premier rock 'n' roller of the 1950s, and Mary Alice's secret love, while toe-tapping tunes to dance to, recordings both slow and fast, were features of "sock hops" where dancing was done in socks rather than shoes to avoid scuffing floors. Variety programs like *The Ed Sullivan Show* often featured the latest hit singers among similar programming from other networks that became America's favorite evening pass-time, often eagerly awaited by families. Afterward, the networks signed off during late evening into a television test pattern, signifying bed time in many families, to begin broadcasting again the following morning. In the Garvey and Zell home, homework had to be completed before TV time.

Television broadcasts of adventure and mystery shows became one of the gateways to the wider world for Mary Alice. She particularly liked reading books of these themes, and as a member of the high school Library Club, many more books were available to her, to the extent that her mother complained that she always had her nose stuck in a book. Television broadcasts of thrilling shows such as Boston Blackie, the crime detective who was "friend of those who have no friend," and mystery programming, in particular *The Inner Sanctum* that began with sounds of a creaking door slowly opening followed by a sinister voice asking, "What evil lurks in the hearts of men? Only The Shadow knows."

In Elkin stood a tall Victorian house of dark coloring with surroundings of hiding shrubs. Well kept but with a mysterious aura, Mary Alice always thought of it as her "mystery house". With mystery show TV programming and books that she liked to read, especially the Nancy Drew series of mysteries, her "mystery house" inspired her to take pencil in hand one summer day before beginning high school to compose the following story:

Have you ever been so scared, that your back felt like some one was dripping ice cold water down your spine, or an old Tom cat ran up your back with his toe nails out? That is how I feel now just looking at it. It is my Mystery House. Mystery House, because no family has lived here for years, just an old care taker. The house is three stories tall with little dog house kind of workings on the roof. There are four large chimneys on the steep slate roof. The house is totally covered with bushies and vines and an icky green paint. The drapes are all pulled giving it even more an aura of mystery.

Here I am grown and on my first big job and I am just as scared as I was when I used to ride by the house as a child and later drive by the house when I got older, but you see I have never actually been inside the house.

I am working for my daddy's big real estate firm and my job is to appraise the value of this big old monster. Mr. Allen the owner,

19

who lives back east has decided to sell and the firm of Squires &
Weston are going to represent Mr. Allen.

As I stand on the porch looking at the door I can't remember
if I have knocked on the door or not. My heart is knocking so hard in
my chest that I can hardly hear - when the door slowly starts to open,
and just like in all the stories that I had made up as a child, and heard
told about the house, it was scary, and the care taker must be at least
100 years old, his skin was old and wrinkled but his eyes were clear
and sharp as the eyes of an old wise owl.

Here I stand like a school kid, I can't even remember my
name, finally I stammer my daddy, I mean, I'm Miss Squires, Billy Jo
Squires, I am here to apraise the house. This is my associate Al
Weston, we are just going to have a look around and make a few
notes. The old care taker, Mr. Grimley was his name just looked at us
with those wise old eyes and said sure, look to your heart's content,
but as we started up the stairs, I thought I heard him mutter, but
watch out for the ghosts, or was it just the stairs creaking.

The inside of the house really did look like a classic murder
mystery house, with all the furniture under dust covers and cobwebbs
in the corners, however much to my disappointment, not a single ghost
or sound was seen or heard. Al and I made our notes and left, thinking
how silly we had been to let child hood fanticies work us up into such
a frinzy. I look back toward the house and start to smile, when, did
that curtain at the top window move - was someone there or was it
just the wind, but ah! yes there is a hand holding that curtain open.
Come on Al lets get out of here.

Mary Alice liked to write and use her imagination. Through
the following years she kept many of her compositions. Also having a
flare for art, but with little in the way of art supplies or tutoring, she
was never satisfied with her compositions, keeping only a few. One
still life charcoal was framed and placed on a wall in our home when
it was discovered rolled up in her Hope Chest, having been there well
into her married life.

Home life on the farm included reading magazine stories when time permitted, and especially for her, the advertisements of ladies fashions that instilled many ideas of what she could make while also inspiring her own drawings of fashions. TV time, especially for such special events as broadcasts of the Winter and Summer Olympics, piqued Mary Alice's interests in the world beyond her own experiences. And, among many on-location travel series, *Route 66* was an early '60s program that further expanded her world with adventurous travels by car. In a few years, she would travel the real Route 66 on adventures of her own in her own snazzy roadster. *The Dinah Shore Show* with its catchy slogan, "See the USA in your Chevrolet", instilled more get out and go among "boomers" everywhere that contributed to Mary Alice's steady involvement with school and friends. Film spectacles of classic and religious themes made huge impacts on audiences, but the cost of theater tickets were most often avoided. Life on the farm rarely included spending beyond essentials, except on special occasions.

Still, Mary Alice was growing up, becoming her on person with interests that were most often held quietly within as she participated in the needs of home life with two younger brothers, the second who became "her" baby when she was about twelve years old. Caring for a baby brother contributed to her own developing instincts of motherhood. What she learned during those few years was to be applied with her own two boys during years to come.

Sundays were always reserved for attending Primitive Baptist churches, always attended in her Sunday best, perhaps a new outfit that she had made. Singing of hymns by voice alone led to long sermons that ended with another song and sorrowful walk-around goodbye handshakes. Conclusion of services often came with invitations to a preacher or two and their wives to stay for lunch of meals prepared by Zell and Mary Alice.

Although a staple during growing up, the Primitive Baptist precepts of predestination never fit firmly in her religious considerations. All life simply acting out a pre-ordained cosmic order

21

put love, in particular for her, in an unacceptable sequence of no other choice, simply a blind unfolding of a pre-determined sequence with no alternative. That was always a source of doubt for Mary Alice whose thoughts of love were paramount in her life, her most ardent pursuit; to love and to be loved remained the single most important aspect that gave her life meaning, an inclination that never changed.

Her father tended to accept interest in his daughter among boys from other church families but gave little, if any, consideration to any boy he did not know. His protective posture was never an issue for Mary Alice who knew his concern was for her well-being, and that gave her a deep and lasting sense of fulfillment of her core need, to be loved. To "go home" remained a long held, guiding desire that was always reassuring and certain when there, a feeling of her father's never-ending love for her that almost always welcomed her home.

Her growing up years involved sorting through continual wonderings, particularly about maturing years later than her classmates. She described herself to me saying that at sixteen, she still looked like a boy, a stretch, I thought, having seen her 9th grade school photo... already a beauty, definitely not a boy. Then further consternation about having intense abdominal cramps each month when maturing began. Her mother was less help in such matters than her friends who gave her the benefit of their experiences, but when bent double with pain at night, it was her father who sat up with her. This aspect of maturing was not welcomed by Mary Alice whose tom-boyish rearing as her father's tag-along, whether hunting or fishing or working on the farm, meant leaving that life behind to be a young woman. That change long remained a source of sadness for her; wonderful memories of childhood with her father that the passage of time would never allow to be repeated tended her toward melancholy moments.

As the 1959 - '60 school year came to a close, leaving another favorite part of her life behind, Mary Alice had made many friends. Among them was Carolyn Blackburn who wrote in her annual:

Mary Alice, It has been a real pleasure knowing you and going to school with you. I have known you all my life and so I can say with true honesty, you are one of the sweetest and nicest girls I've ever known. Good luck and Best wishes thru the following years, A friend always.

That friendship did last through the years and was often recalled as favorite memories among her high school friends. By then, sweet and nice was who she had always been, the person she remained through the years, never with a harsh word against anyone. Even in circumstances that brought her to tears, Mary Alice never allowed herself to utter harshness or condemnation on anyone.

Another classmate noted with underline in the yearbook advertisement section, *You are as fresh and pure as mountain air.* A fitting description. How Mary Alice became sweet and nice was grounded in her core desire for good for everyone, and she believed that being sweet and nice to everyone she met contributed to spreading good. Wearing her heart on her sleeve, as the old saying told for people like her, meant that she was, occasionally, a pin cushion for barbs from other people. Those pin pricks were often taken deep and heartfelt, though never to produce retaliatory anger. Harshness against her often became lasting memories, her reward for being sweet and nice and expecting the same from everyone else. Some of those pricks took her to tears in quiet moments that she kept to herself. More than anything, she did not want to cause bad feelings in others or to be a burden for anyone, and being sensitive meant enduring what most other people dismissed as incidental.

The following summer meant more picking of blackberries, sometimes sold adding to her small cash on hand. Most of the berries were cooked and sweetened and filled jars of jam and jelly that later topped buttered biscuits that she learned how to make at her mother's side. Farming meant field work such as springtime planting and fall-of-the-year harvesting. Fresh corn for their table or ground into corn meal for corn bread remained an annual routine. Late harvested corn also became barn yard livestock feed during coming winter months. Summertime "priming" tobacco for curing was the only significant source of income when sold to makers of cigarettes. Coming to grips with an allergy to tobacco was another troubling aspect of her physiology, so her contributions became cooking meals for those who worked the fields, keeping house in her mother's absence, doing laundry, sewing and mending, cleaning... daily activities. Issues of spring and fall hay fever allergies were additional sources of consternation resulting in questions like, why me, that would haunt Mary Alice with swollen eyes and her runny nose from time-to-time throughout her life. She was by nature a gentle person who loved the pleasures of simple living, especially being among people she loved, those whom she always found when she could "go home", back to where farm life had given her lifelong pleasant memories that caused troubles to fade away.

The following school year, 1960 - '61, was another step up the ladder to the future and into the wider world, as the theme of her yearbook expressed. Among eighty-five or more Juniors, she achieved grades of A or B in her five main subjects, English III, U.S. History, Home Economics, Typing, and Spanish. Never tardy, she did receive the negative, "Does not make good use of time" for being absent eight times during the school year. Each of those absences was due to severe cramps when the morning school bus arrived, another source of consternation that maturity gave her.

Mary Alice was always comfortable among friends, especially at school where she pursued topics of interest among other courses of lesser interest but deemed necessary additions to her capabilities, although Typing and Spanish classes proved sufficiently demanding that she was not satisfied with her B grades.

A classmate, Peggy Hemric, wrote in her yearbook:

Dear Mary Alice, I have truly enjoyed going to school with you for the past three years. I think we have had good times at 'Good Old East High'. In a few years we can look back and remember the endless trips up and down the hall. Let's don't forget our experiences in Home Economics III either; maybe the food wasn't 'up to par' but it was fun. Remember that terrible picture of us in the newspaper! I'm trying to forget it. What a picture of me! I really had a good time visiting you at your home. You were a very good hostess. Maybe the bed was a little crowded, but it is something to remember. I think your parents are very nice. I hope you are always as close to them as now. I hope you don't have any scars from those falls you had when running to lunch. I hope you always have as many admirers as you have now (Boys I mean). Be real careful when driving your Ford and keep it in one piece. And you! I hope to be remembered in the years to come. I wish you the best of luck in whatever you undertake to do as a career. A good friend.

Carolyn and Peggy among others of favorite memories remained lifelong friends, and into her scrapbook went that Home Ec photo cut from the newspaper story.

Those "falls when you were running to lunch" were another limitation, a concerning aspect of her physiology, the kind that made her aware that she had little tolerance for exertion in physical activities. Why she would suddenly faint remained an unanswered concern from then onward, perhaps first signaled to her during high school with those "falls", hints that something was just not right with her because she could not do physical activities like her friends.

In "Home Ec", Mary Alice excelled due to doing what she wanted to be. Broad studies of foods, their nutritional value, costs, and making of menus was a lengthy project promoting in-depth understanding of food that received an A+ grade. She also received an A for her composition;

My Philosophy Of Homemaking. It takes many things to make a house a home. There are many more things to do besides just living there; for example there are childcare, homemaking, housekeeping, and, at first, one of the most important things is the selection of

25

furniture. There are not many young couples that have enough money to pay for the furniture they get, so that brings in financing. The next things are family relations, food, clothing, and something that goes with all of these - safety.

The selection of furniture is one of the major things to make a home beautiful. But before buying furniture there are many tests it must meet. For example if a person wants to have children - and most young couples do - they wouldn't want to get velvet or something hard to keep clean. Another thing to remember is that a person buys furniture for a purpose not for its beauty. If a person buys at sales don't buy just because it is a bargain or because it is pretty, buy it if it serves a purpose. Before buying furniture check it inside and out. Look for corner blocks on chairs, dove tailing at joints, and smooth insides of drawers. The best thing to remember in buying furniture is to buy as you need it.

The buying of furniture brings up another problem. Most young married people can't pay cash for their furniture; therefore, they have to finance it. There are many different ways of financing and there is no one way right for every one. A person should study the different ways and decide wheather he is going to mortgage something, borrow from a bank, or pay to the place where he bought the merchandise. Two things to remember in financing something is to keep up with the payments and make as large a payments as possible in order to cut down on the interest.

The crowded years come next from the time the couple have their first baby to the last. But before the first baby is born there are many adjustments for the young couples to make. The first is - can they afford to have a baby at this time? Second is 'are they willing to give up some of their own pleasures in order to support a baby?' The third thing is - do both the parents want a baby? There are also many other arrangements to make, such as what doctor to go to and what hospital. Make sure you will be able to get a room at the hospital at the time you will expect to need it. After the baby is born there are many things that change. The parents will have a larger grocery bill,

26

more clothes to buy, and they will have to fix a place for the baby to sleep. There will be much more work for the mother to do after the baby is born. She will have to feed the baby about every four hours, give him a bath at least once a day and keep his clothes clean and his dipers free from germs. The mother should stay close by so she can keep an eye on the baby. When the baby is twenty months to two years old his toilet training should start. The mother should stay with him for the first few times, then if he does not cry she can leave him alone. These are a few of the problems in bringing up children and there are many more. The parents are faced with every one of them.

The mother is not only faced with the problems of feeding the family, but she has to select foods that are high in nutrients. She has to select foods that are good for the family and at the same time stay within her food budget. Douring the time when there is a small baby the parents may find that it is hard to select the foods the family needs, buy milk for the baby, and stay within the food budget. In order to do this most families find that that it is necessary to cut down on some of the other expenses in order to add money to the food budget. The expenses that are most easily cut are recreation and pleasure trips. While there are small children in the family it is hard to add very much money to the savings account, but it is still easier to live on a budget than to live and worry about where the next money is coming from.

Clothing is also a problem when there are small children in the family. The mother will probably have to buy for the baby instead of herself. It would be much easier for the parents to stay within the budget if the mother knew how to sew, because it is much cheaper to make some of the clothes than to buy all of them.

The parents should make the home as safe as possible for their children. They should keep all sharp and dangerous object out of the childrens reach. The parents should keep all medicines or poisons locked in a medicine cabinet or out of the childrens reach. To be good parents the mother and father should take all the safety precautions necessary to insure their famil 's health.

27

These facts and ideas make up my Philosophy of Homemaking. Mary Alice Cheek.

Although a school assignment and clearly influenced by marriage and parenting guides widely available at the time, for an 11th grade girl in Home Economics to compose such an outlook meant that Mary Alice had a clear vision of her future. Among her friends, such topics were every day conversation due to the norm of girls getting married while still in high school or shortly thereafter. Her best friend Carolyn married Vernon that year and brought a real life change into Mary Alice's outlook. Such were the thoughts among classmates who wrote messages for the future in their annuals.

Another classmate wrote:

Mary Alice, May the best of everything come to one of the sweetest girls I have ever known. Be Good, Lynda Baker.

And Ima Jean, wrote in her yearbook;

Mary Alice, I have enjoyed going to school with you all these years. You are really a nice girl. May the best of everything come your way - you surely deserve it. I will always remember your friendly smile.

That friendly smile was hers for life, always with pleasantries upon greeting someone, a smile that was the expression of her outlook of always wanting to instill "good vibrations" in people around her, an attribute that excluded complaining. She had read Norman Vincent Peale's little book, *The Power of Positive Thinking*, that helped solidify her notions of how she wanted to live her life, whatever it was to bring. Her smile and beautiful eyes were to capture a husband during years to come.

1962

As Mary Alice grew into her teens among cousins and high school friends, her father became increasingly unwilling to accept courting of his daughter. Being self-motivated with many friends and family nearby, she did not fret over such limitations due to her secure home life, but when they arrived for services at a church far from home one Sunday and the boy thought to be chosen for her was there with another girl, it shook her very being. Putting the pieces back together took some time, and what was put together was a different outlook; Mary Alice became determined that who she loved was to be her choice. Guarding her emotions was her new commitment that prompted the question; did she really love that boy? Or did she let events disguised as love dictate to her? That would not happen again. Such re-alignment in her personal life was to remain her guiding principle, hand written in a few sentences on a small piece of note paper placed in her scrapbook:

I will greet this day with love in my heart, and I will succeed;
I will persist until I succeed;
I am nature's greatest miracle;
I will live this day as if it is my last;
Today I will be the master of my emotions.

With deep and continued respect for her father, Mary Alice gradually came to setting her own course in decisions of what was heartfelt to her. Such a harsh and vivid revelation resulting in a new awakening did not inhibit her continued quest for personal and academic excellence in school or to inhibit her out-going personality among boys, one who wrote in her 1962 yearbook;

Mary Alice, I have sincerely enjoyed going to school with you these past four years. You are one in a million. Remember me in later life. Think kindly of me. Your friend always, Tommy Holleman.

Mary Alice did remember Tommy, recalling him among her favorites that time and circumstances left behind.

Classmate Larry Shore wrote;

Mary Alice, I have enjoyed knowing you for the past year or so. I think you are a real nice girl, who can make friends with almost anyone. I would just like to say that I wish you all the happiness in the world. And hoping that we can always be good friends.

Wanda C. wrote in her annual;

Mary or (Miss Alice), I have known you as long as I remember and you are a very good friend and a sweet cousin. This is your senior year and I'm sure although you'll miss East High, you'll enjoy going somewhere else and working. Best of luck to you and Robbie. You're already having some luck to have him. Best wishes to a dear cousin.

Brenda Joyner wrote;

Mary Alice, You are the one girl I will never forget. You are so sweet, cute, and most of all irresistible. You are All of them tied into one. Keep your sweetness and be yourself, and you'll have success in anything that is your goal. I have really had fun this year with you and Spencer in English. He really is cute. Ha! I'll always remember you as one of my very best friends. I'm sure you will get that special one. You deserve the best. You have been a nice person to know these past 4 years but more this year. I'll always remember you. So, I hope the best comes your way, and I'm sure it will. Be sure and remember me. Love always.

The coaches wife, Joanne Hales wrote;

Mary Alice, You are a bright star in all your classes. My wish for you is that you find a niche in life where your talents will shine the brightest.

The end of high school was the senior class trip to Washington D.C. during June, 1962 when she roomed with classmates Linda Durham, Ella Mae Ray, and Evline West. Among many sites seen in the capital, perhaps the highlight of her adventures was meeting Joe. He was handsome, in the U.S. Air Force, and was soon to be stationed in England. Their impromptu encounter flourished into romantic feelings, especially from him that resulted in exchanges of letters and gifts. While he was in England, a gift sent to her included a color portrait of him in uniform and two Beatles albums recorded in "the Cave" at Liverpool, the band's first albums. Later, her middle brother gave them away, claiming a loan. Joe's seriousness toward her was clear, but letters and gifts alone did not lead to... Did she love him? Really love him? That was the question with an unsettling answer. Upon his return to the States, he arrived one day at her home driving a new Corvette with a ring in hand and matrimony on his mind. Asking for her hand in marriage came with whisking her away with him back to England. The combination of marriage with someone she hardly knew, leaving home, and soon to be in another country brought that unsettling, insecure feeling to a disappointing answer for him. Afterward, ridden with guilt for having broken a heart that professed undying love for her, Mary Alice became an emotional recluse even more reserved in committing her emotions. That required further sorting out.

With return from her Senior trip, graduation was past, and neither Joe nor Robbie were in her future. By then, Mary Alice had many suitors, especially another young man from Elkin that she had met who also professed his undying love for her, although they never dated. His rejection led to drowning his sorrow in alcohol and arriving

31

at her home one afternoon, on his knees in the front yard begging her to marry him. She left another broken heart in the wake of seeking the bond with a boy that she felt was right for her, and her unintended reputation of being a heart breaker was bantered around, that she was "stuck up", although none of her suitors knew of her father's tight constraints on her. A third proposal of matrimony came from a young man she knew who was soon to be sent in uniform to Viet Nam and was desperate to marry her. Another decline and no dating other than visits at her home remained her lifestyle, to her father's satisfaction. If she stayed home forever, that would be okay with him, but such a pretty girl unmarried at her age and widely sought after brought comments that she thought herself too good for the boys she knew. Her father continually reinforcing the notion that what people said about her, her reputation, was of utmost importance, to always be guarded, remained significant guidance for Mary Alice, but many of her friends were married or on that course by then, and she still had no boyfriend of her choosing.

The combination of her sense of being burned by love that she came to recognize was probably not love at all, and her unwillingness to marry without the feelings she sought, along with her father's protective influence, her future with boys was not at all clear. Still, her future lay before her, and what to do next was also not so clear. Her future seemed to dictate a career of some sort, but what? A first job was sewing belt loops onto boys pants for about a year, a job at a factory involving travel to and from with her mother. Among the first things she did with her income was to repay her father for the cookware set that remained in its box tucked away in a closet, the box too large to fit in her Hope Chest. Making about $50 each week, Mary Alice decided that she wanted a car of her own. With her father one day, they visited a local Oldsmobile dealership where she saw an English roadster that she liked. Her father advised against buying such a car for lack of available service and suggested a recent trade-in, a blue 1962 F-85 coupe. She could afford that purchase, and with a second car in the family, her own car gave Mary Alice a new level of mobility and independence. Her blue Oldsmobile was soon to change her life.

She left her pants factory job to go back to school, but not before breaking another heart. The son of a co-worker became so enamored with her that his mother was concerned he would harm himself because Mary Alice did not return his affection. That led to a broken friendship and a reason to find another job. Registering for nurse's training at Catawba College became her first step away from home, but a few months of home sickness combined with nauseating medicinal odors ended upon her return home. What to do now involved getting another job. The time was September, 1963.

The new regional telephone exchange in Elkin was hiring, and the man she interviewed with knew her family. Her credentials showed that she had been a good student and was reliable. When hired, the job renewed her income, $1.25 an hour that later went to $1.85 an hour. By then, both Garvey and Zell had regular incomes with jobs of their own.

Jobs meant that home life changed. Garvey continued farming on a smaller scale; tilling an adjacent plot led to growing a large garden that remained an annual undertaking. The garden produced a broad variety of vegetables, and with an assortment of apple trees, a corn field next to their house, peaches bought by the bushel from roving South Carolina growers during late spring, cherries picked in Virginia orchards, summer and fall canning continued as in years past, preparation for the lean winter months ahead along with selections of fresh fruits and vegetables holed in the ground below the frost line. A chest freezer in the small concrete lined basement he had built received portions of home grown beef for freezing among similarly frozen fruits and vegetables. Also home grown were varieties of pork, including ham that Garvey sugar cured along with bacon and side meat salted, and sausage ground, bagged, and hung with hams and shoulders in the barn. Home life on the farm was busy and needed continual preparations for what was to come, whatever the time of year. Upon arriving home after each work day, tending to the needs of

33

the farm remained unrelenting. Gradually, farm work declined as time consumers were done away with for easier evenings.

Mary Alice's telephone operator work schedule was second shift, 5pm to 2am, the night shift, and she drove the distance home to sleep late during following mornings. With her mother continuing her job that required leaving home early, Mary Alice had a new daytime routine that she knew well, housework, this time with evening meals prepared by the time her parents arrived home from their jobs, left for them when she drove to her job. With little to do at home during that time, Zell often commented later that she "had it made" as long as Mary Alice lived at home.

The holidays that year came and went with Christmas gift giving among family members of all store bought items. With the new year, Mary Alice had a boy's romance in her life, a boy among other suitors who continually called for dates. She accepted few of them, mostly daytime outings, perhaps a picnic or a weekend afternoon movie, or just sitting on the porch talking. Her work schedule did not permit the usual dating routine, and, her schedule at the exchange often extended into overtime during weekends. Being single, she filled in for other operators who needed time off for some reason. Her extra earnings, however, meant buying more clothes and shoes, a luxury in her life for the first time, although her father continually encouraged her to add to her savings account at a local bank. That done regularly, her savings steadily grew. Home life with a regular routine was reassuring, but a sense of being unfulfilled was growing within her.

The Beginning

On an unseasonably warm and bright Sunday afternoon during March of 1963, when there were no visiting preachers for lunch after church, Mary Alice set out to enjoy the afternoon with a drive in her Oldsmobile. The day also coincided with 16 year old first cousin, Phyllis, having recently gotten her driver's license. A girl going for a drive by herself was not acceptable, and neither was driving around just to drive around, but Phyllis, being three years younger, had become rather like a little sister to Mary Alice and had traveled on vacations with Garvey and Zell so that Mary Alice would have someone to pal around with. Phyllis was a known and accepted companion for Mary Alice, so saying that she was going for a drive with Phyllis was acceptable. Crossing the gravel road to Uncle Robert's house came to these two pretty girls setting out to enjoy the sights of an early spring-like day. Theirs was just a Sunday drive, something to do on such a nice day, and neither suspected what was to come. This was to become an eventful day for Mary Alice.

Also that day in Surry County east of Wilkes County, a telephone rang. Tommy called to ask if Alex, a long time neighbor and classmate at Surry Central High School, would like to ride around. I am Alex, and that offer suited me. To Elkin we went as did Phyllis and Mary Alice. Tommy's white with red interior Corvair was a nice ride and flashy, just the sort of car to get attention at the Tasty Freeze or the Little Rebel, the two main places that catered to teen clientele with rock 'n' roll music blaring from loudspeakers. Both offered selections of burgers and fries and malts in abundance.

Noticing a car with two pretty girls off the street, stopped in a parking area, Tommy boldly drove his Corvair to stop door-to-door with Phyllis behind the wheel of a blue Oldsmobile coupe, and boy-girl banter between them began. Their talk left the other boy and girl simply observing. Tommy was good with boy-girl banter while I said nothing. The other girl also said nothing, but she kept looking at me, paying no attention to Phyllis and Tommy. I kept looking at her thinking, "Dang, that girl is good looking, really good looking!"

That girl kept looking at me, completely unusual because girls did not make eye-to-eye contact in my experience, and I kept looking at her, our eyes constantly meeting that produced the most engaging smile I had ever seen. No more than about ten feet apart, I had no idea who she was or what she was thinking, but I was overwhelmed to have such a completely unknown girl, such a pretty girl looking straight at me. Eye-to-eye contact was not at all normal in first time boy-girl encounters; girls seemed naturally to be coy, to avoid eye-to-eye contact, but this girl looked at nothing but me.

When the banter subsided, that girl, still looking straight into my eyes with her captivating smile, said, "I like that quiet one over there." I was speechless, nearly stupefied; never before had any girl said anything like that to me or paid any attention to me. Tommy saved the awkward moment by asking if the girls would like to get milkshakes. We arrived at the Tasty Freeze parked side-by-side, my door next to Phyllis's door. I had yet to say anything. I kept looking at that other girl, really good looking! my continual thought. Phyllis was a beauty of her own, but I was captured by eyes and a smile by another girl I had never seen before.

With only about three dollars in my pocket, I gathered enough composure to get out of Tommy's Corvair to get closer to that other girl. As I walked around the front to her side of their car, I noticed that she watched me the entire way, then our instant and lingering eye contact became as capturing as her smile. I asked her, "Would you like a milkshake?" At that moment, I would have done anything for this mysterious beauty, and I did not know her name or anything about her.

That Sunday encounter was unlike all the previous boy-girl encounters of my life. I had turned seventeen just three months before then and a junior in high school having had no dates, no experience with girls other than in classes, church functions, and sock hop dances that my very musical Mom chaperoned and took me to. This new girl

36

was unlike any girl I had ever met; everything she said was reassuring and said with the most beautiful of smiles and... she seemed interested in me. In my mind, that did not fit; she was so pretty that I was certain that she wore the class ring of some quarterback from somewhere, but nothing about her indicated any attachment.

When I brought her choice of milkshake to her, I asked, "What's your name?"

"Mary Alice Cheek. What's yours?"

Names exchanged, I asked, "Where do you go to school?"

"I'm not in school. I'm a telephone operator. I graduated from East Wilkes."

Now I knew why I had never seen her before, we lived in different counties. But already graduated meant... Holy Moses! It suddenly dawned on me... She's older than I am. Suddenly my hoped for quest to get better acquainted with her was dashed; she surely had a boyfriend, maybe married already.

"Where do you live?" she asked.

Now resigned to a lost cause, I told her.

"So, you're at Surry Central?"

My affirmative answer came with Phyllis changing the moment by suggesting that we congregate at one of the picnic tables nearby. That gave me the opportunity to see the form of my mystery girl whose trim figure was immediately alluring. Everything about this girl was so captivating that I retained little memory of anything of that day but her, especially her eyes, those beautiful eyes that entranced me, and her smile that captured me, her expression completely lacking in coyishness. Nothing about her was shy... I had never met any girl even remotely similar to this girl whose completely open manner toward me was as if she had known me all of her life. Long conversation with Phyllis years later filled in gaps in my memory, gaps that did not include Tommy asking Phyllis for a date. That question led to her accepting, and that led to double dating during the coming weeks. As we sipped our shakes that beautiful Sunday, my admitting to being a mere junior meant further doubt that anything

37

could come of this, especially when Mary Alice told of graduating the previous year when I had another year of high school to go. I wasn't talking to a high school girl, I was talking to a working woman two and a half years older than me. Where could this possibly go? She made nothing of what appeared to me to be insurmountable differences. My thoughts went beyond her innocent openness to wondering if she was married and out "playing the field", but she wore no ring or displayed anything even hinting of being betrothed. With nothing more than her charming manner, this beauty was taking me into a completely unknown aspect of my young life, my very own boy-girl encounter akin to the many rock 'n' songs of the time about love, particularly the Ricky Nelson hit that told... "There'll never be anyone else but you...." I had learned the lyrics of that song from listening to the radio, and while looking into those beautiful eyes across the table from me, those words seemed to fit perfectly. I had known Mary Alice Cheek for no more than a few minutes and sat there looking at her completely entranced, entirely captured, perhaps ensnared is a better word, as never before or since.

Small talk led to Phyllis suggesting that we follow them to their home so that we would know where we should go for future dates. Phyllis recalled driving Mary Alice's Olds, then stopping prior to her home so that a driver change could be made and suggesting further that we lag behind their car. The reason was to avoid the potential of getting into trouble if it became known to their protective fathers that they, two girls, had been driving through town and brought two boys home with them.

Returning to our homes that day, as Tommy drove along, the thought struck me; dummy! You didn't ask for her phone number or address. But, oh well... I was certain that her capturing eyes and smile were for someone else. Still, I had never met anyone like her, a beauty who conveyed interest in me with eyes that... I could not explain what that interest could be, but I was lost in her eyes, her smile, and her natural beauty without a hint of makeup other than tempting lips of pink. I was sure, however, that I could not possibly be competition for whoever was her boyfriend.

The next morning, I woke up thinking about Mary Alice Cheek, knowing nearly nothing about her, and rode the school bus to and from school, Tommy driving, resigned to never again seeing her beautiful eyes. Several days went by as I thought a lot about those eyes. Then, near bed time one evening, our phone rang. I answered to a hushed voice that I did not recognize.

"Is this Alex?"

"Yes," I answered, wondering what the cloak and dagger was all about.

"This is Mary Alice. I'm on duty, and I can't talk long. Could you come to town Sunday?"

The light came on, brilliantly lit. It's her! "Sure!" was my immediate answer.

"I'll be driving my blue Oldsmobile. See you there." And, she hung up with me still holding the phone, stunned. My mystery girl called me to set up a date. Such short, clandestine phone calls became late evening regular features when Mary Alice was on duty that week and weeks and months thereafter. Come Sunday, another pretty day, I borrowed Mom's Studebaker Lark that I cleaned to sparkling and drove to town in search of her blue Oldsmobile. The two "in" spots in Elkin meant that my search quickly ended at the Little Rebel. Not nearly so adept at boy-girl banter as Tommy, my attempts at conversation stumbled along from being absorbed by the light fragrance of her perfume, her smile, and those eyes. Mostly, we exchanged questions and answers to get better acquainted mixed with small talk. After a while, she said that she was scheduled for an evening shift at the telephone exchange and asked if I would follow her home so I would know where she lived... so I could meet her parents.

Her parents! Her home! This was going somewhere for sure, and I was not at all certain that I was up to what I imagined was to come. I also did not realize the enormity of courage Mary Alice had to

39

muster for her to bring home a boy, especially a boy that her father did not know. After introductions with Garvey and Zell remained casual, I was at a loss when her father told me in his stern manner that, "Lust is a sin." I was only vaguely familiar with the word, thinking that lust had something to do with sexual appetite, so I was stumped in a fanciful way. Her father was clearly unaware that his daughter was lusting for me. I did not think that to be at all sinful, and I was certainly well dialed in to her physical beauty. Our attraction to each other was clear to me.

Mary Alice invited me to sit with her in the metal chairs on her front porch. And, we talked. As time neared for her shift, I said my farewell with a smile for a most interesting afternoon. We had not yet touched as Mary Alice walked with me to Mom's Lark. As I began my slow drive away and looked back with a wave, I noticed that she stood in the yard watching me. My every thought was, "this Mary Alice Cheek is really something." I was glad that I looked back and kept wondering as I drove, "Wow!... Wow!...." That first springtime meeting, then this day with her led to infrequent meetings as our schedules permitted.

Phyllis also recalled that during our picnic table gathering, Tommy initiated double dates for the two of us that lasted into that summer. What brought those double dates to an end occurred when she told Tommy that she and her long time boyfriend had made up. Tommy was told that he was out. On that occasion, the two of them were seated in the back when Phyllis gave Tommy his class ring back. Taking their break-up deeply, he promptly threw it out the window. Later, his harsh words about our Wilkes County girls led to fracturing our longtime friendship, from grade school, because I continued to date Mary Alice as occasion permitted through that summer.

Returning to school for my senior year led to a request one day. The football homecoming game was to showcase the court of the Homecoming Queen, and one of the candidates did not have a convertible to ride in. My older sister, Charlene, had recently bought a new and beautiful white Falcon convertible with aqua colored interior, and the request was to see if her car might be available for the homecoming game. Charlene agreed, and as I slowly drove in the parade, I kept looking in the rear view mirror at my rider perched on the rear deck in a flowing gown. Sharon could easily have been selected Queen, in my opinion, a very pretty and friendly girl who was one of the football player's girlfriend. My overtures toward her led to an occasional date that came abruptly to an end after a few months when her family moved away.

Another date was with a friend and his date, a double date. She stood me up at her door. Those two girls comprised my total of high school dates until Mary Alice. By then I had kissed only one girl, due to playing spin-the-bottle at a birthday party years earlier, a girl who made it clear that I was of no interest to her.

Mary Alice and I had seen so little of each other that I did not think about giving her a Christmas gift that year, 1963. As the new year unfolded, I was increasingly drawn to memories of her friendly smile and... those eyes... that came with another clandestine phone call, and another.... After casual dates in her home, a warming fire adding to wintertime's ambiance, slow dancing to her Hi-Fi in the front room brought her into my arms and me into hers. Our bodies in close contact for the first time was enduring. As we perfected various moves and routines for the dance floor, her initial reluctance to dance, I learned, was due to a church taboo, but with her father's acceptance, we went to occasional church dances that my Mom chaperoned. Our dates at her home helped hone dance floor skills into show winning performances later. By my Senior Prom, we had routines to really show off.

That spring we actually were able to arrange a night time date, the first being a Saturday night drive-in movie. Having a girl alone in a car, in the dark, was new to me, especially with her gentle fragrance continually toying with my senses. While she kept to her side of the Lark's bench seat, as I did on my side, our chitchat was more interesting than the movie. Afterward, on the way to her home, along an out-of-sight stretch of the gravel road, she told me to stop the car.

41

With the Lark motionless, only its dash lights illuminating us, she reached for me. I went ever so willingly into what became - the kiss -, her kiss, a tight arm around kiss that I had waited for, a kiss like never before, a kiss so filled with emotion that I was carried away by her soft lips and her fragrance, with affection that I had never felt before making a banging in my head. Still suspecting that I could not possibly measure up for a girl more than two years older than me, I asked if she would be my date for my Senior Prom. When she accepted, I felt like I had hit a home run out of the park; this beauty was going with me to the Prom. How was that even possible?

The Prom

Through that following spring, Mary Alice and I dated infrequently as our schedules permitted. By Prom time, I had come to envision only Mary Alice Cheek in my girl affections, but not yet a girlfriend because I was still convinced that she surely had lots of other dates. I still had no inkling of how restrictive her life at home actually was. My Mom put up the money to rent a tux and shoes for me. I could not do that because of being on a trip with the Surry Central Marching Band and arriving at the High School with hardly enough time to go home and dress for the Prom. Mom and Charlene did yeoman duty getting everything ready for me, then following a quick sponge bath and a splash of Aqua-Velva, I was dressed and out the door to pick up my date. Arriving at her home, Mary Alice presented herself to me, her parents, and her little brother dressed in a white satin A-line gown to the floor, her golden hair up with curls above her eyes, those eyes that absorbed me, and her little smile with pink lips... She was gorgeous. Charlene had bought a wrist orchid of pink and white for me to give to my date, and as I slipped it on Mary Alice's gloved hand, I was in disbelief that this was actually happening. I had been unable to secure a date for my Junior Prom the previous year, and this beauty was my Senior date? On our drive to the High School we decided not to be wallflowers; we were going to show off our dance routines. As I held her hand up in mine when we entered the Prom, I overheard mutterings of, "Who is that?" It dawned on me that no one in my high school knew Mary Alice Cheek, my date... MY date! Among all the pretty girls in my senior class, all dressed in their Prom finery, I saw no one but Mary Alice and retained no memories of other girls from that occasion but her.

When the first record was played, we were the first couple to begin dancing. Our rock 'n' roll routines of spins, turns, twirls, and dips were put on display as the gathered stepped back to give us room. We were showing off, and it felt good. When I noticed another group

43

watching other dancers, we worked our way over to discover that my Mom doing the Charleston had drawn a crowd, a dance of her era that none of us rock 'n' rollers knew. Mom received resounding applause for her performance. That was another satisfying moment for me.

Mom was the Regional Supervisor of Music for the county school system and drove from school to school to school for many years to end each school day at Surry Central while I was a student there, and one of us drove her Lark home. Mom had conducted all musical events, including chorus, throughout each year and ended every year with ceremonies for the graduating class. When I crossed the stage as she played an appropriate piano processional piece, I heard her sniff, a signal to me that a significant moment in her life was passing, too.

With graduation as a good but not a scholarly student, although a Beta Club member, I did not have a clue of what I was going to do next. Growing up on Grandpa John's farm with work constantly driving each day, I was busy going into that summer, 1964, working the fields and hiring my labor to other farmers. That was how I had earned the money to buy clothes for school each fall, but now there was no more school. What was I going to do?

With enough money to go places, I had the occasional use of Charlene's convertible and Mom's Lark but could afford only infrequent dates with Mary Alice if they did not include dinner out and a movie. Mostly, our dates were at her home and only then when fitting her work schedule. That meant only a few Saturday night drive-in movies, but usually no more than a Sunday afternoon drive, sometimes with a cousin or friend along who happened to be visiting her.

During that summer, Mom's younger sister Lucille and her husband, H. B. Wolfe, inquired if I would be willing to come to Charlotte and live with them for the purpose of painting their house. I did not realize what a big job that was to become, but the offer of two hundred dollars was incentive that I jumped at. It took a month to scrape off the old paint down to bare wood to the roof.

44

While painting one day, Aunt Cille approached me with sorrowful eyes, then said that Mom had called for her to relay to me that Daddy had died. Painting abruptly ended as Uncle B drove me back to the farm with the agreement of returning to finish the job. Daddy's demise was within a few weeks of his mother's, a favorite grandmother who had told me many stories about growing up in the wilds of eastern Kentucky's mountains. Daddy died just eight years after his father, Berea's dentist who dropped dead unexpectedly one Sunday morning and put the family into an unrecoverable tailspin. Being a teacher raising four children on her own, Mom had no money for a funeral, so the situation seemed to dictate that Daddy would be interred in a pauper's grave somewhere. Grandpa John saved the situation to be a decent funeral and burial for Daddy in the Berea City Cemetery with his parents. Unknown to Mom, Grandpa John had taken out a life insurance policy on Daddy years before and gave it to her for funeral expenses. We traveled to Berea for Daddy's funeral with Mom riding in the hearse with an empty casket for him. His funeral drew a number of home town attendees who had known Daddy, many from his youth and school days. Mom's eldest daughter, Michaela, "my Big Sis", had remained in Berea while we four of Mom's younger children had lived with her on Grandpa John's farm in North Carolina, her birth home, and had gotten on with our lives since their separation during 1954. For me, Daddy's unexpected death came with emotional impact since I had spent several school years in the 1950s with him and his mother working the small restaurant business that his father established to be an enterprise following retirement from his dentistry practice. Later, Mom was able to buy a granite grave marker for him, just him.

On a Sunday afternoon following our return, I sat on the front room couch with Mary Alice holding me as tears of remembrance fell.

Returning to Charlotte, I continued house painting. Uncle B helped when off duty as a taxi driver, and when I ran out of paint near done but before all the surface was covered, he exclaimed vociferously about the cost of another gallon of paint. I offered to

45

reduce what was to be paid for my work to buy another gallon, but he instead drove his taxi longer hours to get the money.

On one occasion of going into Charlotte with Aunt Cille, we happened by a clothing store that had in its window a below the knee length denim winter coat with fleece lining. I was certain that such a coat would be ideal for the coming winter, a notion that proved correct due to having to ride a motorbike, my only transportation. While in another store, I saw a matching set of dog and cat caricatures, wood framed wall hangings that entirely captured my attention as matching how I saw us, Mary Alice and me. The two pieces became my gift to her, her the cat with capturing eyes, me the dog ever devoted to her.

The demise of Taylor Price Gabbard brought to a close his family as residents of Berea since the before World War One. Over time, all holdings were lost in foreclosures that left nothing for his wife and children. What Daddy could have done with his life as a young man, the first son of a well-to-do family in a college town, was no more than pursuing business interests. I, as a young man with high school behind me, faced the same decisions of my future that he did but without the resources that were available to him. What was I to do?

That was a question asked of me by Mom's brother, Uncle Ben, during another Sunday when he and his elegant wife, Sadie Draughn, came from their home in High Point to visit the farm of his youth, where he and Mom and Lucille were born and grew up. He had been with IBM since shortly after returning from World War Two when he and Sadie married. She was his high school sweetheart. I did not have an answer to his question and muttered about going to the U. S. Naval Academy. He told me that no one simply goes to the Academy, they have to be appointed, and that preparation should have been done a year or two passed for me to be accepted.

That idea dashed, he proposed that I go to college. With no money or financial support available, that seemed impossible, but he thought it was possible if I was willing to work to continue my education. My mother was a graduate of Berea College in Kentucky, where she met Daddy, and why attending her college never occurred to me remains a mystery. I liked learning, and my experiences on the campus while a boy when living with Dad and his mother could easily have made Berea College my destination, but....

By then I had read a number of books and had enjoyed high school, but that was the past, and I should think of the future, Uncle Ben told me. He encouraged me saying that a college education would open many opportunities for a career, an idea that I thought was no more than a passing fancy. What to do had always been dictated by the circumstances I was in. Now I had to make decisions on my own. My older brother, Johnny, had been in the Navy, so military service was a viable option for me as well, but also never more than a passing thought.

Thinking of Mary Alice's transition from high school to telephone operator, I professed that getting a job seemed the likely next thing to do, but the only jobs available nearby were working sporadically for farmers who paid no more than one dollar an hour. Uncle Ben assured me that such paltry earnings was not livable and that I should learn to do something that an employer would pay me a living salary, and that required education. I had an offer to go to work at the feed mill at Burch Station nearby, but that seemed to be little more than a job with no future. I was looking ahead, even if I had no idea what was in my future. And, Grandpa John often advised to get a public job, that farming had no future, another stimulus for me toward education.

Some years earlier, events began to lead toward my conclusion that farming was not a desirable future for me. Johnny and I were plowing through a large field of waist high tobacco with Grandpa John's big black mule, Bob, on a hot June day. I was sweaty, grimy, gritty dirty, continually stumbling along amid clumps of soil that plowing was suppose to break up to enhance plant growth and keep weeds down. That was another all day job in a succession of all day jobs that was farming and led to the thought, "there has to be a better life than this." Summer work in the fields came to priming the

47

tobacco when grown to about six feet in height, when lower leaves began turning from deep green to yellow, signaling that those leaves were ready for curing. Bent over to strip three or four lowest leaves from the stalk, successively stuffing them under my opposite arm led to my aching lower back. Piling the leaves into a narrow sled that Bob pulled, once full, the sled was pulled to the barn where children sat on the sides of the sleds and handed three or four leaves at their stems to women who looped each hand with twine onto sticks about five feet long. Once all the plants had been primed, the field hands came to the barn to begin hanging each stick on the long tiers inside the barn in preparation for several days of heat curing. Loading the barn was done by straddling the tiers beginning at the top of the barn of six tiers in height, where the temperature was likely to exceed 120 degrees on a sunny day. On one of those days I became further convinced that farming was not for me. For about six weeks of late summer, this was the routine; in the fields before sunrise, home by late afternoon, then do it again the next day except Sundays. Then there were the gardens to tend, canning to do, wheat and oats to harvest, hay to bail and pack into Grandpa John's big barn, the orchard... Cows to milk morning and night, and... sorting, grading, and bundling cured tobacco for market was often unfinished by Christmastime.

I liked school, and going to college was an immediately intriguing idea, but how to do that was not at all clear. Uncle Ben told that a new Technical Institute had been established in Winston-Salem, and with costs just $30 each session, I should surely be able to find part-time jobs to pay the tuition. Where to live was another issue, though. He offered to help, and soon I had a letter of acceptance to the Institute and half a room at Mrs. Phelps' boarding house that supplied two home cooked meals each day except Sunday, breakfast and supper that were served to all her boarders on the large table in her dining room.

I was set, but neither of the three drivers I lived with were willing to drive me the hour or so to Winston-Salem. I loaded a nylon flight bag with what I thought I would need and walked up the gravels to the highway and stuck out my thumb, my first hitch-hiking. I was seventeen. Four now occupied our house where five had lived, and when Charlene went off to business college in Lexington, Kentucky, there were three. Johnny was soon to follow for an IBM job also in Lexington. That left Mom and Nick until he finished high school and went off to college. Mom was now there by herself until Jacob, a friend from way back in Berea came along, and they married to live out their lives on the farm.

Mrs. Phelps' boarding house was my new home, but how to get to and from campus remained an issue since I had no car. When Bill from Virginia's Tidewater area arrived as my roommate, another student at the Institute, he brought a small German motorbike with him that became our transportation. My schedule for Mechanical Engineering and his for Automobile Mechanics coincided, and we traveled by his motorbike until he negotiated purchase of Mrs. Phelps's 1949 Ford convertible that sat neglected for years in her garage. That car became his project at school, and within a month or so, he had the car's engine running well, then progressed through the car to make it roadworthy. With the Ford his regular driver, the motorbike became mine as I negotiated with Bill for its use.

That motorbike cost so little to operate that a fill-up lasted a month. I kept it operating properly through that academic year, my long denim coat a great advantage on cold winter mornings. I also borrowed Bill's convertible for the occasional visit with Mary Alice. His work on the engine, however, had left a small water leak that was easily managed by topping off the radiator when needed. The drive to and from school of only a few miles made the leak of no consequence, but on the long drive to and from Mary Alice's home, I carried a ten gallon container of water to top off the radiator about every twenty minutes to avoid overheating. That worked without a hitch, but I had to leave early enough in the afternoon to make it back to Mrs. Phelps' before dark due to the car's poor nighttime lighting that was barely visible. Mary Alice's work schedule fit my driving schedule that gave us only an infrequent Sunday afternoon at her home.

49

Due to working two part-time jobs to pay for school, Sunday was my only day off, and when I could, I wanted to spend them with her, but paying for school and for boarding took income from both jobs with little to spare, my savings rapidly depleting as well. Then, checks of about $36 began arriving each month from Social Security due to my Dad's passing. I did not know Social Security existed until then, but those small checks made it possible to get by and were made to last with spending only a nickel on a pack of nabs, crackers and peanut butter, for lunch when on campus. Saving money for using the motorbike and visits with Mary Alice kept my reserves nearly depleted all the time, but each day seemed to progress into the next. I was getting by.

Toward Christmas, 1964, I resolved to give Mary Alice a gift, my first Christmas gift to her. My only possession was a nicely crafted hunting rifle bought from a gunsmith friend of my Mom's. He agreed to give me what I paid him for it, $60, and all of it was spent on a beautiful pink sweater and matching skirt that I bought in a department store. While shopping for her, I noticed a carved wooden laughing Buddha necklace, an inexpensive item that fit her up-beat, friendly manner that so captured my thoughts of her.

Our opportunities to be together were so limited that, on occasion when I arrived at her home, another suitor was there ahead of me. I kept my distance and never challenged for her hand, thinking that other guys with more means would likely be her choice. I did not know about Joe and Robbie or any of her other suitors until years later, and it was not at all clear that she had deep feelings for me due to her commitment to guard her emotions. I believed, however, that her kisses so passionate expressed her innermost feelings... for me. However, if she did not choose me, I was already comfortable with the notion that her happiness was more important than mine.

Without a single date other than Mary Alice while living at Mrs. Phelps' that academic year, another of her boarders invited me to spend a late spring day one weekend with him at his family farm in Yadkinville. His was a horse family, horses being entirely new to me, so that day was an entertaining learning experience guided by his younger sister. She was pretty, trim, a senior in high school, and enthralled to have a college boy to spend the day with. All around their farm, perhaps ranch being a better description, she took me on riding excursions while telling me all about horses and their equipment. Her vivacious, out-doorsy manner was confidently expressed; she knew what she was doing. That was a day filled with new adventures for me, and as evening shadows grew, her brother drove us back to Winston-Salem while she sat on my lap in the back seat talking to me. As darkness surrounded us, she began kissing me with lavish attention. My immediate thoughts were of betraying Mary Alice, although we rarely dated and had never advanced to going steady or beyond. When his sister and I parted at Mrs. Phelps', she made her interest in me clear. During following weeks, I did not respond to her requests, even those extended by her brother, and soon she stopped trying to get my attention. That day with her so unforgettable caused me considerable anguish; this new girl exploded into my consciousness while Mary Alice's reserved manner was of such contrast that I was thrust into being torn emotionally. My feelings for Mary Alice had already turned protective, and I had unknowingly resolved to never hurt her. That meant no other girls in my life. I stuck with that resolution while wondering if she felt the same toward me because there were other boys in her life.

After classes ended that school year, I returned home and worked for local farmers, and Grandpa John, to gather enough cash to visit with Mary Alice more often, although still fitting her work schedule that usually precluded night time dating. We spent several Sunday afternoons on drives to picnics or for scenery, once to Lake Alpine where my trick diving skills from a spring board allowed me to show off for her. Or, just being together at her home, talking or dancing was our date. On one occasion, I was not able to get the field work done as anticipated and had to hurry to our date, only to arrive significantly late. I had not thought to call to let her know, I just went on to her house. She came to me sobbing. Once again, I was

51

unprepared, especially for such an emotional display. I recognized that I should have called, and apologized, but thought she would be understanding of the circumstances. She voiced worry that something disastrous had happened to me because I had never before failed to be on time, and without a phone call, her imagination had run rampant. My response was simple to me; I was there in front of her, shouldn't that be reassuring?

Later I wondered about her emotional display, having never before seen that aspect of her manner and resolved that her concern for me was real. How I figured so strongly in her thoughts remained a mystery, another mystery that began with our first sight of each other when I did nothing to attract her attention. Was love at first sight actually real? Seemed so. Years later when we reminisced, I asked why she picked me from among all her suitors. Her answer; If there is such a thing as love at first sight, I was that sight for her. She had no other answer and neither did I, but I had learned by then that loving and being loved set deeply within her consciousness was THE purpose of her life. That was all that mattered. I was certainly captured by her, yet always of the mind that many other boys had far more to offer than me, but what anyone had to offer did not matter to her. What felt right to her was entirely the source of her interest in me. Me, a boy she had never seen before that first day, a boy who had done nothing to get her attention, a boy who she was instantly willing to share her life with from that moment, a boy who gave her fulfillment upon first sight. That was story book, love song lyrics. How could that have happened to me?

Mary Alice had been to my home on occasion when she drove her car to see me, and with four of us and Mom in our small share-cropper's house that Grandpa John had built from a store building he bought many years earlier, its careful disassembly the source of materials for building the 4-room house we all lived in. I was concerned that my home would not measure up to hers, a nicely built and appointed farm house that was much larger. She never made an issue of the differences.

On that summer's birthday, 1965, when Mary Alice turned 21, I was yet to turn 19 the following December. Shortly after her birthday, I headed back to the Institute for my second year, again boarding with Mrs. Phelps. Bill's motorbike was again available to me and was in steady use to and from school, to my Monday-Wednesday-Friday afternoon job at the Farmer's Dairy Bar and to my Tuesday-Thursday-Saturday part-time job to closing at Burger King. Usually arriving late, I was concerned about its loud exhaust waking sleepers, so I became adept at negotiating the stoplights to allow coasting from the last one, silently to park in Mrs. Phelps' garage, then into the house.

During September, a date with Mary Alice was another warm Sunday afternoon at her home. Nothing seemed unusual about this occasion, a repeat of some two and half years of our infrequent dating, that became extraordinary when she asked, "Why don't you ask me to marry you?"

Our letters exchanged that spring while I was at college included references to marriage, but nothing approaching a firm commitment, just ideas of what marriage ought to be. Standing there looking into her eyes, I was speechless. Suddenly thrust so unexpectedly into such a serious question, I stumbled for words. "Get Married!?" My thoughts rolled from my mouth; "I'm working two jobs trying to go to college, I can't get married. I don't have anything to offer. I don't even have a car."

Mary Alice looked at me eye-to-eye and said. "I want you."

I knew those eyes, and I knew that she meant every word. Recalling past thoughts, I mumbled, "Maybe after I get through school and get a job... and a house... maybe then. Maybe then."

Still looking me straight eye-to-eye without the slightest doubt, she said, "Whatever happens, we'll do it together."

This beauty looking at me within kissing distance, her light fragrance toying with my senses as usual, making such a statement was more than explosive. I was dumbfounded... and, overwhelmed with wonder; where did that question come from? We had never gotten beyond passionate kissing. I was very much a virile boy thoroughly dialed in with admiration of the female form, but beyond seeing her in a bathing suit at Lake Alpine, I had taken no liberties with her, even with desire for more swirling in my thoughts. *Playboy* foldouts and a vivid imagination were the extent of my involvement with girls, and this one wanted to marry me. "Get married?" I managed to say. "I don't have anything to offer, nothing."

"That's okay," she said. "I'll help."

Ever since a girl in my junior class married, I had been stumped by girls. It was a mystery to me that a mid-teens girl would leave everything she had known throughout her life, her home and her family, for a boy and wander to who knows where with him. Many songs we danced to spoke of love, boys and girls singing about love to each other, that big hit "I Will Follow Him" characterizing many boy-girl relationships throughout time, even her parents' time as told by Zell's travels across America to be with Garvey during wartime, and now, this very thing was happening in front of me. I was not ready to be that boy because I was certain that I could not support Mary Alice in the manner of her life at home to that point. I had no home to take her to, no steady income, no car, nothing.

Ricky Nelson's song that I had sung to Mary Alice and we danced to, "There'll Never Be Anyone Else But You" was how I held Mary Alice in my heart. "A heart that's true and longs for you is all I have to give," is literally all I had to give. I wanted good things for her, and I knew that I could not provide them. I had thought about marriage but considered it well into my future when better prepared to bring a wife into my life. I imagined carrying Mary Alice, a blushing bride as portrayed in movies, across the threshold of a nice home, our home, our love story according to me. She did not see our love story that way; our future was simply love, to fulfill her innermost desire; to love and to be loved, wherever that love might take us, to who knows where did not matter, we would do it together. That was how she saw our future. Mary Alice had taken my rendition of Ricky's lyrics to heart for she knew that I had nothing but aspirations of a future that I

54

talked about. Uncle Ben's advice had taken hold; I wanted a better future, and I knew that it came with education, even if I did not know how to achieve it other than remaining in college. And, by then, Mary Alice was always in my imagined future, but always with better circumstance. Her proposal to me was clear, circumstances did not matter to her. She wanted me, and if I wanted her, that was all that mattered. I did, but I was genuinely concerned that I could not provide for her as I thought a husband should. My own parents' story was known to both of us, a broken home in which Mom had taken on the unending hardships of raising four of her children in conditions that most everyone would regard as poverty. I also had learned from my Mom that perseverance works, that getting by was achievable simply by adhering to honesty with a willingness to work to achieve goals. I had goals; Mary Alice and I often talked about the future that I was positive would unfold while she always reminded me that now, rather than just the future, was important, too.

Her view of our future was to become ours when I agreed to marry. What I did not know was that no one but her knew what was about to happen in her life. Among many admirers and pursuers, Mary Alice had set a secret course to marry me. Why me?

A Big Change

With literally nothing to offer her, her pursuit of me has always been an unanswered question in my mind. To set about marriage so secretively was clearly not the norm as everything I knew about marriage was that her wedding day was the bride's biggest day and lavishly spent upon with extravagance to make it the most memorable day of her life. I did not have the cash to pay for a marriage license; Mary Alice acquired it on her own, knowing that there would be no lavish wedding to remember. The short time from her proposal to our marriage, no more than three weeks, told me that she was committed to our union without question, but I wondered; was I to move into her home or was she to move into my small apartment recently taken with a friend? Neither route seemed do-able or acceptable, and many such questions had no answers.

Why Mary Alice wanted so intently to marry me continued the perplexing question, why me? Any of her other pursuers had more to offer than me, I was certain of that. And, why so secretly? I had notions of an answer; she was fearful that her father would nix another proposal. There may have been doubts in her mind about those past, but now with me, she had fixed her intentions, choosing me for marriage and did so recognizing that secrecy was the only way that her intentions could be protected. I did not recognize what a big change was occurring in her life, an emotional upheaval that was slow to abate once set upon. Yet, Mary Alice had determined her course, wherever it was to take her, her path was with me, a poor college boy. I was certain that I was the poorest of the boys in her life, and the question, "Why me?", remained a topic of conversation for decades to come, and no answer other than love at first was offered.

On Thursday the 1st day of October, 1965, I composed the following letter to Mary Alice, postmarked that day to her home address.

Dear Mary Alice,

So far, everything has lined up really well. Don Annas has talked to his boss who is a preacher, and everything seems to be ready. So, don't forget the license.

Kessler really has troubles. The courts annuled his marriage and he owes all the court costs. Quite a bit. It's all still going and it may turn out worse. But, his ex-wife will be 18 in April, so they will probably get back together then.

The way things have been developing, I feel like we will be just fine. The reason is this: Annas and his wife just bought $700 worth of furniture for the apartment they just rented. To sum it up, he has payments on the furniture, apartment, all other small expenses and keep his car up. If he can keep all this going on her check from Western Electric, I feel sure about us.

I don't think you have a cold any more because I have it all now. I'm not worrying about it; It will probably be gone shortly.

Well, what are we going to do with the girl that is coming with you? She probably wouldn't want to stay at the hospital for several hours. The fair will be here, so if she wants to or if someone comes with her, she (or they) could go to the fair for a while after doing their visiting. Nobody but R. J., Don Annas, and Mr. Fishel know I'm getting married.

If you would like to stay with me longer than the few hours we will have, tell your family that you might go to the fair and that you might be late.

I hope my Social Security check comes this week because I don't have enough money to pay rent and it comes due Oct. 4. I don't see why they have to wait so long anyway.

I'm making a little money from my cars. I sold 1 car and 1 body for $8.00. I've got 2 more bodies in the showcase at Old Town. I have bought another car for $7.00 but I'm going to try to sell it at a profit.

You don't want to read all this stuff so I'll write something that might interest you. You are my one and only love. Both of us are going

57

to try very hard to be the happiest over the thick and thin. And we will
be happy if we do this. Right?... Right!
Be Good
A. Gabbard

The following Tuesday, the 5th, Mary Alice arrived at my apartment with long time friend and confidant, Irma, and her sister who had been asked to be witnesses of our marriage. I was not free of the cold and ran a low-grade fever, sufficient for me later to chide Mary Alice that I was delirious and did not know what I was doing. She saw no humor in that, coming to tears saying that was a sign that I did not really want to marry her. I was quick to learn that Mary Alice had ventured far out onto emotional thin ice with matrimony, especially with me being entirely outside her family's experiences. The secrecy that she had undertaken was not at all like her normal outgoing, care-free, confident personality that I had come to believe was the real Mary Alice. Her newly revealed insecurities were to remain continual sources of tearful interludes as we entered upon our period of adjustment together. Such adjustments ranged from minor to major, the latter especially regarding her father whom she felt deeply that she had betrayed his trust. Not at all comfortable with how he would take her being sneaky and secretive, even dishonest about hiding her marriage from him, her concerns were real to her and soon proved to be real to him.

The five of us, Mary Alice and me, the preacher, Irma and her sister, Lois, gathered at the prescribed time in the preacher's church (my mother having requested that I marry in a church rather than by a JP as was her marriage). Completely naive about marriage, ours being entirely irregular compared to notions of the time, we had made no vows, no rehearsals, no pre-marriage functions, no bridal shower, no fanfare. There was no ceremony, no photos, no celebration... I was down on myself because I thought our proceedings so unfair to Mary Alice. She was so pretty that I imagined her to be a magnificent bride deserving of a celebration long remembered, a celebration that I could not provide, a celebration that she was convinced her father would not provide. This was supposed to be her biggest day and it wasn't. She wore a business woman's suit, not a bridal gown. I wore a cheap, grey suit chosen off the sale rack of a department store. The preacher recited the usual, we kissed at his direction, and then signed on the dotted line. Each "I do" exchanged, in a matter of minutes we were married and walked out of the church to her car, both as quiet as a church mouse; no feelings of celebration because Mary Alice was so fearful of what she imagined was to come. She was convinced that when her father found out, it would break his heart, a feeling that she had never before encountered, now torn between a new life with a husband and a loving father who had always been there for her. Mary Alice was more deeply troubled than I was aware; where was our new life together to take her? Her entry into this new aspect of her life was clearly driven by her love for me and her desire to be with me, that very mystery of the female mind that had befuddled me in high school. I knew that she was giving up everything of her past life for me, and I was not at all sure that I would measure up to her expectations, not realizing that her only expectation was to be loved.

Within the hour, Irma and her sister arrived from visiting a friend in a nearby hospital, and Mary Alice went back home with them. I did not see her again for over two weeks when her work schedule allowed a Sunday afternoon visit. She drove alone, coming to me, then returned to Elkin to her shift at the telephone office as usual. She had not told anyone that she was married. I encouraged her to do so, saying that she should tell her father rather than him finding out by hearsay. She resolved to tell her mother first, whom she was sure would tell her father. That happened, and Mary Alice's life at home changed. I was unaware of just how drastic and emotionally rending the change for her actually was. Our union caused severe repercussions.

The Break Up

Her inhibitions were unlike anything I thought I knew about females, largely gleaned from *Playboy* magazine photos and features I read. I wanted to see Mary Alice like that, for her to be like a *Playboy* bunny. Features I read presented the *Playboy* model as adult behavior with each being a plaything of the other, exciting, fun, and for the female to be sexy, alluring, to show off her beauty as enticements for male attention. Mary Alice had an abundance of alluring qualities, but she had never seen a *Playboy* magazine or any such material due to all things sexual being strictly taboo in her home. She knew that her new life being married involved sex, she was fairly certain how babies were made, but talk of sex or watching sexy movies or showing off sexually was not within her willingness to participate. She had never seen a nude adult male, and my first exposure brought fright; my male organ was so large that she believed me to be abnormal. It took some convincing her that I was normal, but she was not convinced that her anatomy could accommodate me. Our first encounter became bloody and painful for her, so much so that she cried, and I hated myself for hurting her. This was all new to me, too, and my model of a *Playboy* bunny as a wife was unfolding nothing like I thought marriage was to be. Both of us were troubled, much more deeply for her than I recognized, as I continued my routine as best I could.

When Mary Alice told me that she had found a furnished apartment for us in Elkin, rather than a more expensive apartment in Winston-Salem near school, I thought that move to be exactly what was needed, but what was I going to do about school? She had a ready answer; I could drive her car back and forth. The apartment was within two blocks of the telephone exchange, so she could walk to and from work. I did not like the idea of her walking alone at two in the morning, even if a short distance, especially with winter coming on. She had another ready answer; she had requested of her supervisor, Flossie Johnson, to have her shift moved to daytime. That done, I could drop her off at the exchange on my way to school each morning and pick her up afterward

A letter from me to Mary Alice post marked October 29, 1965 included my apartment address in Winston-Salem to her apartment in Elkin. She had moved out of her childhood home. I did not know why, and circumstances of that move were never revealed to me. I wrote:

Thursday Evening
Dear Mary,

You don't know how well your letter has completed my week. I looked for one all week. It is a comfort to read your letters, especially now. I never thought any person could mean so much, or that I could miss anyone the way I miss you. Most people would say that it is not right for a married couple to be apart the way we are, but, I feel like it is a definite asset to be apart because I have learned to really appreciate you and being with you. When you are not here, I can't just walk up to you any time and smile and kiss you and say I love you, so this has helped me not to take you for granted like some people would. I think I have learned the meaning of love and happiness in marriage. Probably not as much as time will teach me, but, I have a very good start. With you in my heart, you can be here or away and I'll be happy, lonesome and blue maybe, but very happy. SHO 'NUF

I hope I will be able to study well when I'm with you. (I know my mind will be on other subjects (you)). Right now, I am top in shop, automation, and metalurgy. I am coming up in electricity and physics. I hope my grades will continue to climb. I'm really proud of them and you must help me stay this way. I think I can be top in my class if I try hard enough. I'm going to try harder, because I want it. Here again you must help me. I will want to have you in my arms all the time; but please don't get mad at me if I study all the time. Now, I am studying from the time I get home until about 11:30 - 12:30. This has resulted in good grades. Top grades means I get the choice job offers, and probably highest starting wages. All these will benefit us, in that we could do and have more of what we want. If you want me to be good

61

in my field, then you must help me. It is for you and myself that I am trying so hard.

Please understand how much school means to me, and please don't ever say I think more of school than I do you. That hits hard and hurts deep.

You are what I have wanted, I want the best for you with much love and happiness.

For the Sweetest Person in the World, My Darling Wife, Good Night
W.A.G.

This change smoothed a number of concerns and worked well, but I had given up my jobs and their income. Mary had to pay for my education for me to continue. Also, I soon learned that marriage brought the end of Dad's Social Security checks. I had no income at all. When I learned that another student drove from Elkin each day, we began carpooling that reduced expenses. Mary Alice had use of her Olds making our situation work even better. Her income and savings were all the financing available to us, and while our togetherness was getting better and better with more time to be newlyweds, our living expenses were a continual source of worry for her.

On a visit with my Mom one day, she had a ready answer of her own; I was now a married man with a wife to support. I should stop school and get a job. With that thought in discussion, Mary Alice would have none of it. I wanted to go to college, and she wanted to help me do that. We would keep on the same track. Her unwavering support of my interests in college, a profession, a career, remained steady thereafter, for which she earned my continual admiration and gratitude. Amid the frequent statements from pricks, that she would work to put me through school, then she would get dumped, were other statements from girls saying they would never do that... husbands were supposed to support their wives, not the other way around. Mary Alice ignored all such warnings although such nagging remained a concern that was held unspoken, concerns that she continually offset with her notions that ours was true love, that we were on a life course together, wherever it was to take us. She knew that she had set our course, saying that she would help me achieve my goals, and she never wavered from that commitment to herself and to me.

During this time a hit radio tune became haunting for me. It's main line, "I'll never find another you..." resonated in my mind. Mary Alice was by far the most unusual girl of my limited experiences, and she seemed completely devoted to me no matter what anyone said. My time was consumed by school, studies at home, and attention to her such that I was completely unaware of the turmoil she was living. She never complained or demanded anything of me, no expressions of expectations other than being a good student. She knew that strategy well from her own academic excellence and its requirements. Even during these deeply troubling times, she revealed nothing of the dramatic struggle that she was quietly enduring until....

Moving into the Elkin apartment on Church Street involved no more than our clothes and personal effects. We had nothing more. Being furnished, Mary Alice and I simply adapted to what was there and began regular rent payments to the two old ladies who owned the house and lived below our apartment. Ours was a rooftop abode with outside entrance that gave us free access. Things seemed to me to have settled into a do-able routine that gave us pleasantries, but Mary Alice was not settled. My first exposure began during a pleasant late afternoon one day just after we moved in. Her kitchen abilities had produced a tasty and satisfying meal, and I offered to clean up, but she declined. Thinking that she would be occupied, I stated that I was going for a walk, then headed for the front door leading across the roof and down the steel stairway. Not yet to the door, Mary Alice tackled me from behind. With her arms tightly around my ankles, her hands grasping my legs, she sobbed.

"Please don't leave me. P-L-E-A-S-E don't leave me!"

My first thought was humorous, that she was acting out a playful melodrama, and that I had to be quick to come up with a

63

suitably playful response. Looking behind me to see that she was face down, prostrate with her arms clutching my ankles and convulsing with sobs, I immediately recognized this quickly unfolding drama to be more than serious.

"What are you doing?" I asked. "I'm not leaving. I'm just going for a walk."

"P-L-E-A-S-E don't leave me. P-L-E-A-S-E. I don't have anybody. P-L-E-A-S-E."

"What are you talking about?"

"Daddy hates me," she sobbed. "Mama doesn't want me around. P-L-E-A-S-E don't leave me. I don't have anybody," she begged again.

This was clearly a drastic situation, my first challenge as a husband, and I did not know what to do. I had never seen Mary Alice so emotional and immediately recognized that an immense upheaval with her parents had occurred. She had not mentioned anything of that sort to me, not a clue, and trying to grasp the moment so beyond my experiences in life, I could only ask, "What has happened?" She would not, or could not answer my question.

"Daddy hates me," she sobbed. "I can't go home if you leave me. I don't have anybody."

Searching myself for reassuring words that fit the moment, I told her, "I'm not leaving you. I'm just going for a walk. Come on with me. Let's go for a walk, okay? You and me, okay? It's a nice day. Let's go for a walk, okay?"

Mary Alice continued to clutch my ankles, sobbing as I grasped for something appropriate to say. Fleeting thoughts ran through my mind, one in particular; I had not been sufficiently reassuring to her that simply going for a walk tipped her insecure feelings into this drama. I had clearly failed my responsibility as a husband. Somehow, I had to reassure her. I slid down the wall to sitting and caressed her hair, patting her shoulders and back, talking to her, saying; "Your father doesn't hate you. Think back, all those stories you've told me about growing up, all the things you did together. All those good memories. Your Dad doesn't hate you."

"Daddy hates me," she sobbed again. "I can't go home anymore."

"Oh, I don't think that's right. I haven't known your Dad long, but I don't think he hates you. I guess that he just wanted more for you than me."

Determination gripped her. Mary Alice got up to her knees, her eyes filled with tears, both hands holding my face, and said, "I love you with all my heart. From the first time I saw you, I always will. I don't want Daddy to hate you, too."

I thought some humor might help, and said, "Oh, I'm sure that he doesn't like it, that his pretty little girl is all grown up and got married, to any boy. None of us were good enough for his little girl. I'm sure he's like a lot of fathers, really picky about their little girls."

Catching her breath, Mary Alice continued to look into my eyes. I hoped that she saw what she needed. All I could think of to say was, "There'll never be anyone else but you."

She snickered and smiled. "I like this Mary Alice better," I said.

She snickered again. I drew her lips to mine. We exchanged deep feelings amid salty kisses, then hugged. "How about we go for that walk, okay?"

The anguish that she presented was clearly deep and entirely unanticipated. She thought for a moment, then said. "I've got to clean up the kitchen. You won't be gone long will you? You will come back, won't you?"

"How about we go for that walk, and I'll help clean up the kitchen when we get back. Okay?"

We went for that walk, holding hands, a nice evening of gentle breezes whipping golden leaves in abundance, and with unusually tight hugs, we kissed again under the low branches of an evergreen.

Our Period of Adjustment

Mary Alice never told me the source of her emotional crash. Not a hint. As I slowly learned who she really was, the person she kept within, I recognized that she just could not utter anything disparaging about her father, and never did. And, she clearly did not want me to harbor any ill will against him. Whatever was said or done, she kept it to herself for the simple reason that she knew the cause, her secrecy, although feeling that she had to be secretive because of what she anticipated would be his response to her marrying me, clearly the poorest prospect among the boys in her life. I was also to learn, as time went on, that she applied that guiding principle to everyone; she would endure whatever barb was thrown at her without ever retaliating, and I quickly learned that even good natured barbs in jest were to be avoided. She saw no humor in jest. Her life at home had always been serious; spontaneous humor was unknown to her. Her crash revealed that her insecurities ran much deeper than I had any reason to suspect. I also learned rather quickly that she was much more sensitive to what people said and did than I thought good for her well-being. She easily saw "signs" of this or that, "signs" that I often opposed as insignificant, meaningless, or just plain normal, ordinary, but her interpretation of those "signs" was always that they pointed to trouble yet to come.

I became aware that her deep need for continual reassurance was firmly set in her religious foundation, troubling to her for her sense that she was violating religious tenets with me. She had heard her father's admonishment to me, that lust was a sin, and whether her interest in me was lust, a sin, or love, as divine; doubts overwhelmed her thoughts; was she a sinner, wicked to love me? If so, did that make her mother wicked for loving her father so much that she traveled across America to be with her new husband when they were young? Were they sinners to love? Did that make love wicked? For Mary, to love and to be loved was her core desire that drove

66

everything else. Love was the ultimate good, not bad or wicked in any way, but deeply troubling doubts lingered due to lifelong teachings.

Her feelings for me brought new ground well beyond comfortable for her, as had been her life at home before me. I was soon to learn that she was as emotionally dependent on me as she had been with her father, a relationship entirely new to me; I regarded marriage as a partnership. I was not at all sure how to handle these revelations of our new lives together and bought a book, *The Ideal Marriage*, that provided many answers to my wondering what happened to the out-going, confident, carefree Mary Alice whom I had come to know with such admiration. Something deeply meaningful within her well-being had been shattered, and I knew that I was the cause.

What I said and how I said it took on new guidelines to avoid another of her "signs". I became convinced that she was scared for the first time in her life, frightened about the unseen future without the protective cocoon known throughout her life before me, afraid that what she had begun in defiance of her father would not continue, that what was ahead would not be as good to her as the life she had known at home, that she had ruined her life for love. It would be years before she was comfortable with the real me, not the imaginary me in her mind, the real me. "Signs" of this or that kept getting in our way.

Reading about The Period of Adjustment gave me insights into what was happening to Mary Alice, but why she was so deeply conflicted had no answer that I could see. What seemed obvious to me was never obvious to her because of doubts, her interpretations of my behavior that were "signs" of.... My own naiveté, not yet nineteen, meant that adjusting to life with Mary Alice was entirely new to me, my own period of adjustment in which her needs were often a hindrance to meeting my schedule of classes, studying, exams and such that involved two hours of travel each school day. Our limited time together was not magical due to the practical needs of daily life, and I was often tired by day's end and unresponsive to her grasping for attention, the source of more "signs."

67

Bed time brought another adjustment. Mary Alice was so pretty, her trim form of such great interest to me, that I always wanted her to parade her natural form for me to admire, for her to be my bunny. She could not do that. Everything sexual embarrassed her. She confided to me that her grandmother had once told her that she had not been naked since her birth, yet she had become a mother. That was how Mary Alice thought she should be, always clothed, nakedness hidden, saying that unwrapping the present was the best part. I was simply entranced with her beauty and wanted to see her bare form, every inch of her. She could not do that. She bought a long white nightie that she thought to be inviting wrappings and willingly paraded before me, rather like fashion modeling, but every attempt to disrobe her was so distressing to her that I soon stopped trying. She did, however, welcome my attention, my caresses, my time with her under the bedcovers, in darkness. Our first encounter having been so frightening to her, bloody and painful, had led to a settling of our relationship with no further such problems, even becoming pleasurable, but I also knew where babies came from.

A *Playboy* feature and other similar sources had instructed me in the rhythm method of sexual activity to avoid pregnancies. That was easy to determine due to Mary Alice's severe cramps that I was continually unable to provide any help to alleviate. Someone suggested that birth control pills would be a benefit to her toward easing her cramps. Once acquired, they did reduce the severity of her cramps, giving her more freedom from her worries that I was unhappy with her. Such pills were new to society and I was not at all certain that she should take them, but they helped. That alone was reassuring.

Being a college student, I kept aware of campus activities and noticed a flyer one day about a dance competition at the armory near campus, a holiday season affair. Mary Alice and I had not danced in some time, and I thought going to such an event would be a good night out on the town for us. She was not enthused, but we put her portable Hi-Fi back into service and practiced our moves, much to the disdain of our landladies who complained about the noise we were making. The day of the competition arrived, and we were entered, Mary Alice with her hair in a pigtail, dressed in a red poodle skirt and a white blouse, red neck scarf, white bobbie socks and saddle oxfords. She was beautiful. What I wore is lost to memory, but I was really proud to get on the dance floor with her. Among the list of tunes available, we selected a Dave Clark Five hit that we especially liked, *Can't You See That She's Mine.* We put on a show like we had danced together forever, great fun, and we won the contest. Our prize was a $25 US Government E-bond. It was worth less when cashed a day or two later, and I spent the money on a fine dinner out with Mary Alice, our first opportunity to dine with a white table cloth and candle light. She expressed fear that we were wasting money that would be better spent paying a bill. I was learning that issues of money were a constant worry for her, a worry that never subsided.

The arrival of the holiday season posed a difficult situation for her; what had always been a happy time was now strained due to having a husband that her parents hardly knew. She gathered her courage with purchase of Christmas gifts as in the past, then wrapped them beautifully to place under the family tree awaiting the arrival of Christmas morning. Rather than spend the night before in her home that would likely not have been received well, we stayed in our apartment and arrived early for the big day, just as a sumptuous breakfast was being served. Both Garvey and Zell were noticeably cool toward me with little conversation, none from him, giving me the sense that my presence ruined their Christmas, but everyone was civil as good will was cheerfully distributed by Mary Alice who treated the day like those past. She made it as much a happy day as could be achieved, and once the gift exchange was completed, we left to go to a similar affair at my home.

Just as I had felt uncomfortable in her home, Mary Alice was uncomfortable in mine, not from actions addressed toward her, but my Mom making it clear that I was not handling my husband duties correctly; I should get a job. Being careful to avoid confrontation with

Mom, Mary Alice assured her that she expected me to stay in school to achieve what I wanted, that she supported my interests. That established, the issue was never discussed again. Charlene expressed her sentiments that getting married so young meant not getting a chance to live. Johnny said nothing, but he noticed Mary Alice and knew that she was his age. That day, Mary Alice became tearful and came to me saying that I was going to be a father. I was not convinced, believing the rhythm method worked in addition to her recently begun regimen of birth control pills that had eased her cramps. My judgment proved correct.

Following Christmas came my birthday that had always been combined with Christmas during years past. Mary Alice baked a birthday cake for me, nicely decorated. I turned 19 that year, 1965, and celebrated with my first birthday cake of memory.

The New Year followed with some bad weather that made living so far from school precarious. I was not able to make it to class on occasion, so we decided that we should relocate to Winston-Salem. Mary Alice found a job as bookkeeper and babysitter for an upscale housing contractor who maintained offices in his large home. This new job allowed her to work quietly and listen to local radio stations. Our new apartment was an efficiency in a complex on Northwest Boulevard within easy driving distance of campus. So, dropping Mary Alice off at her work, driving to school, then the reverse in the afternoon became our new routine. Then, finances gradually dwindled into just getting by day to day.

Living in close contact with a female was not entirely new to me. Growing up with Mom and Charlene in our lightly constructed 4-room house afforded little privacy. Charlene was four years older than me, so our time together to that point was through her high school years and first job that afforded purchase of her Falcon convertible and a beautiful cabinet model phonograph with a selection of long playing albums. What I had learned of female routines day to day was that Mom and Charlene lived rather like I lived, more or less the same.

With Mary Alice, her routine was different; most days were

similar, but each month came some days of cramps, headaches, and "female troubles" that often required quiet bedtime and a blindfold to keep light out of her eyes; migraine headaches. She tried hiding her difficulties and endured quietly for her job and for me, but all I could do was keep things quiet for her. That was a benefit to my studies as I neared finishing, with final exams looming ever larger

As springtime melted away the trappings of winter, an exciting opportunity presented itself on campus one day when a recruiter from the Newport New Shipping & Dry Dock Company arrived. He was signing second year mechanical engineering students into his company's on-the-job Marine Architecture program that paid a salary while including education leading to a Bachelor's Degree in that field. The salary was eye opening, and education, too? I signed on with the firm intention of building warships in Norfolk, Virginia as my career, if we could make it through the next few months and my exams.

One day with no money in my pocket, I went to our apartment for lunch. Holding both doors of the cupboard open, a single can of beans presented itself for lunch. As I thought about having a third for lunch, leaving two-thirds for Mary Alice and me for supper, I wondered what we were going to do for food until her Friday payday. As I stood there, I heard a car come to a stop at the curb outside, two doors slam, and the voices of a man and woman talking glibly. The thought crossed my mind, "Wouldn't it be odd if they came to my door?"

Footsteps became louder, and the knock at my door startled me into wonder, "Who could that be?"

Opening the door to a nicely dressed young woman and man, she asked if I might be Alex Gabbard. My affirmative answer brought a huge smile and her raised voice asking, "How does it feel to win a thousand dollars?" I thought this a ruse of some sort, some kind of sales gimmick, until she presented me a sheet of notebook paper that I recognized.

Mary Alice listened to radio station WTOB, Thirteen-Eighty, that was broadcast just a mile or two away. The station began a contest of giving listeners cryptic clues daily that described a villain's hideout somewhere within the city. Whoever was first to discover the hideout would win $1,000 cash. She thought it worth a try and wrote down each clue that we discussed in the evenings, then drove around trying to match the clues to what we saw. I had written our findings on that sheet of notebook paper, stuffed it into an envelope addressed to the station, and forgot about it until seeing it again.

Time slowed down to a crawl. They whisked me to the station for interviews that were broadcast during following days, presented me with a check for $1,000, took photos, along with handshakes and congratulations among station personnel. I told the lady who had presented me with the news my bean story. Her reply was that she was pleased that their money went to a needy couple. I did not think of Mary Alice and me as needy, we were just doing what it took to get by. She delivered me back to our apartment, and once in Mary Alice's F-85, I arrived on campus with time to spare before classes resumed after the lunch break.

Discussion among classmates was about the contest, a very popular invention by the radio station. I sat listening, then said, "I know where the hideout is" and said so. No one agreed, but when I showed the check, everyone was dumbfounded. The instructor had arrived by then, and he was so enthused by my winnings that he called off our next class to discuss investments and the stock market, saying that thousand dollars invested would grow into many thousands of dollars over time. I did not mention that I had no lunch, with a few beans my planned supper to be shared with my wife with nothing left in our cupboard afterward. Memory of the remainder of that afternoon is lost in the blur of time, until I picked up Mary Alice at her office. We rode home quietly as I thought through various scenarios to find the most fun way to tell her, until she said, "I heard you on the radio."

Rats! My planned fanfare when presenting her with the surprise was spoiled, more so than I realized. She was serious. That was a turn that took me by surprise. "Were you going to tell me about it?" she asked. My presenting no jubilation was taken as a sign of alternate intentions. "Of course," I reassured her. "I just wanted to make a big deal of it. We don't have to worry about money now."

Our evening was quiet, no celebration. We had beans for supper that night because we had no cash for anything else, and I had studies. The next morning, we went into the day without breakfast. During the lunch break, I deposited the check and went shopping to re-stock our cupboard. That weekend, the first thing we bought was a black and white Magnavox portable TV that was to go with us for years to come. It cost less than eighty dollars, and after groceries, the balance of our winnings remained in our bank account.

I was unaware that Mary Alice was unhappy with her job that included babysitting her boss' tattle-tale spoiled brat who produced confrontations. She applied for and was immediately hired by a downtown insurance company located in a large office building. Her new job suited her much better in that she was around other young women who brought her into their group, including their socializing that included lunches in local restaurants. This kind of camaraderie was reminiscent of her high school good times and contributed to improving her well-being, the happiest that I had seen her since our marriage.

With her increased income and a sizable bank account, our lives changed. We were the most free in spirit that we had been in our half year together. I was thoroughly pleased that my future seemed to be working out to my satisfaction, a good paying job waiting for me with more education to boot, money in the bank, and a beautiful wife whose worries seemed to have subsided with a job that she was happy with. It paid $260 each month that went to $285 per month after six months, the most income that Mary Alice had ever had.

The next day, after picking her up at the entrance to the tall building where she worked, our newly acquired sense of financial freedom began leading to all sorts of outings together in and around Winston-Salem. Her Oldsmobile proved to be excellent transportation

73

requiring little maintenance, and we discovered new attractions as our togetherness took us on a variety of outdoor pursuits, although any of them requiring extensive walking or exertion were of no interest to her, another thing I learned about her. Short, leisurely walks were okay, but no hiking, nothing physically challenging. However, our period of adjustment had smoothed into routines that were comfortable, her job and my school, that looked to be a good interim until our anticipated move to Norfolk. Our world was expanding and included my continual interests in college activities and, especially, cars and racing.

Drag racing at Farmington and other drag strips the previous summers were entirely new to Mary Alice and gave us more long remembered weekend adventures. At Farmington, our chosen spot in the bleachers for spectators was the top row at the corner overlooking the entrance to the paddock where I could see action in the pits, the staging lanes, and the starting line. On one bright Sunday, I heard a rumble below us and looked down upon a silver 427 Cobra pulling to a stop on a patch of grass at the end of the bleachers just before the gate leading into the paddock. Instantly intrigued, I recognized the driver, Zac Reynolds, whom I had gotten acquainted with as a college boy tagalong during motorcycle outings. He had shown interest in Bill's German motorbike.

That low-slung, silver roadster had magnetism. I was drawn to it like no other car I had ever seen. This was my first Cobra, my initiation to the top of the mountain. That was a time when every American nameplate sold muscle cars that could turn 15 second quarter-miles with just a little tweaking beyond showroom. So, picture a paddock filled with loud, fast cars of all sorts, all of them with big cubic inch engines with open pipes blasting down the strip with thundering basso profundo sounds amid billowing clouds of staging lane tire smoke, the scene during the time when Jan & Dean and the Beach Boys and their car songs heard regularly on radios were the rage. Then there was that tense moment as the flagman held everyone's attention just before he flashed the green flag (there were

74

no staging lights in those days). THAT was an exciting era, a time before flopper style funny cars, a time when A/FX (A/Factory Xperimental) cars were the big guns. They were the cars anyone could buy through a dealer and go racing. Such youthful imaginings did not include the cost of racing and the time commitment - very different than being a spectator. All this was new to Mary Alice, a step far beyond her sheltered life before me, but following me was her new life and drag racing proved to be memory making. Racing became a new adventure for her.

I had known Zac for about two years and immediately recognized the car as something really special. I just had to see that car up close. It was silver, black inside, chrome side pipes, fat tires on sensational cast alloy wheels with real spinners. We exchanged greetings, then he walked off with a flick of his hand to close the driver's door. It did not close, then slowly swung open as if greeting me with, "Come on big boy. I'll take you for a ride." While I continued to admire the roadster, Zac returned with the track promoter. Zac raised the hood to reveal... two 4-bbl carbs on 427 cubic inches. What a sight! I was impressed and continued to be impressed with growing numbers of stories that began that day, stories about Zac and his fast Cobra.

Zac Reynolds was a millionaire, an heir to the R. J. Reynolds Tobacco Co. fortune. He lived a life of total freedom from workaday that most of us only dream about. That roadster, the ultimate in my mind, became the subject of many stories making him legendary among us motorheads in the area. Another set of stories emerged from the Reynolds family estate, a huge tract of mountain terrain with a stately house located about twenty miles from my home, about mid-way to Mary Alice's home. When Zac stayed there, he frequently shattered cool mornings by "qualifying" the Cobra down the narrow country road to a little store about a mile away. It was win or break against the nothing more than patches of low-lying fog. That's the way Zac was; he lived very fast.

75

He launched out of the Reynolds estate, then hammered a ninety degree left across a little bridge followed by an abrupt ninety degree right, that 427 engine bellowing its announcement to the morning. Arriving at the store, he'd slide sideways into the lot, spraying gravel and pop bottle caps everywhere, then spin the thing around a time or two just to let everyone know he had arrived. Shutting down the Cobra, Zac would saunter into the store for breakfast, usually an RC and a Moon Pie.

Many such stories accompany Zac's Cobra, CSX3038. His Snake was meant to go fast, and Zac drove it that way. He was the gunslinger with the fastest draw and, so far as I know, he was never outrun. Shortly afterwards, he met an untimely end in a light plane crash, and I lost track of the car even though I tried several times to locate it in hopes that it could be mine.

Among that sort of warm weather activities with cars, Mary Alice and I frequented local dealerships to admire showroom models. With our earnings settled and our winnings insuring some degree of financial freedom, our showroom visits took on new interests; the notion that one of those beauties could be ours steadily grew in our ambitions.

By then, with my future as a Marine Architect secure, I imagined Mary Alice and me tooling around Norfolk in our own E-Type Jag. Those that we looked at were expensive, but I was certain that one was worth the stretch to own such a beautiful car. Mary Alice agreed; she liked those roadsters, too, but all that money...? My assurances of our future getting better and better were not entirely reassuring when money was the topic.

One day during a revisit to our local Sunbeam dealership, we gazed upon a red Alpine and a white Tiger on display. I was intrigued by the Tiger with its V-8 engine sure to be an exhilarating performer in league with the E-Type but much less costly. While I imagined the two us motoring along in a Tiger as shown in posters on the dealership's walls, Mary Alice imagined us motoring along in a red Alpine. When she said, "I've always wanted a red sports car", that

76

sealed the deal. With papers signed and her perfectly suitable Oldsmobile traded, for payments of $72.79 each month, she became owner of that roadster. That day, May 6, 1966, she drove it off the lot the proud owner of a snazzy British roadster that was to take us on adventures far beyond our wildest dreams.

Better Times

With our new roadster parked outside our apartment, our cupboard full, her job rewarding and keeping pace with monthly expenses, we were getting by nicely as newlyweds with anticipation of our move to Norfolk. Our period of adjustment seemed to be resolving issues as we began participating in weekend car activities beyond drives to no place in particular, just another drive together in our new car. Then, our first outing at a car gathering produced a concern. On this springtime picnic that involved other sports car owners, mostly young couples, we arrived in Tanglewood Park to enthusiastic greetings and compliments about out new roadster. Upon exiting the car, Mary Alice stood for a moment listening to the enthusiastic welcomes, then said, "I'm ready to go."

"What?" I responded. "We just got here."

"I'm ready to go," she repeated.

I managed to convince her that we should stay and enjoy the day, make new friends and such, but she was noticeably uncomfortable. I never learned why, only concluding that she was ill at ease among people that she did not know, perhaps an artifact of her upbringing. That seemed odd to me; she had never mentioned anything similar about her jobs, the people she worked with, or the people I was associated with at school or work, our dances. I was stumped, leading to asking what concerned her. Her answer was another puzzle; "There were pretty girls there... I don't want to share you... I want to put you in my pocket and take you with me... just to look at you...."

I was learning more about the real Mary Alice and thought of her timidity as one of her charms, the sort that brought hugs and kisses as reassurances, occasions for me to recite my favorite ditty; "There'll never be anyone else but you for me."

As our period of adjustment continued through the end of that school year, she slowly became more at ease to the extent that our weekend outings were anticipated fun things to do. We were enjoying our snazzy roadster and the culture it brought, including gatherings for long weekend drives with groups that a local Mercedes dealership hosted.

Our springtime had become fun, until a letter arrived one day. Reading it, I sat down with a new load of concern. I was to report for examination. I had been drafted into the Army at a time when televised evening news about the Viet Nam conflict told of increasing numbers of body bags and downed helicopters. Mary Alice cried.

The good life that we had just entered upon came crashing down. That summer was a repeat of the summer before; car activities, drag racing, outings and picnics with other young couples, her job and my work once out of school, but with heavy overtones. My phone call to the Newport News Shipbuilding and Dry Dock Company, thinking that job would likely exempt me from the draft, came to a disappointing end; my name was not on their list of employees. Explaining that their recruiter has signed me on to join their program of work and education came to nothing; the lady I talked to had no such information. That exciting opportunity was suddenly a dead end, and I resolved that my dead end was waiting for me in the jungles of Viet Nam.

During examination day, I looked at all the young men in our white skivvies lined up in front of a drill sergeant type examiner and imagined that some of us were near to the end of our young lives, to end in a place far away, far from everything we knew. My own fate, too. The turn of events for me was so dramatic that I approached this new future for me with dread.

Being a two year college boy, I was instructed to talk with a recruiter who told me that I was perfect for flight school. Just sign the paper he presented to me, and I would be guaranteed training as an officer in the Army. When he answered my question about what would I fly, a Huey Cobra, I recognized that such a gunship meant jungle warfare, the same that was reported during evening news broadcasts about downed helicopters. I did not sign. Instructed to talk

79

to the Marine recruiter, I was told that I was perfect for the Marine Corps that was looking for a few good men. Both recruiters gave the same pep talk to get us newbies to sign up that day. Again, I did not sign.

Upon returning to the recruiting station very late that night, I called Mary Alice to come pick me up. When she arrived, concern was in her voice. I told of signing nothing and that I was given no idea of how long I had until having to go in the Army. On the way to our apartment, a large dog leaped from the darkness. Mary Alice drove our little Sunbeam into direct contact. The next morning, I removed the bent bumper and noticed some front end sheet metal damage. Why we did not get the car repaired was likely caught up in resignation to a military assignment that could arrive any day. That heavy overtone was to cloud everything we did that summer. I worked a full time job waiting for the notice, and, it arrived, telling me to report for the draft on a specific date in October.

With such promise of being in Norfolk learning to be a Marine Architect... that date so ominous to me meant somber hours slowly passing toward my fate. I had no choice. Mary Alice stuck close to me during our evenings and tried to hide her tears. I noticed.

While we sat watching television the Tuesday evening twenty days past our first anniversary, with no memory of celebration having taken place, our phone rang.

"Is this William Alexander Gabbard," a man's voice asked.

"Yes."

"Are you still interested in joining the Navy?"

Instantly recalling my attempts to volunteer for the Air Force and the Navy, neither with open billets, I was heartened. "Yes!" I answered.

"If you can be at the bus station at seven in the morning, I have a billet open. One of my recruits is in the hospital... wrecked his car. If you don't want his billet, I'll contact other..."

"I'll be there!" I said with enthusiasm, leaping at the prospects of avoiding the Army and Viet Nam.

80

Our evening instantly changed for me, a most favorable turn, but Mary Alice endured her anguish with silent resolve; into whatever uniform, I was leaving her, the most dreaded outcome for her... to be alone, alone into coming months. That evening could not have had more contrasts for us; I was exhilarated, certain to be avoiding a death sentence; Mary Alice was forced into facing her worst fears. The next morning, we got to the recruiting station about half an hour early, and I checked in to make sure that I had the billet. I did, and before climbing onto the bus, I gave Mary Alice hugs and kisses, saying that I would stay in touch. She was nearly in shock at this sudden turn of events so drastic; worst of all, I was leaving her.

I took a seat by a window, lowered it, and continued to say reassuring things to her, but I could tell that she was devastated, tears streaming down her face. Standing quietly looking at me, unable to speak, her lip movements a simple "I love you" was our parting. I smiled and waved, our eyes in constant contact until the bus motored away. The sight of my beautiful Mary Alice thrust into the very thing she feared most remained a lasting memory.

She had never been alone. Endeared to her protective father while growing up with abundant good memories and now me that was emotionally rocky from the outset of our marriage, she was entirely on her own for the first time. Getting into the Navy was an enormous relief for me, but I knew that she was thrust into what was for her a host of foreboding unknowns. Neither of us had family locally for support, and we had made no friends sufficiently bonded for her to call upon. She was still convinced that her father hated her, her mother not wanting her around.... What was she to do but face each day without me?

Once in San Diego, day after day was filled with things every Navy recruit was ordered to do, marching hither and yon, tests and training with little time available for anything else. At lights out, each day was done, and we were tired. As soon as I was able to make connections, such as my new address, Mary Alice and I began exchanging letters. I was in sunny southern California in Basic

81

Training that was little more than a four month vacation for me, and I constantly imagined that those same four months were far more than difficult for her. I also recognized their benefit to her in building her confidence that she really could make it on her own.

In my first letter to her, post marked 31 Oct, 1966, I wrote:

San Diego, Calif.
Saturday [29 October]
Dear Mary Alice,

Please excuse me for not phoning you tonight, but I'm not going to be able to phone anybody for about 6 more weeks. I came into San Diego Wednesday about 1:30 am your time, all the other guys on my list at Raleigh went to Chicago. It wasn't very cold there (70°) but it will get colder later. There are 56 in my platoon. We have been assigned everything but uniforms which we will get Monday.

All we have done up to now is march and eat, marching taking the most part. My Company C.O. is a Chief Petty Officer Smith, directly under him is a Seaman Apprentice Baggett, both being pretty good guys. We haven't been hollered at much, which seems to [be] quite different [from] all other drill officers.

In the last week, I have come 2460 miles. That's quite a distance between us. As it stands now, I don't think that I will be home for Christmas. We will have training up into January, then we will be shipped out to various posts. We won't [know] where we will go until we graduate from basic training. I plan to take some correspondence courses where ever I am. I don't even [k]now what I will be doing, job that is.

I don't have much time so I will have to close for now. I am in the Navy for 4 years only and I don't plan to enlist for any more unless I can get my commission as an officer.

Take care and sleep well tonight because I will be thinking of you.
William Alex Gabbard
B323862   638-16

USNTC San Diego, Calif. 29133

Another letter written 31 October but postmarked 2 November included:

... I just got called down this afternoon for smiling; all the other guys say I have the same expression all the time; my face feels the same as it always did; so I've got to remodel my mouth, or get called all the time. (Funny how you always wanted me to smile, now with the same expression I get chewed out for smiling.)

... you probably want to know what the Navy is like, so here goes.

Up every morning at 4:00 AM

Dressed, bunk made up with everything in its place in 15 minutes. March to the chow hall for breakfast. Eat in less than 10 minutes and run back to our position and fall in at attention. March to get our cloths (only ones while we are here.) Take 3 hours to get them, try them on, count them all. March over to the print house with these (75 pounds). Spend 3 hours and 15 minutes to put our names on, march to lunch and/or go to class... march everywhere.

Go wash clothes;

go clean up:

and; and; and; and. You name it, we do it.

...Sleep well tonight because I'm thinking of you.

Here's loving you. Be Good

W.A.G.

P.S. Please excuse my first letter. I had 6 min.

My letter of 7 November was another short scribbling, only:

Sunday 6

Dear Mary Alice,

I think you are the sweetest most wonderful person in the world.

Be Good and Keep Pretty for me
W.A.G.

In my letter composed on the 7th day of November and post marked the 9th, I wrote:

Dear Mary Alice,

I received the cookies and book this evening. I had to go to battalion headquarters to open it. The petty officer in charge made me throw the book away. I only ate one of the cookies because he decided the can would take up too much room in the locker. (The RCPO of my company said to tell you they were good. He went with me to H.Q.) So, if you would like to send me another small package of anything you wish to send. The cookie was very good.

I found out today that I am listed as Seaman Recruit High School instead of Seaman like Chief Keller said I would be. That means less money. So, I'm going to try for a hardship discharge if my rate don't change quick. This place bothers me; and all the petty shit everybody slings around here is about to gripe me. But, I'll try to stick it out for a while.

I think you are very sweet to send me cookies, but I still haven't received a letter. (I think we will pass in the mail.)

Would you send me some Air Mail stamps. I have only 2 stamps left which I'll use on this letter.

We go on schedule tomorrow, meaning I have about 9 or 10 more weeks which will be over sooner than we expect. We'll have our first inspection tomorrow morning for initiation. Everyone is in a great havock, but it will be over.

One of these days I'm going to surprise you with a letter you can understand . With all this noise I can hardly think much less write.

Be good and stay pretty for the man that loves you with all heart. And I do. W.A.G.

On the 9th of November, I wrote:

84

Dear Mary Alice,

You know, it makes a person feel very good to know that someone loves you, and that they always are thinking of you. I received 9 letters today and they all said the very same thing, that you love me, wish I were there, you want to hold and kiss me or just to see me. This all made me very proud to have you....

In one of her letters, Mary Alice wrote of being startled to open the door to our apartment one day to two stern Army MPs. They were there to arrest me for being AWOL, that avoiding the draft was a serious offense subject to prosecution. Her explanation that I was in San Diego in the Navy was not well received and that I was subject to prison time for not doing my duty. She countered that I was doing my duty, to their disbelief, and continued explanations took her to tears, whereupon they left with a stern warning that I was in deep trouble. I took her letter to the legal branch on Base where the officer I talked with laughed heartily, saying, as usual, the right hand did not know what the left hand was doing, and that he would take care of it. That was the last we heard from the Army.

Her letters were disturbing because I envisioned her wasting away with heartaches for me. Our separation was much more difficult for Mary Alice than I realized, as expressed in deep emotions that I envisioned leading her deeper into.... All I should have written to her was reassurances, instead I berated her to be strong. She expressed deepest love for me in the most vibrant words that she knew; I should have responded in kind, but I used my example of having to reply "Yes Sir" in all cases regardless of what I thought without recognizing that she had the same challenge; having to put up with what she did not want.

With my loss of income to a paltry military salary, her finances soon forced a change; she moved in with a roommate in a nearby apartment to help defray the costs. With another girl, Debbie, to share living time together, she was finding her own way for the second time in her life, and it was working. I wanted Mary Alice to send me photographs of her without letting her know that I was looking for reassurances that she not wasting away, and Debbie took camera in hand to do just that with a sequence of photos that Mary Alice sent to me.

As Thanksgiving passed into the Christmas holidays of 1966, having known Mary Alice since introduction during March of 1963, my sage advice for other recruits thinking of marriage was more along the lines that dating and marriage were very different; what was kept hidden while dating was revealed in marriage. During those discussions, a notion began to form in my mind that would not mature until years later. Our first year together had progressed beyond newlyweds toward a relationship that the guys thought admirable, especially since I told of having a flashy sports car and an eye catching wife who continually sent tasty treats. My status as a college guy among other recruits remained high, especially being selected Color Guard Regimental Commander with a voice part in the graduation ceremony when all the training companies gathered on a huge parade ground and marched before the brass and a crowd of visitors.

I had done well on the tests administered early on to determine best fit in the Navy and became exempt from normal duty upon being assigned to Color Guard. This duty involved marching, marching, marching in preparation for graduation ceremonies. Along the way, I had occasion to investigate my rating as a seaman and was promptly elevated to Seaman-JC (Junior College) due to my two years that brought a modest increase in salary. Arranging for most of it to be sent to Mary Alice, I believed that I was doing my part as much as I could.

Early on the 10th day of November, a Thursday, I wrote to her noting my concern for having written things that caused her anguish. I was learning more about her and myself, particularly that being dictatorial did not help her, and neither did lavishing my feelings of love for her because the day to day practicalities of her life kept getting in the way. She wrote of bills to pay and no money to pay them and how she was being squeezed for payments. Citing the Soldiers and Sailors Civil Relief Act that was supposed to keep debt collectors away did not help. That was her reality. I tried to help financially, and wrote that;

I filled out your allotment papers today. It will be at least 6 weeks before [you] receive anything. You'll get $55.20 a month plus $10.00 from my check. I'll be paid $90.60 on payday. The way it is set up here is that you get $40.00 of the total (leaving $50.60). I'll receive $35.00 and have to pay $25.00 for the personal articles the Navy supplied (leaving $15.60 which the Navy will hold until my graduation, to keep me from spending all I'll make.) All paydays will be like this. When I finish up I'll receive $46.80 savings from the Navy to help in traveling. If I'm to be stationed anywhere around here, I may not get to come home at all, because they'll pay only to my next duty station (based on miles.) I don't know where I'll go as yet, so we'll just have to wait and see what develops. (It'll cost almost $300 to get to and from N.C. from here.)

Tomorrow is Armed Forces Day here, so we may not have to do much. It'll be a sleep in for the morning; we get to sleep all the way up to 5:00.... We just got chewed out for not having this place cleaned up it's 7:40. Got to get to work.
Be Good and Stay Pretty for me.
W.A.G.

That evening, I sat down to write a letter of apology to Mary Alice for berating her. Some of the guys had helped me see better, that her expressions of love and caring for me was special, the sort that they hoped to find... and always described as such a beauty! And, a beauty who was a terrific cook who loved me and liked cars and racing, too!! What more could any man want? Mary Alice had never been to a race or around racing cars before me, the very things that interested me the most. I brought her into the car scene with young friends having fun with their cars. She was uncomfortable at first as

87

noted earlier, but weekend after weekend of drag races among loud, beautiful cars amplified by the steady blare of the announcer's voice was infectious. Radios constantly playing the Beach Boys and Jan & Dean with their car songs, also cited earlier... that was all in our past. They were the good times, new and exciting adventures, and we were in the middle of it. Now there was no money for fun. I knew from her letters that she was deeply troubled, and I was not helping. With genuine concern for her well-being, I wrote;

Dear Mary Alice,

Last night I wrote you a letter that I am rather ashamed of. I always feel bad after writing like that because you are so delicate and so full of love for me, but, if you would only think like me we could be so much happier. Both of us have plenty of love for the other, but it seems that our thinking is so different that it always causes a conflict.

Myself, my lips and my body is just as far from you as yours is from me. I'm lonesome, too.

I know I seem very head-strong, and set in my ways to you, but I do enjoy life more than you do. And life is so short that you may cry yourself out of any reason for living. One of these days you are liable to find yourself left behind because you weren't ready for it when an exciting life came your way.

I am not everything in your life but I do love you and that alone should be enough to make you glad to face another day each morning.

In the Bible there is a statement like: "He helps those who help themselves."

You can take care of yourself, so why don't you try. Don't wait for someone else to make you smile. Just Be Good and Enjoy Life, you only get one.

Take care of yourself. Please Be Happy.
W.A.G.

My concern for her prompted five letters to Mary Alice post marked the 10th and 11th. In one of the 11th, I wrote in part:

... I know you are feeling lonesome and kind of blue right now so I'll try to make you feel better by saying I wish I could hold you for just a minute... it does make me feel better to think of the fun we've had together. I'm hoping that this absence the Navy is providing will help us to become closer together, because we have too much in common to let ourselves become married enemies like we were for a while. I think I could cherish you, your feelings and your body 'till the end of time if we could have more trust and faith and allow each other to live his own life.

I enjoy the fun and love with you and I hope we can have it for the rest of our lives.
Be Good & Stay Pretty for me.
W.A.G.

Remembering her attitude toward me that was expressed frequently in telling me what I was not, a sticking point in our adjustment, I countered her comparisons of me to her father by defending, saying that I am just a husband, that I could never be her father. She seemed never to understand that, and I further defended saying that it was my intention to be a good husband, but husband and wife could never be the same as father and daughter. Her intentions were expressed in saying, if I would just... a "sign" of this or a "sign" of that, each being uncomfortable predictors deeply troubling to her. I believed that I was doing all I could, and it was never enough, but I remained completely captured by her, her ever loyal.... Later that day, just before lights out, I composed another short letter saying in part:

... I think of you about all the time. I find myself feeling your nude body gently against mine when I'm thinking. Sliding my hands over your superb body and feeling greatness in your passion and

beauty. The tenderness of your touch and majesty of the feelings
conveyed offers only the finest in love.

It's bed time now, so I think I'll retire with a dream of you.
W.A.G.

The reality of greatest concern for Mary Alice was that love did not pay the bills. Regardless of what I said or wrote, she saw the "signs", that she would soon be unable to pay her own way, and she had no one to turn to. By mid-November, she faced a stark reality; her only recourse was to mend her relation with her father and ask for his help. Knowing that he had no means for supporting her financially, she resolved to move back home. We had been married well over a year on our own, but the drastic changes due to my military life clearly showed that I could not support her. Our income simply was not enough to pay the bills. I had done everything I could, but it was not enough. Even letters from the Navy to creditors did not help. Mary Alice had kept her job and pared down expenses to bare bones... there was nothing further that either of us could do.

I wrote to her saying that I would graduate on the 2nd day of February (1967) and that it would take 3 to 5 days to make arrangements for departing San Diego, although I still did not know where I would be stationed after Basic. What that meant was clear; she was on her own for months to come. Moving back home was her only choice, and that choice went surprisingly well. She wrote that her change of address would take place early in December.

Changes in her outlook were expressed in her letters. I responded on the 16th, a Wednesday, writing:

Dear Mary Alice,

Today, I received a letter and a package of cookies. And I think you're wonderful, you're the greatest, you're the sweetest, and I adore you with a love I never knew I had. You've made me the happiest I've ever been. You write that you are gaining weight back and that you are growing up and accepting life; and I'm thinking you

90

have decided to love me without question or doubt. I hope I'm right. You write that you are sorry about what you have said in your letters, I accept it graciously; but you'll never know what you did to me. I'm also sorry about what I've written but, all I've ever wanted from you is a love pure and simple. You've never given me this; it's always been so cluttered with your expectations.

I know it's been [a] big change for you but you didn't even try for a while, I hope I've given you reason to. About the car, just let it go and I'll see what I can do when I get home.

Dearest one, my love is strong and pure, so please keep it worth giving. You're with me always, I just wish I could touch you. My heart is filled with joy to know you wait. You are my love, my life. Care for it tenderly.
Be Good, Be Strong, and Believe
W.A.G.

My letter of the 18th, a Friday included musings about my Navy future.

...I still haven't chosen what field to go into. Everything that will benefit me and our future is 6 years. I've decided against the Nuclear field, but there is one I like. It's called Data Systems Technician. They teach how to operate, maintain and repair all the workings of electronic computers. This would be a good field to know if someone wanted a top training. The A School is 32 weeks long for Electronics Technician then advanced school is 42 weeks for Data Systems Technician. I seem to be qualified for everything the Navy has to offer, but I want to make a choice you will be satisfied with because you'll be with me. For the length of time I would be in training you could go to school too, and I wish you would sometime anyhow, because I love you and I want you to have the life you are made for. Such beauty shouldn't be wasted in a slaving life.
Good Night and Be Good
W.A.G.

91

I had decided only four years in the Navy was for me, and during Basic one day, we recruits were to chose three ratings that we would like to pursue, presumably to get one of them. I expressed interest to my interviewer that I wanted to be assigned to the Naval Research Laboratory in Washington, thinking such an assignment would advance my education and experience. Anything at the Lab was acceptable to me. However, choices had to be made from those presented to us, and NRL was not among them. My second choice was anything scientific, anything that involved more education. That led to the most unusual interview of my Basic Training.

I was instructed to meet with Mr. John Smith at a particular building for an appointment. A reason was not given. When I opened the door, the rush of cool air in my face, air conditioning, told me that I was in the wrong place. Saying so to the young receptionist dressed in civilian attire furthered my conclusion, as I continued to hold the door knob in hand with the door ajar. She asked my name, then looked at papers on her desk and said, "Yes, Mister Gabbard. You're in the right place. Come in, have a seat. Mister Smith will see you in about twenty minutes."

Seated in a nicely appointed civilian office flipping through an assortment of magazines was immediately odd to me, and I had no idea why I was there. When she got my attention again and instructed me to the second door to the right down a hallway, I entered to another civilian, a man in suit and tie who stood up and stuck out his hand. "Mister Gabbard," he said. "Come in. Have a seat."

For the second time in twenty minutes, I was referred to as Mister. That was strange, not at all typical of Basic Training, and as we talked, he wanted to know about me, my interests and background. We talked for about an hour, I was presented with nothing to sign, and as I walked back to my barracks afterward, I was mystified. What was that all about? What came of it, I reasoned later, became illuminated when I was told to gather all sorts of documentation for a background investigation leading to a security clearance. No one else in my company had such an experience, and I still did not know why.

A follow-up letter written to Mary Alice on Saturday the 26th included more possible choices of Navy training. One, Gunner's Mate Technical, I described as;

...The job is to maintain, operate and repair high level electronic systems for tracking, training on and firing at moving objects with guns, missiles & rockets, with much emphasis on the repairing and building of atomic warheads... as high as I can go in Navy education without signing on for 2 additional years.... I have to have a security clearance....

That last item included a long list of needed documentation about our lives and my mention that F.B.I. would be canvassing everyone we had ever known. That began a sequence of events that set me on an entirely different course.

Each of my letters to Mary Alice included expressions of my love for her, to the extent of saying that I was entirely hers. That was to last through the years and beyond, and now with this writing of recollections, reading half-century old letters and remembering, many photos to draw upon, my memories are as fresh and vivid as when made. To me, Mary Alice was the "you" that I would never find again, as the hit song told, "I'll never find another you"; perfectly proportioned, beautiful, and.... Her trim size seven form of five feet six inches and about one hundred pounds was near flawless perfection, with only a single birthmark hidden on the back of her neck at the base of her hairline. It was never an issue.

But she had so little self-confidence, with fears continually working against her, even with my continual reassurances. I remained concerned but did not know what to do more than I was doing. My hope was that my continual out-pouring of love for her would be up-lifting. She had so many doubts, her "signs", that kept her constantly disturbed with trouble, mostly imagined, but real on occasion, especially medical issues. I believed the changes expressed in her letters were indications of gradually freeing herself from the

93

emotional strictures that she did not know that she had live with her entire life. Her emotions tied to imagination remained a lingering source of tribulations for her.

On the last day of November that year, 1966, I wrote to her:

Dearest Sweet Baby,

Well, here I am again, thinking of you and writing the same things. I seem to have a one track mind about these things, but I forsee our future with much happiness. I desire this, and I'm sure you do to. My thoughts see us in the freshness of springtime, when all life is alive with love, we are always smiling and joyful. I really am proud to have you and your love; you can give me such wonderful feelings.

There is not much more I can write to express my love. So I must say good-night for I am writing in the dark.

Be Good & Sleep Well My Love. The happiness of life and love is yours.

W.A.G.

All of my frequent letters to Mary Alice were, by now, love letters because I wanted to tell her my feelings for her, true feelings. My concerns that grew from her first letters expressing continual anguish subsided with the conclusion that she was okay and would be okay. I simply did not know the details of her daily life, so I usually included details about my life in the Navy, and I composed a letter on the 2nd day of December saying:

Dear Mary Alice,

It's late now and I'll have to make this fast. For the next 7 days, Co. 638 will be pulling Mess Duty. That is, we'll have to cook for Regiment I, with all the other consequences cooking brings. We will be up at 3:00 AM and to bed at about 9:00 PM or later, so if you don't receive any letters for this time, don't feel bad because I'm not even going to have time to read your letters... Right now I'm fighting

94

time, I have yet to shower, shave, wash clothes, clean up the barracks, polish my shoes and anything else they want done....

Anyhow, I'm thinking of you with an adoring feeling in my heart.
Be Good and Be Happy for me.
W.A.G.

One of the packages I received from Mary Alice included a letter and a beautiful color portrait of her with a longing expression that I understood perfectly. When first seeing it, I was..., perhaps mesmerized is a good word, because I kept staring at it; I was captured by her beauty once again with a sense of missing her like never felt before. Several of the other guys exclaimed; "How'd you rate that!?" Among assorted guffaws they simply did not believe that she proposed to me, that we were married secretly - for more than a year before getting drafted; all of that a tall tale straight from story land, but.. maybe not. On Saturday night the 3rd, I followed my last letter to Mary Alice writing:

~~Dera~~
Dear Mary Alice

~~Bob~~ Boy am I tired. 16 hours of mess duty and I'm beat. I suppose you can tell by my spelling.

I've just taken a shower and now I'm sitting nude on the edge of my bed, wishing I could be with you so you could sooth my aching body. (I've been on my feet all day.) You are really wonderful in helping me do things, right now you could be especially wonderful. I look at your picture and see the wonderful-ness in beauty your body beholds, your love of great magnitude.

I received your fruit cake today and it was the best I believe I've ever eaten. I[t] was really good. I feel really good when I open a package from you, it's not that I have a package but the thought from you means so much more.

95

Please excuse me if I close for now but I've got to be up at 3:00 AM so I'm gonna need all the sleep I can get.

Be Good my love for the goodness of joy in love is all yours tonight for my heart is with you. My dreams, desires and feelings belong to you as you dream with me tonight.
W.A.G.

Mess Duty took me places on Base that I had not known about, such as pay phones. One night, I broke the rules. Being Color Guard, I had a "walking chit" on my dog tags that gave me some liberties to be out of barracks. I sneaked off to the phones and called Mary Alice, a real surprise for her and a great pleasure for both of us. Just hearing her voice was a thrilling boost to my well-being that letters did not achieve. While getting acquainted with further reaches of the Base, I also noticed vending machines that displayed large, chilled Washington State apples. With cash in my pocket, I bought several to take back to the guys. That led to regular late night contraband trips for apples that each of us enjoyed, the only fresh apples of that quality we had during the entirety of Basic Training. And, I never got caught. On Sunday the 4th, I wrote:

Dear Mary Alice

Another 16 hours gone and I miss you, your smooth, warm, and tender body; your wonderful, loving affection. My thoughts extend to you the happiness I wish to give you; to see your smile upon your radiantly beautiful face, to help you to be as happy, gay, and joyful as you wish to be. Young people beginning our lives with young thoughts, carefree in a world of springtime freshness. I do hope you can be happy for this is what I want for you, so keep your heart open for the happiness that will come your way.

Please don't be too upset at the shortness of this letter.

I think you should buy a copy of Playboy Magazine and send to me some of the pictures, you won't send any of you.
Be Good W.A.G.

Mary Alice knew well my interest in her natural form, but her reluctance to display for me remained deep; she just could not do that. So when I received a set of color prints of her, I was genuinely surprised. Her roommate used the Kodak Hawkeye to take the sequence of Mary Alice in several poses in various outfits. The most striking were shots of her in the long white negligee I remembered, alluringly on a bed with a white covering. When received, the photos quickly made the rounds among guffawing recruits in my company who promptly elevated me to the admirable position to being married to a beauty. No one else was married, and several of the guys wanted to know more about marriage, so discussions frequently put me on the spot for sage advice that I did not have.

What I offered to other recruits who asked, How do you know for sure if she's the one? foundered on my own concerns about Mary Alice, that our Period of Adjustment was still adjusting, and I had no clear vision of us in the future. My answer was; you are taking a chance with marriage because unexpected things happen along the way that alters what you think is your future. Getting drafted rather than becoming a Marine Architect was my best example, and like me, they wondered how that job did not keep me out of the draft. Also, I had paid for summer tuition, $18 on June 6 that I had a receipt for, to complete my schooling, so why wasn't my student deferment still in place? I had no answers. For sure, though, like all other recruits, I was in the Navy for at least four years; that was my future. How Mary Alice fit in that future was not at all clear, yet would become adventures that we could never have imagined.

Tired from long days of Mess Duty did not stymie my writing to Mary Alice. Somehow I found the time, squeezed into a niche somewhere. My composition on the 5th of December said everything.

Dear Mary Alice,

I think you are just the greatest thing in this great big old world. One of these days pretty soon, I'm gonna grab you up and squeeze with a great big old love hug. (I'm not a bear so I can't say

bear hug, I'm a lover so I say love hug.) I'm gonna nibble at your nose, ears and neck. I'm going to nibble around and on your beautiful, firm, young breasts and make you wiggle and giggle. I'm gonna tickle your tummy with the tip of my tongue and give you a twang with a tingle. I'm gonna caress your legs and torso, squeeze your breasts, hold you tight and kiss your sweet, tender lips. I'm gonna make you feel soooooooooo good you are gonna wiggle and squirm like a baby in my arms. So there!! Smile and think of me.
Be Good
W.A.G.

Regardless of my reassurances, none paying her bills, Mary Alice wrote of increasing financial difficulties. Making car payments of $72.79 each month and paying for gas, maintenance and other car expenses, monthly insurance payments of $25.80, rent at $70 each month, increased to $75/month beginning in October, a phone bill exceeding $22 a month, costs of food and other daily expenses were more than her income, and paying bills was depleting our savings, even with a roommate to share expenses. Mounting financial difficulties were a real problem that she faced with no clear way through regardless of what we did. Going home was the only solution, but that involved having to face her father and mother. What she did not expect was that they were sympathetic from having been in the same situation when her father was in the Army some twenty years earlier.

On the 7th day of December, I answered her latest letter saying in part:

Dear Mary Alice,
...Anyhow I miss you terribly under any circumstances, debts or not. Each night after I take a shower, I sit on the edge of my bunk and look at your picture, look[ing] at me and remember and dream of the times we were intimately together. You are so beautiful and so much to desire. You have the beauty and body many people wish they

98

*had. I only wish you were more proud of your magnificent gifts. I
think you are beginning to open your eyes, thoughts, and life to the
goodness that living offers those that accept what it has to offer. For
this I am so proud of you I almost... My desire for happiness is so
deep that it makes me act or seem strange when I see you unhappy,
and you always seem to be sad, blue, discontented, doubtful or
something all the time. Please don't think I'm being hateful again. I've
just confided in you the secret of my life. I never thought I would;
that's how much you mean. I guess I've been afraid to yield to my
heart before because you said you just couldn't care for anyone (male)
after you found out they cared. But, it's out now and I'm not ashamed
to say I adore, cherish, and love every secret memory of you. I only
wish you could have seen it before now....*
W.A.G.

I imagined that my letters helped her get through each day,
not realizing the resolve that Mary Alice had to muster to go back
home. My letter of December the 2nd was mailed to her home
address. Others that arrived at her Winston-Salem address were sent
on by her roommate, now on her own, too. My letter of the 12th
included devastation news.

*...I've found out that my choices of ratings are going to put
me on a ship most of the time, so I'm going to change (or try) my
rating. In order to do this, I'm told that only a two year extension will
do it. So I would rather be with you for six years than not to be with
you for four years. I think I'll change to the Data Systems Field. This
will make us more money as civilians anyway.*

*I'm going to be stationed here in San Diego for my training, I
think. That means no money from the Navy except regular pay ... I'll
have to save all the money I can get in order to get home. I'll receive
only $134.00 possibly and probably only $54.00 with the remainder
going to you. This means I may not get home after basic. If not you*

99

have to sell everything and come here. This doesn't sound good does it?

My letters through Christmas were not cheering. My gift to her was a color portrait that was inscribed, *Loving you always, Forgetting you never, Yours for a lifetime.* I meant every word. With no spirit at all in a place like no Christmas I remembered, I was offered an adventure; another recruit whose aunt and uncle lived in San Diego invited me to spend time with his family, very nice folks. In civilian attire, he took us into Tijuana, Mexico. Crossing the border took me into a vastly different world, first and foremost, the people beyond poor; many were nothing more than destitute in living conditions far worse than anything I knew. Wandering through a huge market, with my meager cash I negotiated purchase of a rather nice chess set for only a few dollars that I later sold to another recruit at several times what I paid for it, gathering cash for my planned flight home after Basic. Not able to change my rating as planned, on Christmas day, I wrote wishing Mary Alice a Merry Christmas, that she was able to spend the holidays with her family was heartening. My news was not heartening, in part writing;

...Getting into the Gunner's Mate field will probably put me on a destroyer for about all my Navy time so be ready for lots of lonesome hours. I do hope I will be able to make you feel your lonesomeness worthwhile when we are together... I kind of feel like these next four years will be a waste of time because it won't give me much of anything to use on the outside... I think both of us will be rather tired of the Navy when it's over....

Knowing nothing more of the Navy than Basic Training, I had become disappointed to have uninviting prospects ahead and to be separated from Mary Alice for who knows how long... That was more than troubling. I wrote to her on Sunday the 27th saying:

100

Dearest Sweet Baby and Lover,

I received 3 letters from you a minute ago and even though I'm missing you terribly, I feel a lot better. You say some of the sweetest things and make me so proud of you.

I look at your pictures and see your sweet innocence. I sometimes feel sorry for you. Being so sweet, kind, gentle and innocent and married to me. I'm sorry you won't be able to live the life you should have, but maybe I can make your living a happy one if I try hard enough. I guess the reason I feel so bad most of the time is that it's going to take much longer to give you the finer things of life than I had planned on.

You're so beautiful. So much to love; so much to have. I want so much for you. You have such a proud life ahead, I hope you can live it. I've wanted so much for my one and only; now it's you... I've enclosed two pictures you may like....

I was preparing both of us for the worst. Mary Alice was living at home, not where she wanted to be, but she had no other choice because of my situation that showed no prospect of improving. I knew there were many suitors who would step into my role without hesitation, and I resolved that her happiness was more important than mine. Whatever was to come, I was stuck in the Navy, probably at sea somewhere for years to come, perhaps deep in the jungles of Viet Nam on a swift boat. She had far better prospects with someone else. I knew about Dear John letters from one that my roommate at Mrs. Phelps' boarding house received. And with each mail call, I expected Mary Alice's to be placed in my hands. Our exchanges continued through the New Year. I kept writing love letters with heaping compliments. Hers continued to be reassuring of her intentions.

Slack time during the holidays gave us recruits more time to get better acquainted. I wondered about the other guys who had set their courses to get married after Basic, wondering if they had any real idea of what they were in for. My advice seemed to have been received positively, and when another set of photos of Mary Alice arrived, exclamations among them were in the category of; "That's your wife? GAWD!" These photos of various poses were taken in her home, some in tight fitting two piece bathing suits clearly displaying her flawless 37-22-37 form. Another showed her in the Christmas gift from her parents, a fashionable red coat and white boy cap. Seated with a lot of leg showing, her little smile spoke to me, too.

On the 10th of January, 1967, I wrote:

Dear Mary Alice,

I received a very nice letter yesterday. I can tell you have developed into a person who likes to think for yourself. You seem rather disappointed, though, about being straddled with things you have no bearing on. There's 16 more days; I'm sure, even though there is conflict, you learn some of what human nature will be facing you with for times to come....

Anyhow, I'm proud of you because you have decided that childhood belongs with children. You are certainly not a child for if children were put together like you, this place would be all confused.

Sorry to have to quit, but the RCPO says everyone not on clean up--- out!

Take care of yourself sweeety. (Notice the extra e in sweety. That's for excellence. That's you.
Love, Alex

I was putting one foot in front of the other, going and doing each day with anticipation of my Dear John. My immediate future and long term future was in no way promising; Mary Alice was on the other side of America, and my chances of getting to her were clearly slim. Even with fourteen days leave following the end of Basic, the cost of a flight was beyond my cash on hand, even if flying with reduced fare as military standby, and how would I get back to San Diego? My greatest concern was that I might not be able to make it home for months to come. I recognized that she was mingling with old friends and available to suitors. What I did not recognize was that her protective father was protecting her, exactly what she needed most.

Near the end of Basic, rumors circulated that our entire company was to be assigned Swift Boat duty in Viet Nam. My initial concerns about war in Viet Nam returned; to resignation that southeastern Pacific jungles would be the end of me. Running the rivers of the Mekong Delta in a gun boat was not inviting in any way. My seeking more education and worthwhile training for a better life after the Navy seemed pointless, and I thought through the idea that she would be better off with a new love now rather than having to go through the anguish of burying me. The Navy could do that.

The day came when orders of our new duty assignments were distributed. I was assigned Gunner's Mate school at the Great Lakes Naval Training Center north of Chicago. Swift Boat duty seemed to be confirmed. How I got assigned to Gunner's Mate was a complete mystery to me; nothing I requested had anything to do with guns. I thought I would surely get an A School of some kind in electronics, but Ordinance Mechanic? That translated into nothing civilian in my mind. The only consolation with my new orders was that I would get travel pay. I could go home. And, I had fourteen days to spend with Mary Alice, before heading to Chicago. I phoned her with the news while saying that flying military standby meant that I would have to take flights available to me and that I did not know when I would get to a nearby airport; Charlotte, maybe Greensboro. I would call when I had better information.

I arrived in New Orleans without a hitch, and having been on my feet for twenty hours, I confirmed with the airlines that I had a seat; next stop - Mary Alice. I phoned her with arrival information, then went to the concourse, took a seat in the waiting area with my ticket in hand, and went to sleep. My flight came and went; no one waked me; I had missed my flight. I called her again with the change of plan... stupid me. With connections finally made, I arrived. My first sight of Mary Alice was thrilling, but something was wrong. She was crying.

Entwined in exchanged love hugs, I spun her round and round; such a delight to be in her arms again, but I was concerned. "What's wrong?" I asked. "Why are you crying?"

"You're back," she said among flowing tears.

"Well, why are you crying?"

I was learning more about Mary Alice, that her expression of emotions always tended toward crying, tears of joy, tears of sadness. For her to show happiness as cheerful was filtered through her notion that being happy was a jinx; she had told me that as a child she noted that when she was happy, someone she loved died. We had talked about that notion at length from time to time, me always reassuring her that life includes happy and sad, that being happy was okay. There was no jinx; it was all just life. Laugh, smile, play, and be joyful; they were parts of life, too. She remained convinced that she should never show happiness, especially around those she cared most about for fear of jinxing them. That notion was firmly set in her mind along with a second notion I thought curious; she had told me, also as a child, she noted that people are nice to sick people. I took that to mean that her being sick insured that people would be nice to her. Saying so, Mary Alice was offended that I thought her sicknesses were put-on, not real, one act after another. That took her to tears again, sobbing, saying that she could not help being sick.

And, she had been sick a lot during our first year together, at least once a month with cramps along with headaches, then hay fever sniffles during spring and fall, swollen eyes and runny nose, and allergies. Initially, I was slow to grasp that my Mary Alice was of fragile health, that what was normal for other people, such as physical exertion, was taxing to her, taxing to the extent that she knew such activities were to be avoided; no riding bicycles, no running, nothing strenuous. Restricting her activities was not seen as limitations, it was simply normal for her. That was how she lived, always careful to avoid taxing herself, which was, after all, rather similar to all other girls. She had learned in high school that sudden bursts of activity as

104

simple as running led to faints; she had learned how to live with that issue, although not considered a limitation, just normal for her.

With my own robust health and large measures of endurance, it took a while for me to see her as my delicate china doll, and as I came to that realization, I accepted her life without challenge. What I wanted most for her was for her to be happy, and that included expressions of happiness, the very things that she had difficulty doing. All of this contributed to the notion in the recesses of my mind that kept smoldering.

Those fourteen days of leave prior to heading toward Chicago included activities in our typically mild winter weather, even in mid-February. I tuned our Alpine to proper running condition, Mary Alice and I drove it to visit family and friends, and... then the Prince of Darkness struck.

During one late Saturday afternoon we were motoring into Winston-Salem for some reason that was suddenly changed when I flipped on the headlight switch and the engine died. Startled, I flipped off the switch, and the engine began running again. That had never happened before. I tested that sequence again; the engine died when the headlights were on and ran just fine when the lights were off. Stumped, I pulled into a service station. Not daring to turn off the engine that sat idling perfectly, I got out, raised the hood, and talked with the young attendant, asking if he knew what the problem might be. He walked around the car wiping his greasy hands on a equally greasy towel and said, "This here car come from across the water." I knew that. "'Spect that wiring harness'll have to be pulled. I might can get to it Monday."

I was instantly convinced that I knew more about the Alpine than he did, the problem had to be minor that did not require removal of the wiring harness, and waiting until Monday was not possible. So, I lowered the hood, got in, and drove the hour or more back home without lights. Fortunately, the night's moon was bright and shown our way well. Through all of this, Mary Alice sat quietly in her seat without a word. I wondered if she was terrified to silence; the idea of being stuck on the road somewhere at night with a dead car....

The next morning I started with the battery and cleaned every electrical joint up to and including the engine. When I started the car, everything worked just fine, lights on or off. I was dumfounded; what had I done that solved the problem? I did not know.

That episode caused discussion that our Alpine might not be up to a northern winter. Further, I was concerned that Mary Alice might not be up to a northern winter, that she should consider staying with her parents until I finished Gunner's Mate training and was assigned to a post somewhere. We could be together again in about four months. That seemed entirely do-able to me. We had made it through Basic Training... She looked straight into my eyes and said with firm conviction, "I'm going with you."

Another thing caused me concern; one evening nearing bedtime, Mary Alice was bent double with cramps, groaning with pain as she lay grasping her abdomen on a couch. As he had often done over the years, her father pulled up a chair to sit for coming hours to assist her. I, being husband, thought attending to Mary Alice should be my responsibility. Without a word, he got up and went to bed. I sat those hours with Mary Alice, doing nothing of benefit to her but being there. Occasionally, she looked at me through her tears, saying nothing, then hiding her face. That notion smoldering in my mind took on new proportions. As the night passed into morning, Mary Alice felt better, and both of us got on with our new day, although a bit weary from the sleepless night. Again expressing my concern that she ought to remain at home while I went through training, she was adamant; she was going with me.

The day came when we packed our Alpine with what we anticipated needing and headed to North Chicago's US Navy Training Center. I mapped our route to a first overnight with my "Big Sis" and her husband in Lexington, Kentucky. My plan for the following day was through Ohio, then Indiana and Illinois, thinking that should put us at the Training Center well before dark. I did not have the slightest suspicion that we were headed into the most ferocious winter of our lives; bitter wind, deep snow, and ice everywhere!

Worsening conditions the further north we went, as we got nearer to Chicago, the snow was piled along the highway deeper than any we had ever seen before with more thickly falling, with lots more continually blown sideways in the fierce wind. From time to time, I had to stop, get out, and wipe off the headlights that were packed with so much snow that no light was getting through. I also cleared the windshield wipers from ice packed on them. Once in the city, we traveled behind a slowly moving snow blower truck that blew snow to a height well above the top of our car. The truck cleared a single lane, requiring us to remain behind it, and like traveling through a snow tunnel, we moved slowly along until finally reaching the Base deep into the dark, bitter cold night. When I checked in I discovered that Mary Alice had not been included in my orders; I was assigned to a barracks as was normal for singles. The Base had nothing available for us, so the Duty Officer made other arrangements for us to overnight at the Army's Fort Sheridan Guest House several miles back toward the city. Finding our way through the blizzard, we arrived at the Guest House tired and hungry; we had not eaten for hours other than snacks Mary Alice had brought along.

This introduction to a Lake Michigan blizzard began a sequence of car related misadventures that we had no choice but to endure. Our first two weeks or so, at Fort Sheridan until Base housing became available, began our troubles. The very next morning, our Alpine would not start, and I could not make muster. Being a car of southern winters, our roadster had to be winter-ized to the frigid conditions. Completed that morning at Fort Sheridan's auto service center, no further such issues were encountered.

Living short term at the Army's Guest House had two fortunate upsides; one, Mary Alice noticed a job posting, applied for it, and was hired. That was most fortunate in many ways, not the least of them an income that proved pivotal in events to come. At $2.06 an hour, her job classification of General Office Clerk gave her the most

107

income yet received in her life and proved fortunate to have begun so soon after arriving in the area. I drove her to her new job, then went on to my training, then the reverse in the evening. Once Navy housing became available for us, we were quickly moved into a heated two bedroom house with no furniture. Our schedule became opposite; Mary Alice drove to Fort Sheridan and back each work day. With nothing more than a blanket on the bare floor, we resolved that we needed a bed. A roll-away bed, a card table and four plastic chairs for the kitchen soon became our only furniture; all we could afford.

Once on Base, we immediately faced significant issues; with signs covered in snow, a sequence of parking violations led to Mary Alice getting chewed out by the Provost Marshall who revoked our vehicle pass. That made no sense to me; exiling her, a civilian, to having to brave the ferocious winter with long walks from where she could park then walking onto the base, then further to our quarters. Explaining our circumstances to her new boss, the Fort Sheridan Procurement Officer, he solved our dilemma by issuing her a Fort Sheridan U.S. Army vehicle sticker that was never challenged, and we came and went with no further issues.

Howling wind at night that continually rattled the window of our room; each bitter morning of more snow and ice; scrapings from streets piled into mounds alongside; incessant traffic; driving in darkness both ways; Mary Alice faced all this to and from work without a complaint. During weekends when sunlight invited us out, we drove around the area. Thinking Chicago an odd name, likely Indian in origin, I wondered what it meant. Somewhere I learned it was Indian, meaning "place of stinky onions". How the city had grown from nothing to become an enormous, bustling center of commerce was lost on us. We waited impatiently for orders to anywhere, hopefully warmer.

The second fortunate upside while in Fort Sheridan Guest Housing was a newspaper ad that Mary Alice saw and responded to. Vogue-Chicago was inviting interviews for fashion models. When she received notification for her interview, she was delighted but unsure of what to wear, what to do, what to say, how to act.... Her evening interview took us into the inner city of tall buildings. My wool uniform and peacoat were not enough protection from the bitter wind off the lake while Mary wore her most dressy outfit that was sufficient only for a southern winter; she was shaking cold when we finally got into the warmth of the Vogue building. The elegant facility of expansive glass, high quality wood paneling, bright lighting, fine furnishings, and beautiful women in a beehive of activity; an entirely new world was presented to us. After introductions, I remained in the waiting room while Mary Alice went with a lady to begin her interview. For more than two hours I waited until asked to join her. Seated in as fine an office as I had ever seen, the lady conducting the interview began what was the most astounding opportunity either of us could have imagined.

The British look in style had taken the fashion world by storm, and Vogue wanted to expand its presence in that market. The type of model they were looking for was the youth look, young, pretty, and trim. Mary Alice fit those requirement perfectly. An additional requirement was being of legal age; she was twenty-two and met all the criteria they were looking for. What followed revealed a completely different life; Vogue's plan for Mary Alice was to send her through their modeling school in preparation for international runways; Rome, Paris, London, New York, Chicago, San Francisco, Tokyo.... She would be part of Vogue's fashion troupe for modeling their teen segment of fashions around the world.

Mary Alice sat stunned to silence as the proposal unfolded. The interviewer was matter-of-fact in her presentation, no doubt whatever that this venture was a go, and they were ready to sign her into the program. This was a career opportunity, fashion modeling with the jet set crowd of a premier organization, and Mary Alice faced the most difficult decision of her life. Both of our WOW meters were pegged; is this really happening?

An entirely new world unfolded in front of us in a matter of minutes... we looked at each other trying to gather our thoughts. The interviewer saw our consternation and excused herself to give us time to digest the situation.

Mary Alice had already been down the road of international travel with Sassa Carter who had firmly planted in her imagination a favorable opinion. She had also been down that road with her scrapbook and the destinations of interest that she had compiled in it, and now the world really was beckoning her. Her interest in fashions that included her own creations was another draw, fashion designer for Vogue. This was real.

Mary Alice sat motionless in deep thought, then turning to me eye to eye, saying nothing, I noticed a slight shaking of her head signifying... no, she was uncomfortable with this. Her decision... thanks, but no thanks.

We and our Alpine survived, but that kind of winter... never again! Four months of training saw me graduating top in my class, Gunners Mate Technical, and one day another student and I buttonholed an instructor to tell us what we were doing, having never set foot on a gun platform that were in place throughout the huge building. Our introductions were only textbook studies to learn gun operation. His response about Gunner's Mate being our "cover" was as stunning as being assigned to the desert southwest. "Shaken, not stirred, Mr. Bond?" took on new connotations. What were we, spies in training? Undercover operatives? Navy moles to be? With graduation, actually my first phase of H-Bomb training, Mary Alice and I were done with Chicago and northern winters as we packed for heading southwesterly out of Chicago on Route 66 in our red but winter grimy Sunbeam Alpine roadster.

My hush-hush training had led to the question asked of that instructor; his answer... "A big door will open in the desert...." That thought echoed through my mind as I wondered what would happen to Mary Alice. Going to Albuquerque was heading into the desert, and I reasoned that the Nike missiles of Fort Sheridan were just indications of the Fort's mission, not my track, although some suggestions were that GMT meant Guided Missile Technician. Directed not to discuss

110

my official responsibilities with her or anyone, and with confidence that the Navy would take care of her in my expected months of confinement behind that big door, I could not help but wonder what Navy facility would be in the desert. Navy meant ships and water to me; Albuquerque was a most unexpected assignment but was accepted as more adventures to come in a part of America that I wanted to see.

We motored our roadster out of North Chicago on Friday the 21st of April, 1967, a densely cloudy day. Our first stop was Fort Sheridan for Mary Alice to say her good-byes and to pick up a letter of recommendation.

Fort Sheridan Consolidated Exchange
Fort Sheridan, Illinois 60037
21 April, 1967

To Whom It May Concern:
Mrs. Mary Gabbard has worked for me as Secretary-Typist. I find her to be very efficient and diligent in her work. Her departure from this office is considered a great loss.
I personally would endorse her to any prospective employer.
Sincerely yours,
WILLIAM A. CLARK
Procurement Coordinator

The sky had blackened considerably by the time we drove through Chicago. I switched on driving lights in mid-day, having confidence that lights-on no longer killed the engine. Still, I sensed nothing unusual. Everything before us was new and different, and we just kept on going toward the narrow band of bright sky at the horizon that spread as far as we could see.

With such unusual conditions still not registering and our Alpine purring onward, we were well out into rural flatlands when I looked over at Mary Alice to say something and saw a tornado funnel beside us, not so far away. Exclaiming the surprise to her, we looked to our left and saw another, then counted seven, eight, the sky was full of tornadoes whipping all around us. We had never seen a tornado before, or the conditions of their making, so this sight was startling; tornadoes were everywhere except in front of us. We kept going, and I kept wondering what might have happened if we had left Great Lakes just a few minutes later and had driven into them instead of leaving them.

The remainder of our drive to St. Louis was uneventful as we drove through town after town, stopping for fuel and lunch along the way but no sightseeing. Both Mary and I marveled at the rapid disappearance of winter the further southwesterly we drove. Out of Chicago, remnants of winter's snow and ice faded away into the stark beauty of leafless trees and grayed undergrowth we knew so well in southern winters. Our arrival in St. Louis for an overnight was to warm sunshine and the spreading of springtime's light green in new flowers and leaves breaking free of their snug winter cocoons to stretch themselves toward the warming sun. The evening news brought sobering revelations; we had told of our encounter with the tornadoes, and we learned from the TV news that we had driven through the worst tornado destruction in Illinois history. The final toll was 59 deaths with over a thousand injuries from funnels that suddenly appeared giving little warning. Damage stretched for miles and laid waste to portions of every town in their paths. A feeling of dumb luck came over me. Later on, I learned that year's number of tornadoes was 40, up from an average of 26 a year, and those of that day in April roared through with category-4 winds up to 260 mph.

We planned to reach Amarillo for our next overnight, and the thrill of traveling Route 66 made famous in the early-1960s TV program of that name motivated us to look for sights along the way while new sights and new adventures greeted us with each passing mile. For Mary and me traveling Route 66, also in a sports car but with only four days to make the trek to Albuquerque, sightseeing off of Route 66 was not possible. Missouri's forested hill country and farmland rolled up and down under us with few curves, so the drive

112

through Rolla and Joplin was no more than just passing through for us. Exiting Missouri toward Tulsa, we rolled into our first toll booth leading onto the Will Rogers Turnpike that Oklahoma put before us. At its end on our approach to Oklahoma City, we left the exit tollbooth to an unexpected flat tire. Pulling over onto the broad apron, I unloaded the trunk and changed the flat for our spare. Now without a spare, Mary and I were uncomfortable about venturing further into the vastness of the southwest that our map indicated lay ahead of us, so we decided to stop in Oklahoma City to have the flat repaired. A clean, modern-looking service station came into view.

The reason that the establishment looked so clean was that it was new. I exchanged pleasantries with the only person on duty, the owner as it turned out, and learned that he was a recently retired US Navy commander of a nuclear submarine. Our conversation was interesting, but I did not associate newly retired with lack of experience in the service station business. All his equipment was new, and he had never used the tire changer. I knew how to handle the machine, and between us we set to removing the tire to repair the flat. I wondered if the $4 paid to the owner was his first earnings in civilian life.

After replacing the spare on the car with the newly inflated repair, we were again back on the road. Then, not more than five miles later, another flat had us parked on the side of the highway in Oklahoma City; the same tire. Off it came and on went the spare again, then we wheeled into the first service station we came to. This one, well used and grimy, was less inviting, but the young man who worked on the spare knew exactly what to do. Once the tire was separated and the tube removed, he pulled out a lead wheel weight from inside the tire that had gone undetected during the previous change. Neither the Captain nor I thought about removing the weights prior to removing the tire, exactly the sequence that my experienced attendant performed. The weight wore a hole in the tube. Once repaired again and reinstalled, Mary and I were on our way, for $5 this time.

113

Overcast, grey skies, and scrublands waking up from winter with a flourish of greenery and flowers was welcomed scenery. In one day, we had driven from Chicago's winter to Oklahoma's springtime that spread to the horizon as flat as a table top in all directions. As we drove from the Turner Turnpike exiting another toll booth, we were greeted with a thump, thump, thump as we rolled away. I stopped our rig and walked around looking for a flat tire. None were flat, and I was mystified as to the origin of the sound. Pulling away once again, we heard the same thump, thump, thump. I stopped again and took a closer look to discover that the right rear wheel had collapsed; not a flat this time but several broken spokes in a tangle that were no longer capable of holding the wheel and tire concentric to the hub. Repairs had damaged the spokes.

Replacing the failed wheel with the spare again put us back on the road once again without a spare, and the wide open spaces of the southwest loomed before us. Our Alpine motored on toward Amarillo where we made our first and only Texas overnight.

Mary and I did not know the highway we traveled out of Chicago would one day be called the Blues Highway and America's Highway, also the Main Street of America. Decades later, Route 66 was described as the Mother Road of America. I was vaguely aware that this highway was the migrant route that John Steinbeck wrote of in *The Grapes of Wrath*, but having come from a background of work-every-day farm life and making do, I did not associate our modern rig of belongings heading in the direction of California with those hard-timers who packed up everything they could carry and headed west three decades earlier on this same highway. They were Okies trying to find a better life while we were young adventurers on the best tour of your lives.

Mary Alice and I were definitely products of the rock 'n' roll era, but its transformation into psychedelic during the late 1960s passed us by, that movement of the time celebrating anti-war, San Francisco and its summer of love, the wearing a flower in hair did not connect with us at all. Our early 1960s was a time of up-beat good

114

times, dancing, and fun ever present in our days back then. The new wave was a downer largely ignored by everyone in uniform. After Chicago, we were on new adventures with the southwest looked forward to with anticipation; rock 'n' roll was in our pasts.

Terrain we saw west of Oklahoma City was dotted with short, flat topped trees of a decided easterly bent, our introduction to the stiff, always-from-the-west prairie winds that pushed every growing thing into a similar shape.

We crossed the border into similar but progressively dryer Texas. Sprawling Amarillo slowly rose out of the horizon ahead, and springtime in the desert brought every growing thing that could be green and in bloom into clumps of color or shoots of blossoms along tall spires of desert plants. The flat scrublands all around were waking up from winter while last year's bent-over and broken dry grass, brown shrubs, and the occasional tumbleweed rolling along at the behest of the never-ceasing wind were fascinating.

Upon selecting a roadside motel for the night, we were soon able to shower and rest before supper. Along the way we had seen signs of a restaurant that offered a 72-ounce steak free, if it could all be eaten, and we decided that was the place for us. It was a Texas-size restaurant with its large parking lot full of big rig trucks. Inside, the huge establishment was open, a beehive of activity with cowboys and cowgirls seemingly straight out of TV and movies. Boots, western hats, weathered blue-jeans, checkered shirts, wide leather belts with big silver buckles were the norm for the guys, and I suspected that our back east look was noted by the regulars: tourists. The atmosphere was brash and loud and the place rough hewn with longhorns on the walls, steer hides, branding irons, too.

Cowboys came here to eat, and did the steaks pour out of the kitchen! I imagined the ranchers and cowhands whose long days out on the range on horseback were rewarded with a trip to town and a favorite watering hole to feast on steak. Big steaks, more than enough for the two of us, were the ticket while Mary and I opted for lesser fare.

115

Up early the next morning, we greeted the faint light of the new day and overcast sky in summer wear. This day would take us to Albuquerque, and I wanted to get underway, but I had heightened concern about the door that would open in the desert. What would become of Mary? I had no clue and trusted the Navy. She had no clue what I was thinking and trusted me.

The morning hours passed in the drone of our westward passage, a stop for gas and a stretch somewhere along the way, and little else. This part of Texas wasn't much to see, but as we neared New Mexico, my interests perked up. I was certain that fascinating things lay ahead; my own interests with New Mexico as the heart of the Spanish southwest inspired all sorts of imaginings. Ahead was the land of gunslingers and outlaws like Billy the Kid, the Santa Fe Trail and wagon trains, big science at Los Alamos and world shaping secrets, wondrous Albuquerque and lots more; all places I wanted to see. They would come, but that Texas morning passed with the gait of the tortoise.

When we finally got to the border, Route 66 disappeared into the horizon straightaway ahead of us. I pulled off onto the gravel to capture the moment on film. Stateline, New Mexico. The rustic wooden sign of stubby timbers inset with a yellow panel sat low to the ground. Boldly written on it in red were the words; *Welcome to New Mexico* and underneath *Land of Enchantment*. I was already enchanted even though Stateline was no more than a dusty stop with a few trees for shade and an adobe building for tourist shoppers among a few smaller outbuildings that the locals lived in. The sign above the door of the largest building stood out against the background of ominous black clouds ahead that spoke of heavy weather. More tornadoes, I wondered?

Driving back onto Route 66 again, whatever the day was to bring, we were headed into it. Then, as the morning warmed, the sky opened into increasing blue overhead with dark bottomed clouds billowing high into the sky, their tops boiled up into picturesque white pillows highlighted by the brilliant sun, their moisture laden bottoms

116

flat and parallel with the desert. As we motored on, we noticed an especially dark cloud off to the right ahead. It was dumping its contents onto a swath of desert, a ribbon of moisture pouring onto the thirsty soil, another new and interesting sight. I speeded up a little. The cloud was on a southwesterly path that would cross Route 66 ahead. Could I get past its rain? I speeded up a little more. Our paths drew to a focus in the distance, and as we watched the cloud move across the desert beside us, our race with it took on comical proportions, another fascinating New Mexico moment.

We rolled along in perfect conditions of warm southwestern sunshine getting ever closer to converging with our cloud. The faster I pushed our Alpine the more I realized that the cloud would win. It did. At that point, the downpour suddenly turned on and dumped an intense shower on us. Our respective paths crossed, then separated, and just as suddenly, the downpour turned off. Our cloud moved on southwesterly as we drove westerly from under it back into the marvelously sunlit day. As the morning warmed further, the sky became a deep blue accented with white filaments floating lazily along in the dazzling sunlight. Our introduction to New Mexico became a long enduring memory.

The enormity of the sky with clear views to far distant horizons gave proportions of vastness to these ancient lands in ways I had never before seen. I imagined the land changing so little over time that when I envisioned indigenous tribesmen trekking its landscape eons ago, followed by Spaniards seeking golden riches in the Seven Cities of Cibola, then wagon trains of settlers rumbling slowly along, and finally Mary and me in our Alpine heading the same direction, the scene did not change. New Mexico was timeless. From Santa Rosa, the whole world seemed to be flat and never ending, but ever so slowly the mountains ahead loomed larger. We came to a huge sign describing Clines Corners as THE place to stop on Route 66. Mary and I decided that it looked sufficiently inviting to do just that. More miles of dry grass went by, then another huge sign about Clines Corners sailed by. OK, we'll stop. Miles and miles more droned by, and another huge sign welcoming a stop in Clines Corners emerged. We began to muse; Clines Corners must be some place, but how far away is this place?

Finally, after what seemed to be hours, Clines Corners stood before us. With all the billboard hype, I expected far more than a tourist stop, but there it was, Clines Corners, a large stucco building with its white exterior painted with tourist-inviting graffiti dominating the landscape among a few scattered companions. That was all. Mary and I chose to buy nothing more than topping off our Alpine's fuel tanks.

Albuquerque WAS just ahead, but in New Mexico terms. It was a long way to go in real terms. Moriarty came first and with it a long remembered surprise, the Longhorn Ranch. Our introduction to the Old West of our imaginations was just a turn off Route 66 into a gravel parking lot. The day could not have been more perfect, but I was surprised that so few cars were parked there. In no hurry, Mary Alice and I strolled through the town and settled in at its restaurant for a lunch of sandwiches, fries, and cold drinks.

After refreshing a bit, we walked the town to discover the assembly of stuff to be just like a movie set; each establishment was stocked with everything any set would need, a saloon that fit every notion of a dry gulch barroom, a general store stocked floor to ceiling with late 1800s needs, a Wells Fargo office, everything straight out of the Old West. I was amazed at the quantity of items on display and the effort all of it must have required to collect.

At the General Store, a museum in real terms, I encountered an artifact of the real Old West, a singular throwback to the law west of the Pecos that has maintained a place in my memory ever since. Sitting on a glass-topped counter filled with all sorts of interesting items sat the strangest pair of well worn brogan type work shoes I had ever seen. They were made of an eerie, translucent kind of leather that I could not identify. With no other patrons in the store, I struck up a conversation with the proprietor who was filled with southwest lore and enjoyed the opportunity to tell me about this item or that, another

118

historic piece here, a fascinating tale there, and the lives of famous characters entwined with the displays. He was loaded with fascinating facts of the area, and my inquiry about the strangely pale shoes brought a smile under his broad mustache. I could tell that a favorite story was about to be told.

His tale began by describing a despicable character with a pronounced nose. Big Nose George Parrott was not just a gunslinger, he was a bandit of malicious intent wherever he went, a man who dispensed the same contempt for civility on whoever crossed his path. Two lawmen faced him and died, and the peaceful citizens of the Black Hills territory southward into Wyoming came to fear not only his presence but his name as well, and no one felt safe if Big Nose George was even hinted at being nearby.

The time was the 1880s, a time when action was swift and decisive and carried in the holsters of those who kept their fast draw hands near six-guns. Their barrels of cold steel dispensed final authority in those parts, and George used his to further his path of lawlessness that included stagecoach holdups. He and his gang filled their pockets with loot taken from other people traveling the stage routes.

Big Nose George was a desperado known to shoot up the place and make off with whatever he wanted. His notoriety spread far and wide at a time when verbal descriptions of outlaws and sketches of them on wanted posters were about all anyone had to go by for identification unless they were photographed, which was rare. Such anonymity protected outlaws, but George's nose was a dead give-away; he could not hide among the anonymous. People knew him on sight, and word spread fast.

When Big Nose George and his gang of cutthroats rode up, trouble was in the making. His was the sort of lawlessness that caused great contempt for him among honest citizenry to the extent that when he was captured, the populace readied for a hanging; but George cheated them and death by escaping. During 1881 he was back in the Dakota Black Hills where he was captured again. Extradited to

119

Wyoming, the local people prevented another breakout and to finally rid themselves of him, an angry mob stormed the jail. George was taken to a nearby telegraph pole and strung up. Frontier justice was served by the hands of the frontiersmen themselves.

Among the witnesses was the town doctor, a future governor, who recovered the body, skinned George and cut him into pieces. Parts of him went in various directions while his hide was tanned. Among the items made from it were two pairs of shoes, one for a lady and one for a working man, the brogans on display at the Longhorn Ranch. Another item was a doctor's bag. The legacy of Big Nose George Parrott remained among the dusty relics of the Longhorn Ranch all those many decades later. I was thoroughly engrossed as the narrator completed the tale matter-of-factly, leaving me with a clear image of Old West life and times that transcended all the movies and TV shows I had seen.

After walking the breadth of the town, Mary and I were back into our Alpine and headed for Albuquerque. Out of Moriarty the terrain became rocky and hilly. Route 66 actually made some noticeable curves, and as the highway approached a pass between two ranges of abrupt hills ahead, a surprise awaited us.

That day was perfect; warm, sunny, and filled with adventures among new and fascinating terrain. Then, as we rounded that last turn, behold, there in the valley before us lay the most beautiful city we had ever seen. Spectacular fit nicely; both Mary and I uttered a WOW! each. Then the thought of that door in the desert presented itself.

Albuquerque

How was I to find Sandia Base? The destination of our journey was that elusive door, a secret door in the desert. How was I to find it? My first thought was simply to stop at the first service station, fill up our Alpine and inquire, certain that none among those I would encounter had ever heard of Sandia Base. When pulled to a stop at the pumps, a young man trotted out and provided service, this being a time before self-service. Casually, I inquired if he knew how to get to Sandia Base, expecting him to decline any knowledge.

"Straight on into town and take the third left."

I was stunned. How could a local service station attendant know of things so secret? Now more confused than ever, I drove back onto Route 66 to the third left, went a few blocks and drove into the entry lane of Sandia Base. Long, nicely prepared matching plinths of sand colored stone on either side of the entry rose from near the ground to about head high and extended back toward a guard shack between the in and out lanes. No sentry was on duty; no one was there to provide directions to the secret door in the desert. Tall trees lined the entry way as I drove slowly past the empty guard shack with its large sign proclaiming Sandia Base, U.S. Army, expecting at any moment to have gun-toting MPs jump from hiding to thwart my incursion. I kept going slowly looking for anything suggesting directions. Beyond the entrance, the military installation looked like others I had seen as I recognized WW-II structures, barracks, and buildings with Army personnel going about their day on foot and in drab green vehicles. Civilian vehicles of many varieties were among them, and nothing at all seemed secret. Then, off to my left, I noticed in the distance down a street another guard shack with a gate and tall chain link fences. This was surely the entrance to the secret door in the desert. I turned our little red Sunbeam Alpine onto the street and traveled nearer to the guard station when a uniformed guard emerged and flagged me down. I handed him my orders.

121

"You're in the wrong place," he said. "You need to turn around and go to the Navy barracks."

With his directions, I re-routed our path to the appropriate barracks and took my orders inside. I was a day early. My second phase of H-bomb training soon began, and I was certain that I would be shown the way to the big door. There wasn't one.

Presenting my orders to the Duty Yeoman began a sequence of time consuming things to do in the checking-in process. Meanwhile, Mary Alice was stuck; her Alpine had motored along much of Route 66 without a hitch, then stopped running once on Sandia Base. Out of necessity, both of us had become adept at sorting out whatever problem the car displayed, and she knew what to do. That became an often told recollection beginning with using the wire wheel lead hammer to tap on the starter when it did not work due to a dead spot, an easy technique that never failed to solve that problem. Another problem was burning the distributor points to non-working condition. We had learned to keep two sets of new points as spares along with tools to install them in the car, and she knew how to replace the points and set the gap. That also never failed to solve the problem.

This occasion became a damsel in distress story that she loved to tell. Putting on one of my shirts and stuffing her long blond hair up under a cap, she was under the hood doing what was needed when an MP vehicle rolled to a stop next to the car.

"Hey buddy, you need some help?" the young man asked.

Upon raising up, she knocked her cap off that caused her hair to cascade around her shoulders. Not a "buddy", this beauty clearly needed a man's assistance. Actually, she didn't and said so, but he warmed to the occasion to assist her. Having already replaced the points and needing only a few starter taps, she was nearly done, but the MP insisted on helping her. So, she stood back and let him tinker. His every attempt to correct the problem failed, resulting in his recommendation to have a service truck come and take the car to a garage. At that point, Mary Alice gave the starter a few hammer taps, got in, and twisted the key. The car immediately started. His consternation was resolved when she told him about its idiosyncrasies. Her Alpine was not quite a year old and had taught us it needs, what to do to keep it running properly.

My orders included her this time, and married housing complete with furnishings was ready for us. With our own bed linens and little more, we settled in quickly. I was immediately scheduled for barracks duty and stood a succession of night watches, particularly the mid-watch from midnight to 4am that the low man always gets. After that first watch, I was tired when I arrived at our new home. I had to be back at the barracks to begin school in a few hours and wanted nothing more than sleep, but I detected from her manner that Mary Alice was deeply concerned.

"Is something wrong?" I asked. She was slow to respond.

Looking straight into my eyes, she asked, "Are you in trouble?"

"No, not that I know of. Why?"

Gentle tears slowly emerged from her eyes and cascaded down her face. "Two men came here today. They were F.B.I. They scared me to death."

"Oh," I replied, passing it off as inconsequential. "That's just clearance stuff."

It was consequential to her. It was worrisome among everything being entirely new and different. "I'm not supposed to talk to you," she said with deep concern. "Why can't I talk to you?"

"Oh, I'm sure it's okay to talk about anything except what I'm doing. That's all. We can talk about anything as usual."

"That's what they said," she confirmed with concern. "I'm not supposed to talk to you about anything like that. They scared me to death." She hesitated to continue. "I'm a threat to you, being here... aren't I? And KGB... They talked about KGB everywhere. What's KGB?... What's going on? How can I be a threat to you? What's going to happen to you?" I recognized that she was set uncomfortably adrift from her one firm anchor, me, and that thrust her into familiar but unwelcomed insecurity of being alone again. Just the two of us far from home, with no one to turn to was what she feared most, being alone in an unfamiliar world.

"I'm not supposed to be here, am I?" she lamented. "I'm a burden to you"

Now isolated from me with fear of getting either or both of us into deep trouble with government authorities, my Mary Alice needed reassurance more than anything. I gave her hugs and kisses that everything was okay, that her presence was not an issue, but in following days I noticed that she was even more reserved than usual. We talked less although I made efforts to enliven her outlook with talk of adventures in the area. My positive outlook did not include worrisome thoughts.

For the next several months, Sandia Base was our home and operations center for venturing out to see Albuquerque, its Old Town a favorite for romantic strolls, with weekend jaunts to Santa Fe, one taking in Taos, among other destinations throughout northern New Mexico. Our longest drive was westward into Arizona's Petrified Forest, but having no spare, worries that a flat would leave us stranded remained a real concern. That was a source of constant worry for her, getting stranded somewhere. Inquiry of Albuquerque's Sunbeam dealer about ordering a wire wheel was not heartening; it would have to be ordered from England at exorbitant cost, and it would take weeks to arrive. And, we did not have the money.

Every day brought new training for me deeper into the US arsenal of enormously powerful weapons. Every day for Mary Alice made her a sun goddess. Unlike Fort Sheridan, Mary Alice was unable to get a job because of my short assignment. So, she spent much of her time poolside at the NCO club or other no cost activities due to our limited income and our gathering of funds to buy a spare wire wheel, if I could find one. After hours and on weekends, we melded into entertaining adventures among all sorts of new things to do and places to see, especially Old Town and its ambiance of romance. Occasionally we splurged at its old restaurant, La Placita Dining

124

Rooms. Our favored seating was near a large tree grown up though the floor of an outside dining area. I was intrigued with everything. More than two hundred years old, this adobe construction began as the Spanish governor's home and held many fascinations.

Just strolling Old Town with Mary Alice was fun, her tending toward the romance of it, me tending toward new adventures. Seated among willows in hidden recesses we exchanged hugs and kisses while sampling newly discovered delights; sopaipillas in variety from honey to pastry filled that cost just a nickel each.

It took a while to locate a wire wheel; I was told one day that Nine Mile Hill Garage west of Albuquerque on top of the mesa, up Nine Mile Hill, was a likely place to check. Straight as an arrow I went along Route 66, and upon arrival, I noticed the place to be a high end racing facility rather than a grease pit garage that I had imagined. I inquired of the young parts man who investigated inventory and returned to place a new Sunbeam wire wheel on the counter. I was amazed, and its price was well below what I anticipated, another pleasant surprise. Our spending was constrained to just my sailor's income, so buying a new wire wheel was a substantial outlay, but saving a little along for its purchase covered the cost, paid in cash.

Further surprises followed my inquiry about the facility. "This is the Unser brother's place," the parts man told me. "The Indy 500? Bobby finished 8th last year. Al finished 9th the year before. They're up there testing." Afterward, paying closer attention, I learned that Al finished 2nd the next month.

That was just one of the many delights that Albuquerque and New Mexico held for us. The most engaging was that Mary Alice was the healthiest I had seen of her; no allergies and as time went by, her poolside days in the sun turned her hair golden while giving her the tan of her life. She was vibrant and more beautiful than ever. As time went by, those troubling first few days faded as she became increasingly comfortable with our new environs, especially having to deal with attention she drew from young men, soldiers, sailors, and airmen that were everywhere. Both of us liked Albuquerque and the region, and her new found willingness to explore led to conclusions that we should, some day, live the New Mexico life. Repeated drives to Santa Fe to stroll its historic streets reinforced that perspective. One excursion had us standing at the table where Civil War Union General Lew Wallace, territorial Governor after the war, sat writing his great novel *Ben Hur*. Years later, every attempt at career employment for me came to nothing, even Los Alamos and its big science that was, at that time, of great interest to me.

My training involved close contact with three other guys, all single. Each foursome was called a hook, and with Mary's consent, I invited my hook to spaghetti dinners and such at our apartment. These gatherings gave these barracks bound guys home style cooking along with leisure for getting to know each other beyond training. Mary's cooking prowess included cakes and pies that were completely consumed once the spaghetti pot was empty, always chased by beer that they stacked in our refrigerator. Their gratitude was expressed in financial contributions that lowered our costs while giving all of us good times with hours of relaxed association.

We also made friends with other married couples, one in particular who also had a Sunbeam, a sedan suitable for four while our Alpine was a two-place roadster. Our wives, both named Mary, produced kitchen treats for our tables and for growing numbers of participants in weekend grilling time. Mary's tendency of being reserved was soon abandoned; she had become her old self, her out-going personality of free expression with smiles and laughter became her new normal.

On one outing with two other couples early in my assignment, we chose a recommended restaurant as our introduction to the area's cuisine. Upon entering, the aroma of the place was mouth watering with fragrances completely new to me. The ambiance of the place was equally delightful, a mix of brightly colored Spanish, Mexican, and native Indian motifs. Mary Alice and I schemed to order different selections to share, and when ordering, I was careful to warn our server that I wanted very mild sections, preferring the sampler on the

126

menu. When our selections arrived, our table was filled with large plates heaped with more food than I thought consumable. Before each of us also sat a small pitcher of cold water. Delving into a red sauce covered item, my first taste of the southwest was... this is really good... then the southwest heat took hold, and I became the comic relief of the evening. I instantly learned about my sensitivity to peppery hot food; my lips, mouth and throat were on fire. I simply could not eat it and down went my pitcher of water, then down went Mary Alice's pitcher... and my five alarm antics enlivened the evening for everyone. Rather than share, she could have all of my food, all I wanted was more water, and none of it put out the fire. Mary Alice snickered about that for days to come.

We Sunbeamers, in particular, went on occasional weekend outings due to their car accommodating four. One excursion was to Blue Water Lake on a fishing expedition. Our friends, especially the guy being an avid fisherman, had everything needed for two. With no fishing skills, I followed his lead of baiting and casting. Meanwhile, Mary raided his tackle box for line, hook, and bait. Wrapping the line around her finger, she walked along the boulders at water's edge dangling the bait into niches of water and caught six fish, each about a foot long. We guys caught nothing.

Mary Alice's clearly demonstrated fishing prowess being vastly superior was a source of compliments to her that were satisfying and led to recalling how her father had taught her how to fish the mountain streams where she grew up. The fish were prepared for the campfire skillet and produced a tasty meal, but she declined saying that she had never liked the taste of fish, although fishing with her father was among her favorite memories. Her aversion to eating fish was another limitation that she had become accustomed to, not yet recognized as an allergy but one that was to become known in a nearly fatal encounter years later.

New Mexico adventures in abundance were continual attractions for us, all of them astounding compared to our Appalachian experiences. Driving through massive lava flows; driving along the

127

Santa Fe Trail; seeing Inscription Rock where people on wagon trains heading west had carved their names; jack rabbits far larger than our eastern bunnies; scraggly coyotes after them; and spindly legged road runners scurrying among scrub growth; native Indians and their handiworks of beaten silver, beautifully crafted ceramics, and dolls of their ancient motifs displayed with equally beautiful weavings; sun drenched high desert as far as could be seen in dramatic landscapes; adobe construction amid southwestern lore in every direction; an ancient land where people once eked out their existence as at places like Bandelier; and astounding sites like the Ice Cave.

That adventure took to an unsuspected natural wonder and back eons of earth time. In the warmth of the summer sun day after day, Mary and I prepared for our Ice Cave adventure in summer wear. As we walked the trail through tall pines we came to a giant depression in the earth made from collapse of the roof of a gigantic cavern. After traversing long steps down into the enormous depression we came to layered ice of varied thickness that were clearly differentiated by color change in shades of light blue and green, all frozen solid. An underground river of ice? How could that be?

Our guide told that this feature extended for miles through the earth and was due to ancient volcanic activity making refrigerating conditions eons ago that froze the river. When liquid water found its way onto the river, it froze as another layer, each layer building up over vast expanses of time to become more than seven feet thick that we could see. When the roof collapsed, it sheared the frozen river leaving an ice face exposed to morning sunlight that did not melt the ice because the freezing conditions continued. This fascinating geologic feature prompted many questions with interest in further investigation, but in shorts and a light blouse, Mary Alice was shivering.

Once back into sunlight, she warmed, particularly so when back in our Alpine that was rather like a furnace on wheels in the southwestern heat. That meant early morning and late evening drives, the latter often ending in Old Town for another stroll that included those tasty sopaipillas. Evenings amid lingering light due to Albuquerque being in the valley of the Rio Grande River made for long together times of walking and talking, holding hands with hugs and kisses in the shadows; the most heart filling, romantic times that we had ever had, the warmth of arm in arm in our summer place.

Being frugal, Mary had put away some of her earlier earnings that became our carefully managed travel funds, rarely buying anything more than gasoline for our Alpine. The only thing of significant cost during our New Mexico months was that wire wheel. Sandia Base proved to be a low cost place to live, and we frequented the NCO club and base cafeterias for meals, the theater for 10-cent movies, and we parked for top down outdoor movies among the three screen drive-in theater. One long remembered film was about a no name desperado in the most entertaining western we had ever seen, our first Clint Eastwood film.

On one of those outings, we had walked to the theater with another couple. While enjoying the film, an enormous clap of thunder got my immediate attention. Running to the entrance, the ferocious downpour meant ruining our Alpine. Like many days previously, I had left the top down. Telling Mary Alice to stay put with our friends, I ran through the deluge. Upon arriving at our roadster, what I saw was staggering; I had parked between the corner of our 2-story apartment building and a huge tree. A limb of the tree blowing in the wind had beaten in a section of the downspout that broke from the adjoining section, and gushing rain from the roof was spurting out the broken joint directly into the cockpit of the car. Not just rain, a rooftop deluge, too. I could not have parked the car more perfectly. When I opened the driver's door, collected rain water gushed out over my feet. That meant the seat bottoms were soaked along with everything else. I was certain that our car was ruined.

Erecting the top and rolling up the windows first, I ran completely soaked into our apartment for a cup to bail with and an arm full of towels to dry with. Quickly tending to those needs, once the interior was free of standing water, I was surprised that the car started. Getting Mary and our friends back home was achieved with no further incident, but both Mary and I knew that we had real trouble now; our Alpine was certainly ruined.

The next morning was another of Albuquerque's bright and sunny days. Before walking to school, I opened everything in the car that could be opened and laid the top out across the trunk. The entire interior was saturated; I hoped it would dry out but had little confidence that our car would ever be free of creeping mold. Upon arrival from school that afternoon, the first thing I did was to feel the foam padding under the seats. It was completely dry. I was pleasantly astounded. Peeling up the carpet and feeling everywhere, having been saturated that morning, there was no moisture anywhere. The car was thoroughly dry. Our Alpine was not ruined, it wasn't even damaged. Our worries became nothing more than another New Mexico adventure story of lasting memory.

Another unanticipated adventure boiled up across the western mesa one day to become a giant black cloud of desert dust that swooped down upon Albuquerque. Mary and I closed all the doors and windows tightly and waited it out. How that dust storm found its way into our tub, past two closed doors was baffling. Throughout our apartment a layer of fine, gritty dust was on everything. We cleaned and cleaned and vacuumed and vacuumed and still found dust. When I opened the door to our Alpine the black interior was grey. Covered in dust, I vacuumed and cleaned repeatedly but the gritty sound when turning the steering wheel never went away. Forty some years later when I disassembled the car to restore it back to showroom condition, I discovered grit in several places. Much of the original interior was retained, and from a section of carpet I shook out more dust that I have kept in a vial, a memento of our one and only dust storm.

Clarksville

My assignment after Albuquerque was Clarksville Base, Tennessee. Checking a map and finding Fort Campbell the only military installation near the town of Clarksville, I was puzzled; another landlocked Navy Base? Where? No map or contact information was included with my orders, so Mary Alice and I packed our Alpine again and headed for another mysterious destination. Knowing our roadster to be a hot mid-day traveler, we dressed as lightly as possible and headed eastward in the cool hours of morning well before sunrise. To aid in more comfortable travel, I had bought a pair of wire wound seat cushions so that our skin was some distance from pin prickly black vinyl, with additional protection of bath towels over the cushions. We climbed into our loaded Alpine again and headed east, this time with thirty days leave giving enough time to go home prior to reporting in at Clarksville Base, if we could find the place. Mary Alice looked forward to celebrating her birthday at her home.

Retracing Route 66 toward St. Louis during mid-July with the summertime temperature soaring, we were lulled into doldrums to the tune of the engine's constant drone. Our nearly empty turnpike encouraged high speeds, and our Alpine cruised on and on at eighty-five miles each hour, each of those hours slowly passing as we sat in our stupors. A patrol car went by at an exceedingly high speed. Then a big American sedan went by, its windows rolled up. Air conditioning; at that moment, I determined that my next car would have air conditioning. More miles went by as we gradually closed on the big sedan, now moving slower than before. A long haul truck loomed ahead of both of our cars, so I drove into the inside lane to pass both. Once alongside, the driver of the big sedan also swung over to pass the truck. In a near side-to-side collision, we were instantly roused from our stupors; Mary Alice grabbed anything to hold on to while I gripped the wheel laying on the horn, both of us imagining our little roadster crushed into a ball with end over end summersaults. DON'T TOUCH THE BRAKES! was my overwhelming thought. I let off the gas and kept steering along the median slowing gently as a giant rooster tail of Oklahoma dust boiled up behind us. The driver darted his big sedan back in behind the truck, and I eased our Alpine back onto the pavement, no harm done. Greeted by his apologetic grimace, I waved and continued on while his female passenger lit into a finger lashing and tongue lashing episode that he likely never forgot.

By afternoon and more droning through Oklahoma, I noticed my gym shoe sole was stuck to the carpet. The car's exhaust pipe ran directly under my feet rather than under Mary's side. Hoping her side to be cooler, somewhere along I looked at her to say something and noticed beads of sweat had run down her face, across her eyes taking mascara into black streaks to her chin. As usual, she never complained, not once; that being the only time in our lives together that I saw her sweat.

After more than eight hours on the road, we were done in and chose an Oklahoma City motel for the evening. That shower was the most refreshing of memory, and once in dry clothes, I crashed into sleep on one of the beds. Mary Alice quietly did the same. By evening and refreshed, suppertime took us to a nearby diner, then back to our room for another early-to-bed in preparation for another start in the wee hours the next day.

We made quick stops as needed and laid down many hours on the road, then rolled through St. Louis and its afternoon of slow traffic. Tired, hot, soaked with sweat, hungry, wanting to get on... I complained that St. Louis was the arm pit of the world. It sure felt that way. Taking the route eastward out of St Louis, we were off Route 66 heading for Lexington, Kentucky and an overnight with my "Big Sis" and her husband. Upon arrival, Michaela took some snapshots of us with our Alpine that became treasured moments captured on film, July 1967.

My teen years was growing up in a small house without air conditioning, and I slept many summer nights on the porch because

132

the house with its metal roof did not cool to comfortable until midnight or after. Mike's home with its constantly cooled interior reinforced another determination; wherever I lived henceforth would be air conditioned.

Our overnight gave each of us time to catch up on the events of our lives, then off toward North Carolina the next morning. I chose our route to include Berea, Kentucky, my hometown that held many pleasant memories for me. I drove slowly along familiar wanderings, passing yards I had mowed giving me spending money, crossing the sizable creek where friends and I had carved out a swimming hole, my paper route that ended at a store where I treated myself to a bottle of Frostie Root Beer, then my grandparents home and the house diagonally across Elder Street that was my first home as an infant, then a slow pass of our family home on High Street with its backyard monument commemorating the founding of Berea College during 1855. Our driving tour of Berea College ended at Boone Tavern, the very location that I had been shooed out of many times as a boy. This time, I was a patron of its dining room, the same where my mother waited tables during 1936 while a student. The Tavern was a faculty-student project begun during 1907 that included my great-grandfather's work as a carpenter for the college. "Uncle" Mike lived within walking distance of the Tavern, as did his son, Chester, my grandfather who became Berea's dentist. His office adjoined the Tavern on the second level, and he lunched at the Tavern for decades. Three generations of us Gabbards knew the Tavern well, and that day I added my fourth generation to the list as Mary Alice and I were served at one of the tavern's white table cloth settings. I let my thoughts wander to my Mom serving us, that the tavern had not changed since her time more than thirty years earlier.

This tour was immensely satisfying to me but so much in such a short time was overwhelming to Mary Alice who took in the sights with little comment. She knew my North Carolina farming past, and now all these Kentucky college town elements of my background so different caused concern that I was above her. That was not my intent,

I simply wanted to share my past life with her, a boy on a bicycle in a location of wonders that I explored with complete freedom. I wanted to include her in who I was then, the product of a broken home but with abundantly favorable memories. Her perspective was different, that we would never have met had that breakup not happened and took me to the farm. Without it, I would be sitting there with a Kentucky girl. Wasn't she important to me, too?

I thought I was expressing that sentiment exactly, that she was important to me, that our meeting had given us travels and memories that were ours, shared memories. I was including her in my life, that I wanted her to share the same outlook of pleasant memories as I had of my boyhood in Berea, and that meant sharing my past with her, but saying that we were meant to be there was the wrong thing to say.

I long grappled with why she was often melancholy, and the wrong thing to say revealed her own grappling with deep seated confusion about what events meant, her "signs" of this or that, each of them pointing to an unwelcomed outcome contrary to what she wanted. That little shaking of her head, no, told me that I had stepped on another toe; saying "I love you" with emphasis on "I" was her denial of predestination, feelings that she had difficulty putting into words. Saying that we were meant to be there was the same as saying that love did not exist, and that was not the real world for she knew without question that she loved me with all her heart. That all things unfolded according to a preordained cosmic order meant that love did not exist, that her love for me did not exist. I was still learning that to love was Mary Alice's very essence, who she was, and her love was real to her without question, not some blind cosmic order. She could not accept that a pleasant lunch in a memorable location was a simple predestined unwinding, and neither did I. Her concern was difficult to contend with, causing her to be in constant mental turmoil; being contrary to the very basis of her church teachings, that all things were written in the Book of the Lamb at the foundation of the world was just not acceptable if love was real. But rejecting what she had long been taught was rejection of her father, her very roots, a severe

134

emotional upheaval in her search for meaning. I did not know what to do or how to help other than being upbeat in my outlook that was my normal. I had, however, not thought beforehand the possible impact of what I was to say and how it might affect her. I was learning to tread lightly in conversation of this nature.

For me, just looking at Mary Alice was seeing a natural beauty who was the very essence of contentment and health. She was neither, and her turmoil was a continual source of anguish, a quiet searching that was never completely resolved due to a succession of heath issues that prevented any level of contentment.

During following years, we would occasionally sit at a table in Boone Tavern for lunch or dinner and see through its windows as the world outside went by. I pointed out my grandfather's dental office; we walked nearby streets that I knew so well; we drove around revisiting one memory after another, but I was unable to connect my past to her. The summer street dances held on the short street in front of the Tavern; the scar on my right arm from a dog bite while delivering papers; my grandparent's home and its yard I mowed while marveling at stone Indian artifacts laid along its foundation; its paw-paw tree out back and the droves of bees it drew when the fruit ripened and fell to the ground; my childhood home and its huge back yard where I ran and played; Berea College and its majestic trees with squirrels that would take a peanut from my fingers; on and on for me, memories poured from me. I was, however, slow to learn that Mary Alice was right; what counted most was now. She would shape that notion into the most memorable events of my life and endear my very essence to her, but that took resolution of her own turmoil during years to come.

Back in our Alpine, after several hours of negotiating the curvy highways through the mountains to arrive at her childhood home brought renewed satisfaction to Mary Alice, her safe harbor that dispelled all concerns. She was home. Our surprise arrival was met with hearty welcomes and two more plates set at the table. Like her mother who often talked about her travels to be with Garvey when

135

they were young, Mary Alice talked and talked of our adventures, now looked back upon without the threats that were of such concern to her at the time. We had made it back with many stories to tell, and, her little red Alpine sat outside waiting to take us on more adventures to come.

Her father, being a veteran of the war in Europe, was never talkative of his memories; they were not adventures, they were horror stories that he was not willing to talk about. I was never able to get him to tell me more than snippets of his exploits with the 69th Infantry Division, although he did reminisce about his Army times and the friends he made prior to deployment in Europe. Sadly for him, those horrors of war were to return to dominate his actions.

Our relaxed days of visiting with family and friends, and time spent tuning our Alpine for travel to my next duty station, was a time of smiles and hugs for Mary Alice along with telling of our adventures. When we readied our Alpine for departure toward Clarksville Base, I had a sense that she had fulfilled her need for good moments of home because she was ready to go. With map in hand, once again we headed west through the mountains that took us to US 70, Knoxville, and on to Nashville, then north on 41A to Clarksville.

Without a clue where Clarksville Base was located, I decided that I should do the Albuquerque method: ask a local. When we stopped for refreshments, milkshakes again, I noticed a Clarksville Base bumper sticker on a car parked adjacent to us. When a young man came to it, I got his attention and asked if he could direct me to Clarksville Base. His reticence to answer followed by questioning why I wanted to know resulted in telling him of my new assignment. His answer; go up 41A to the first Fort Campbell gate I come to, Gate Four, turn in and keep going. Once again I was doubtful; Fort Campbell? U.S. Army? I was looking for a Navy Base. But then, my introduction to Sandia Base began like that, simple directions. So, off we went.

I followed those directions and drove Fort Campbell to the point that I became convinced of being duped. Then, beyond an

136

intersection ahead, where I intended to turn around, I noticed the corner of a chain link fence. On closer approach, we saw along the fence tall poles with high intensity lights mounted on them. Inside that fence was a ribbon of manicured grass up to a single lane asphalt road. Inside the road was another ribbon of well manicured grass extending up to another chain link fence. Beyond it was a third fence, but the steel posts of this fence sat on glazed brown insulators about two feet in diameter. I recognized the fence to be electrified, and beyond this fence was another ribbon of well manicured grass up to another fence. Beyond that fourth fence lay another ribbon of grass extending to dense undergrowth among tall trees in a thick forest, one among the trees an especially tall oak that I would come to know when I learned that it guarded histories that were to become fascinations for me.

Expansive barbed wire on four tall fences, one of them electrified? Grounds pristinely maintained? This looked like a stockade to me, a prison, and I reasoned that I had definitely been duped. But, curiosity prevented turning around as I wondered if we might be upon a prisoner of war camp. Mary Alice and I were regularly entertained by the TV series, *Hogan's Heroes*, with its similar setting of captives held within fences and lights, so I wanted to find out if this might contain captured Viet Cong. Driving on for additional miles, we came to a guard post ahead. I decided to stop and ask for new directions, but as we drove to a stop in the barricaded entry lane, the white sign with blue letters read, NAU Clarksville Base, U.S. Navy. Unlike Sandia Base that had been completely open, my new duty station was buried deep inside Fort Campbell and behind a network of fences with guards constantly on patrol. I was soon to learn its mission while men in suits re-visited Mary Alice.

Showing my orders to the Marine guard, we were directed where to go, and the gate rolled opened, then closed behind us. While checking in I learned that the Base did not have housing available for us, and Fort Campbell's Guest House was filled. Advised to find quarters in the Clarksville area, the list provided to us of recommended sites for lodging turned up no vacancies. With no other

137

choice, we checked in at a motel for the night. That gave us time to scan the newspaper for rental vacancies. Only one was available, an older single bedroom trailer among other trailers set up behind a home. We took it on a daily rent basis and moved into roach infestation like nothing we had ever seen. We had to fumigate the place and clean it top to bottom just to be acceptable, then live with musty odors for the next few weeks in marginal accommodations.

Beautiful Albuquerque had presented us with adventures in every direction and a sense of freedom with wide open spaces beckoning us to get out and go. Clarksville was different. My sense of it was confining due to the bustle of many more people, particularly Army personnel, confined in a smaller area. And, our quarters were much less than satisfactory. Once again, I was advised not to wear my uniform off base, and I traveled to and from the base in issued dungarees, Navy work clothes. Meanwhile, Mary Alice cleaned the trailer again and again and scanned newspapers for jobs while getting acquainted with our new neighbors. One couple was from Mississippi, a young Army officer and his wife who had nothing good to say about their experiences with Fort Campbell, especially having to live in less than expected accommodations. He thought it odd that I was Navy assigned to an Army post and had never heard of Clarksville Base. I had to ready my cover story, that being a Gunner's Mate, my assignment was Navy ordinance; the Base being an ammo dump. That cover was effective in a broader context that I soon recognized. When being associated with Clarksville Base was mentioned, its mystery as a secret base generated questions that caused me to stop mentioning that I was part of it.

As we drove around Fort Campbell, particularly to locate the PX, Mary Alice acquired an employment application there and included her letter of recommendation from Fort Sheridan. She was hired almost immediately. Once her skills were assessed, she was assigned to the Fort's large and bustling auto service center, a pretty bookkeeper among a host of guys who could not help but notice her. Our schedules meshed perfectly; I drove her to her work in the

138

morning, then to my work, then the reverse in afternoons. But, rather than working on H-bombs, some aspect of my clearance was not in place, and I was assigned barracks duty. A janitor for some weeks enabled me to learn the confines of Clarksville Base well, especially its small but well equipped auto service facilities that would be of continual benefit to our Alpine. On weekends, we explored the area, driving hither and yon in much more traffic than Albuquerque.

When notice came that a furnished townhouse was available for us in the Clarksville Base Annex, we gladly moved into 8 S. O'Bannon Court, our home for the next two years. Settling in required insuring than no roaches came with us, and now located a short drive to the Base, Mary Alice began driving me to the Base, then to her job. Having our Alpine on her job site proved advantageous in that it received no cost service in addition to attention I gave it at facilities on my Base. And, with our new location nicely furnished, we soon learned Fort Campbell well, then gradually ventured further out.

Now married for over two years of travels, especially gathering shared memories due to my military exploits, Mary Alice had been my constant companion except for Basic. Both of us were comfortable with our new environs, but her inner turmoil remained and soon resurfaced. Attending church had been a constant in her youth, but it had not been part of our lives together. At her request, we began attending the non-denominational church on Base, its beautiful chapel and welcoming atmosphere fulfilling a portion of what Mary Alice was searching for, although services were far different than she was accustomed. Our regular attendance among a modest congregation was noted by the Navy Chaplain who asked us to become youth leaders. Bringing children of Base personnel together for religious teaching and discussion on Sundays branched out to gatherings in our townhouse that Mary Alice also welcomed due to increasing social involvement. This new experience suited her well because, being pretty and shapely with an out-going manner, attention from both boys and girls came her way in the form of questions and conversations that she enjoyed. This new experience, being a teacher,

139

was pleasantly rewarding and became firmly set in her aspirations for future involvement.

The Youth Fellowship was divided into two age groups, and we began our involvement with the teen group who tended to ask penetrating questions about life, such as marriage. Answering such questions put me in a difficult position because Mary Alice was there, and I knew that she was sensitive to such issues. Whatever I said was likely to be interpreted as another of her "signs" that invariably led to doubts about us and more melancholy moments. Recalling the sage advice I had expressed to my Basic Training companions, I recognized with certainty that any such answer was not for this group or for Mary Alice. So, I recommended reading books on the subject and deferred to her to provide answers. She could not and tended to stumble as she was grappling with the same issues due to our relationship still in its period of adjustment. She was not yet comfortable with me due to both of us living secret portions of lives apart, my secrecy that I could not share with her and her secrecy that she had not yet formulated into a coherent perspective to share with me. This was a continual sticking point, and bridging that divide had yet to be achieved. We proved to be inadequate role models for this group, and the Chaplain switched us to the younger group. That worked much more smoothly.

Through that fall and winter, 1967 - '68, we settled into our lives together with a daily routine without a radical change looming before us in a few months as had been the norm previously. Now with a sense of unhurried time, we made friends with fellow sailors in one capacity or another, two in particular who became regular visitors. Sandy and John had the uncanny ability to detect when Mary Alice was taking a pie or cake from the oven and would arrive shortly thereafter. That happened with such regularity that it became an expectation. Always welcomed, we provided a home away from home for the barracks bound and welcomed sharing our table as we had in Albuquerque.

In particular, ours became a lasting friendship of fond memories with Sandy who remained in our lives thereafter. With his camera, he captured images that I now look upon, images that take me back to those goods times with gratitude and appreciation that have no words to describe. He captured those moments of our lives on film, images so precious now that I tear with heartaches when looking at them; my Mary Alice so beautiful, our times so memorable.

Settled for our Clarksville Base time, we steadily expanded our adventures into a variety of outings, some as Youth Fellowship, but mostly on our own. Mary Alice also made female friends who often dropped by, Jill in particular, another natural beauty. As I learned more of the history of the area, my interest grew toward investigating historic sites in the area such as the Civil War Fort Donelson and the nearby town of Dover. Learning details of how the Fort fell to the forces of Union General U. S. Grant, where he became nationally known as Unconditional Surrender Grant, I could not believe the ineptitude of the Confederate command in such a well positioned, well equipped, and well manned strategic fortress. Nashville was also a draw where we strolled among country and western culture and entertainment as never seen before, and we watched summer filler programming called *Hee Haw*, soon to become long lived national programming.

For that Thanksgiving and Christmas, 1967, we traversed Tennessee along Route 70 to be home the for holidays. Each of our Sundays there involved attending services in her father's church with its deep roots in family history. Being the earliest surviving church in Surry County, founded during 1830, many area families and their histories resided in the church's cemetery, including Garvey's father, Cornelius, whom Mary Alice recalled with sadness. Markers of other family members resided there among those of her memories that tended to bring melancholy sighs, occasionally tears, when walking among them. These were mostly quiet moments of reflection that she rarely shared in conversation.

141

During one of our visits, Garvey led a team digging a grave. I went along and participated with pick and shovel to the prescribed depth. As we dug, another man asked Garvey if I was as worthless a son-in-law as his was. That put Garvey in an awkward position; he was aware of the difficulties that Mary Alice and I had encountered since marriage and now having to answer such a pointed question involved knowing that he could make our situation better or worse with his answer. He chose better. His answer also helped focus his regard for me, distant until then. As I helped dig that grave, he came to accepting me as his daughter's chosen without question, his son-in-law.

On occasion when home, Mary Alice and I attended church services that were very unusual compared to our non-denominational involvement with the Clarksville Base Chapel. My experiences before the Navy had always included keyboard music, piano and organ, along with choral singing from hymnals led by my Mom, and sermons were directed in an informational manner. With Navy religious traditions quite different than Primitive Baptist, Mary Alice was exposed to many new traditions. Having already been baptized into the church of my community but without a strong religious drive other than curiosity, I was surprised one day during a sermon when Mary Alice walked from beside me in our pew to her father, hugging him, and crying. The sermon stopped, then shifted into welcoming a new member. Later the following spring on a sunny but cool Sunday, I walked with her to water's edge on the banks of the cold Mitchell River where she was taken in hand to her own baptism. Shaking cold afterward, I wrapped her in a blanket brought for that purpose and took her home to change into warm clothes.

Then, the Prince of darkness struck again; our Alpine exhibited the lights on - engines dies scenario that I once solved without learning what the fix was. This time, I resolved to proceed differently; my new plan was to start the car each time I did something. As previously, I began with the battery, cleaning its posts and cleaning the ground connection to the body. Surprisingly, that first cleaning solved the problem. I had learned another of the car's idiosyncrasies; battery corrosion killed it, but the fix was easy.

Mary Alice was named for her grandmother who took great pleasure riding in our Alpine. Mary Alice took her to visit family, as I did on occasion, and she also took her grandmother shopping. Being unusual, our flashy red roadster drew attention, one in particular... a North Carolina Highway Patrolman. Every time he saw the car, he stopped us with lights flashing on his cruiser. One occasion was that we had no state inspection sticker. There it was on the windshield. Another occasion was that he did not see that we were wearing seat belts. There they were tightly at our wastes. He never gave us a ticket for anything, and I came to wonder if he just wanted to get a closer look at the pretty blond. Fortunately, we were rarely in the area.

Back on Clarksville Base, Command issued orders that spring for me to return to Albuquerque for several weeks of Advanced Warhead Training. Mary Alice had her job and church activities including Youth Fellowship among other friends who frequented our townhouse, and in preparation for my departure, I asked Sandy if he would look after Mary Alice in my absence. We decided that she might need protection, so I bought a western style revolver and a nicely tooled leather belt and holster for her. Sandy drove us out to a range, and with the target fixed, we began showing Mary Alice how to shoot. In her usual manner she quietly took in everything, then with the pistol in hand, she shot a bulls eye with her first shot. "Daddy taught me how shoot when I was little," she said. Sandy and I were awed; there was no doubt, she knew how to shoot a gun.

Returning from Albuquerque, I had no inkling of the depth of impact that events soon would have on me. Mary Alice and I had over five years of association by then, with more than two and half years of marriage, and her initial capturing of me had not changed; she remained my one and only, and I believed that I was hers. Our periods of adjustment so strongly influenced by military hardships had taken us through various challenges and swings of emotion to a day that was to become by far the most memorable of my life. Mary Alice was to

143

turn twenty-four in a few months and had long struggled with how different our lives were compared with her earlier life at home. Ours had remained a relationship driven by affection for each other that always seemed stymied by unexpected events and, particularly, her inhibitions that I had accepted as no longer issues.

Her worries about "signs" foretelling unwanted things to come had gradually subsided in what I came to recognize as her accepting the moment as she had often expressed to me; now is important, too.

She seized the moment again. She had initiated our affair that March Sunday of 1963, then brought us to matrimony more than two years later. She had gotten jobs along the way that repeatedly bailed us out of financial jams. She had turned down a world class career as a Vogue model to stay with me and never mentioned it again. She had been a faithful companion as I continually took her on adventures that revealed great diversity in humanity shown in vast variety. Among our travels, she had struggled through emotional baggage that continually got in our way. Then, on this day, she became free of all that.

I arrived at our #8 S. O'Bannon townhouse following completion of my Advanced Warhead Maintenance training on a beautiful day at the end of May, 1968. With hugs and kisses exchanged with Mary Alice among greetings to Sandy and Jill, I was in need of a pit stop and stepped up the stairs to drop off my grip, then went to the bathroom. Mary Alice followed me. My normal to pee was seated since I did not like the noise and splashing from standing, and as I sat there, I was instantly grasped by Mary Alice's coulats and panties falling to the floor. Stepping her bare legs in boots from them, she reached into my crotch and pulled me to my feet. My manhood now enormous, a few strokes to prime the pump, she straddled me with her legs wrapped tightly pulling me into her. Mary Alice had never done anything like that. My pulse soared in our moments of slow, gentle, deep union as if I was being absorbed by her. Her shoulders pinned to the wall, a buttock in each of my hands, I was so thoroughly entangled with her that nothing in the universe existed but us. With her hands firmly gripping my biceps drawing me closer, her

144

tensed abdomen pulled my very essence into her with such intensity that I nearly went to the floor. Eyes tightly closed, her focus was entirely on us as she held me firm with deep gasps for breath, moments of intensity as never before.

In those moments, my long affection for Mary Alice was sent into a domain that I did not know existed. Those moments so singular, so spectacular were to remain by far the highest moments of my life with her. She opened her eyes looking straight into mine and smiled her little smile of satisfaction, then placed her hands on my cheeks drawing my lips to hers. Our kiss sealed entry of a new entity; us. For the first time in our time together, Mary Alice was completely mine without concern, her inhibitions previously in the way no longer existed. In those moments of union I was her and she was me, bound forevermore with affection that would never be challenged thereafter, my one and only sealed, her one and only sealed in moments of shared ecstasy.

In those moments, another entity emerged. I was so taken by her that just touching her was my singular desire; I placed my hands on her warm cheeks to caress her beautiful face as I gently fondled her earlobes between finger and thumb. That gesture, my caressing her cheek and fondling her earlobe was to remain my "sign" of love to her thereafter. Her response was to press her hands against mine, kiss the heels of my hands followed with her "I love you" and a smile of satisfaction that I knew to be real without the slightest doubt. Only moments had passed, but we were in a different universe.

"Loving you always; Forgetting you never; Yours for a lifetime." In those moments, Mary Alice became my beautiful Mary.

We had guests, and our return to them began another evening of laughter and recollections. One was about John. He had been transferred to another command and was also in Albuquerque during the time of my TDY assignment. We renewed acquaintance at the NCO Club where I went to call Mary. He had been in our townhouse many times and had affection for her that I did not know about. The prospects of talking with her prompted an offer to pay for the call if I would let him talk to her. That seemed odd to me, talking long distance with another man's wife, but he was so insistent that he offered me five dollars more just to get to talk to her. I do not know what was said, but I stuffed the bill into my pocket. More stories and more laughter with friends made that evening a most satisfying day with memories that have endured.

At bedtime, Mary slipped into a nightie and under covers before me, keeping herself hidden until pulling back the covers welcoming me to bed with her. Following small talk, hugs and kisses, our normal tryst led to sleep. The next morning, I was wakened by Mary's hand investigating me, feeling my rise to her touch for the first time, then, another tryst. She had never done anything like that before.

That afternoon, as I entered the front door, I noticed to my right that Mary was standing rather oddly by the kitchen windows bathed in sunlight. I surmised that a concern of some sort was about to emerge. Instead, she reached for the top button of her blouse. Without a word, with eyes fixed on me, she went to the next button, the next in succession, dropping her blouse, then her bra gently to the floor. Down came her coulats and panties again. She stepped from them and stood before me, the very image I had wanted from her from our beginning, to admire her natural beauty. Slipping off her boots she stood before me my Venus, the goddess of love that she was for me, now in her natural glory and so magnificent that this image of her was burned forever into my psyche... Indescribable beauty.

The hit song, *Come Softly to Me,* was exactly these moments. She stood waiting for me to shed my clothes, saying nothing as I also proceeded unhurriedly, completely absorbed with her natural beauty, *Can't Take My Eyes Off Of You* moments, visions seen for the first time. My beautiful Mary was beyond beautiful, her trim form of perfect proportions was... words simply did not apply. With my manhood in full form, she walked slowly to me, climbed me, wrapped her arms around me and caressed my body with hers, her warm breasts moving so delectably on my chest played into another sequence of slow, gentle, deep movements, her shoulders pinned to an adjacent wall, her small buttocks in my hands, her legs and her arms pulling me into her with all her strength; we were once again enraptured in each other.

Those moments completed a transformation in my beautiful Mary. From time before me, cracks had appeared in the emotional cocoon that had long constrained her life, and now she had broken free as if a beautiful butterfly basking in the warmth of radiant sunlight for the first time, pulsing magnificent wings that were to give her flight to anywhere, free at last.

As told in many love songs and verse that were continual boy-girl expressions in our lives, we had become one. We had come a long and often difficult road together, but together we were as never before, just as she had wanted in her proposal to me. My beautiful Mary was finally comfortable with me. Almost. I wanted her to be my nude dancer, to dance for me, and I asked, but that was a bridge to me that she could not cross, and never did.

How to express those moments in words remains a challenge, but since then, whenever a love scene in a movie has the characters hurriedly ripping their clothes off to engage, my thought has always been, that is not the way it's done.

During my Mediterranean adventures, I visited museums that displayed the works of ancient artisans who sculpted their visions of the feminine ideal to become renowned works of art. After Mary's butterfly moments with me, my vision of her feminine form was number 1 on my A-List, and she remained there, her trim figure my vision of feminine perfection that far surpassed ancient art.

Years before, my beautiful Mary had initiated our relationship with her lovely eyes, her engaging smile, and her outgoing personality that captured me like no other girl in my life. She had initiated our marriage with her proposal, then her secret acquisition of our marriage license followed by her incessant desire to be with me wherever I was going. During her butterfly moments engaging me as never before, she opened the door to another summer place that was filled with long hours of simply holding each other. Hugs of delight to be together were ours. She had always fit perfectly in my arms, but now that fit was... well, indescribable.

That evening she made a request of me, a rarity from her. Saying she had read that message causes breasts to grow, would I message hers? More than willing, we began an evening TV watching routine; I sat high on pillows, she sat lower between my legs with her back on my chest. With my arms around her underarms, I watched my hands message her magnificent breasts and gently caress her nipples while thinking how odd the contrast; earlier that day these very hands had serviced a B53 thermonuclear bomb, its yield of nine megatons for one purpose, to destroy Moscow in a single blast, and here my hands were delivering the gentlest of caresses to the most important person in my life, my goddess of love so thoroughly entangled in me that I was, once again, entirely absorbed by her.

I mentioned repeatedly that she did not need larger breasts; her form was perfect to me. She only smiled, letting me know that my attention was what she wanted. The touch, the warmth of my hands, the caress of love became our exchange that always brought the most enduring of her smiles, the very image of her glowing face that remains with me to this day, *The Shadow of Your Smile* always with me.

Mary knew that I was aware of her cycle, and both of us knew that taking birth control pills had almost eliminated her cramps, although with a migraine headache from time to time. Nearly free of such encumbrances that spring, after five years, her outlook had changed dramatically; she was the out-going, confident Mary that had captured me at our first meeting. The gloom brought by her "signs" had faded. Emotional burdens that had haunted her had become resolved to no concern, replaced with smiles and laughter. My beautiful Mary was as free as a butterfly, and we became playmates. Another first came the day that she stepped into the shower with me. My delight in sudsing her everywhere, front, back, up, down, every curve, every nook, was an adventure of sight and feel that was nearly explosive to my pulse. She was so magnificent, so real to my touch

148

that *Playboy* foldouts were no longer of interest. She was my China doll who came alive in my arms.

Along the way, a pretty kitten came to us. Mary wrote of Kit-Kit saying;

Kit-Kit was a mustard colored tabby cat who came into our lives when he was about six weeks old. Kit-Kit started out from the beginning as a very unusual cat; he would rather have beer than milk, and he would rather have champagne than beer.

During this time my husband and I were stationed on a military base, my husband was in the Navy. Many of our friends knew about Kit-Kit's unusual taste, and when they came to visit they would pour Kit-Kit a bowl of whatever they were drinking. Well, that cat would get completely snockered, he would start across the floor and his back end just would not work; he would sway from side to side; he would make it to his basket and literally pass out. Have you ever heard a cat snore? Well, he would lay there all stretched out and snore up a storm.

To go along with his beer and champagne, Kit-Kit loved jelly beans, but just certain colors, pink and purple. (Who knows, maybe if he had lived longer - the White House.) Kit loved jelly beans even before President Reagan declared them a delight.

Kit-Kit had very definite ideas on which cat foods he would eat. One day while shopping the grocery was out of our usual brand of cat food, so I bought another brand. I placed the food in his dish, he took one sniff and pushed his plate over to the his litter box and proceeded to cover the food up. Then he stuck his nose in the air and strutted off.

One Christmas we went to North Carolina to visit my parents and we took Kit-Kit with us in the car. We were driving a small sports car. Kit-Kit would stand in the back with his front paws on my husband's shoulder and look down the road for hours at a time. Or, if he got tired, he would curl up and sleep. When we arrived in North Carolina, my father had killed a beef and he had some fresh meat

149

ground and in the frig. He gave Kit-Kit some. One time was enough. From then on it was love. He would go straight to my father, circle him about twice, walk straight to the frig, pull in his nails so that he would not scratch and stand on his back legs pawing the door until my father would give him some more meat.

Not only were Kit-Kit's eating habits unusual, so were his sleeping habits. If we were down stairs he would sleep in his basket, but if we were upstairs or when we went to bed, he slept in the bathroom sink. He would curl up in it and sleep, but if he heard a noise, all we could see of him was his ears and eyes sticking up over the edge watching everything that went on.

Kit-Kit loved to take baths, but only with me if I was taking a bubble bath. He would get up on the side of the tub and walk back and forth slapping bubbles, and invariably, he would fall in. I began to think that he planned it because, after his bath we put him in my hood type hair dryer, pulled the bonnet up around his neck, and turned it on warm. He loved it and came out looking like a fur ball.

During days, weeks, and months following, the needs of living day to day that budgeting entailed, Mary was the most relaxed that I had seen of her since... well, like never before. Her job at the PX service station and my job servicing nuclear weapons continued unchanged, and during weekends, we frequently ventured further into the area, especially into and around Nashville.

One day after work, Mary came home to excitedly tell me a lengthy tale of the Bell Witch. I had never heard of such and was skeptical, but she went on describing what her boss at the service center had told her. He was a member of the family whose ancestors were haunted by the witch, and he told her story after story that occurred in nearby Adams, Tennessee, where Sandy's wife, Jane, was from. The story was already a hundred years old, but Mary wanted to see where the witching took place, so we drove through the area, even through a rather high covered bridge, another first for us, but never saw anything other than gently rolling farmland. Her boss gave her a

150

little book published many years before that was said to be an authentic accounting of the witching. Mary read it with great interest that led to a long enduring topic of our conversations. She was willing to say that, who knows, it might have happened. One particular aspect of the tale that her boss told was when the witch split and went to two different churches one Sunday and became mean afterward, brought on by confusion. Mary identified with what church teachings could do, her own experiences in particular.

From time to time our excursions were interrupted by our Alpine failing to start. Continually learning the car's aggravating idiosyncrasies had become just more of it. On one occasion I could not get the car to run smoothly and arrived at the auto garage on Base for help. The gruff Chief Petty Officer in charge of the complex diagnosed the problem to be a burned valve. How he knew that from just listening to the irregular beat of the engine as it idled was due to long experience, and he was correct. With a big bill for repairs anticipated at the Sunbeam dealership in Nashville, he would have none of that, what with all the equipment there to do any kind of repair. He was right again, and under his tutelage, I did the repair in a single day that returned our roadster to running smoothly and cost only the price of a replacement valve. In addition, I gained deeper experience with keeping our English car running properly.

Our little red roadster, dubbed the "fast tomato" by one of my fellow sailors, took us into Nashville and surroundings on several occasions, including Andrew Jackson's The Hermitage, the Grand Ole Opry, the Ryman Auditorium, Printer's Alley, and walks along music row where each store of a country music star blared recordings through loud speakers outside. As a throwback to our drag racing days, we even made it to Beach Bend Park for more quarter-mile action with open pipes, smoking tires, and screaming engines. I love it, always have. We went to Bluegrass Dragway near Lexington when visiting my "Big Sis" and her husband. Mike and L.B. always welcomed us, but my go-go-go manner got in the way of visiting.

That summer and fall continued as before, our daily routines. Mary received a raise; I was promoted again; our harmony was the smoothest of our three years of marriage; we had grown up together; whatever came along was as she had predicted in her proposal; we did it together. She turned twenty-four that August; I was yet to reach my twenty-second birthday the following December. Between those dates, we celebrated our third anniversary in early October of 1968 among friends who came to our #8 S. O'Bannon townhouse to party with us. Kit-Kit received more than ample servings of champagne and put on a show of inebriation that had us all laughing hysterically.

By then, a whirlwind romance with a handsome soldier, a Viet Nam night stalker, had taken Jill into an untenable relationship that rapidly disintegrated into parting. Sandy had brought Jane into his life, and... something was missing for us. My beautiful Mary wanted to be a mother. I knew how to do that, and by the New Year she was completing her first trimester, still beautiful, and on her way through a textbook perfect pregnancy. Then....

Early one June morning as we prepared for the day, Mary's water broke. I called in my situation needing the day off and drove her to the Fort Campbell Army Hospital where we had regularly attended pre-natal classes in preparation for becoming parents. Mary wrote her recollections saying:

...we finally were expecting our first child. I had a perfect pregnancy, but when I got to the hospital, everything went haywire. I did not dialate, the baby could not be born. I was hemorrhaging and went into a coma with a rare blood type. The doctors told my husband that they would have to do a cesarean section to save the baby, but that I probably would not make it. But thanks to God and modern medical knowledge, about thirty hours later I came to, to find out that I was mother of a healthy 6 pound, 10 ounce boy.

There was much more to that story. Upon arrival at the hospital, everything proceeded normally until the young doctor assigned to her began flitting around spouting orders, saying the baby was coming breach and that could be deadly. His manner so unprofessional and so unsettling caused me to request another doctor. Soon to replace the twit, Doctor Magandanz came to me with a much more confident manner that was reassuring. The Army nurses were well seasoned with child birth, but I could see that this one was unusual. Morning hours passed into afternoon as I waited, expecting to take my wife and baby home any moment. As time passed I became increasingly concerned and continually pestered the nurses for news. With each inquiry I encountered what I thought was gloom. What was going on? What was wrong? Late that evening as I sat in the waiting room more concerned than ever, the lead nurse approached me. As I stood up expecting good news, her expression was anything but good. "You need to get your affairs in order," she said matter-of-factly. I had never heard that expression before and wondered what she meant. "What?" I asked.

"You need to get your affairs in order," she repeated. "Your wife is... she can't deliver naturally. We are doing a cesarean section to save the baby but it looks like Highland's membrane will take him, too. That's what killed Missus Kennedy's baby," she said with a grimace, then turned and walked away.

I stood there a lump of cold stone fixed to the floor. Her footsteps away were the only sounds I heard as I watched her go through swinging doors, their sounds quickly vanishing. Then, I was completely alone, and had never felt so alone, so empty, so lost in a swirling sea of thoughts. Unwilling to accept that my beautiful Mary was dead and our love child with her, all because of me, I was forced into thoughts as never before. I had to tell her father. How could I possibly do that? I had fulfilled his admonishment that lust was a sin; I had sinned with such adoration for his daughter that it had taken her life. How could I possibly tell him? How could I possibly request of him a place in the cemetery for his daughter and first grandchild? Such thoughts made me completely immobile, only to sit back down in the waiting room wondering what to do next.

Later, when Doctor Magandanz came through the swinging doors, I stood up expecting the words I never wanted to hear to come with final authority, my mouth as dry as a desert. He asked me to sit down as he did, and he began by saying that the procedure went well, that Mary was in intensive care recovery and our baby was doing well in an incubator. Exactly opposite of what I expected, but so uplifting that I had difficulty finding words, particularly words of thanks for his attention at such a late hour. Reassuring again, he said that everything would be okay, that I should go home and get some sleep. I took his word for that.

The next morning I called in my situation needing another day to attend to Mary, then went back to the hospital. Checking with the nurses, I was told that Mary was still in a coma. I thought that unusual for a pregnancy and inquired further. She needed a transfusion due to severe loss of blood, and the hospital did not have blood for her rare antibody blood type. A special flight to Walter Reed had secured what was needed, and Mary was expected to recover, although still in intensive care recovery. Around noon my continual pestering of the nurses raised my concern; Mary was still in a coma. Later that afternoon, inquiry returned news that both Mary and our baby were doing well, that she had regained consciousness and the baby showed no signs of Highland's membrane. Such relief so overwhelmed me that I had to sit down. With deep sighs, I had to catch my breath with my thoughts running rampant.

Later that day, Doctor Magandanz ask me to join him in a room assigned to Mary. As her bed with all sorts of attachments, tubes, bottles, and such was rolled in, Mary was so deep under that his attempts to rouse her were repeated. I watched, hoping, waiting for her to open her eyes. She was slow to come around. Later when recalling what she remembered, Mary told me that the first eyes she saw were brown eyes and she was confused. The thought crossed her mind, Alex has blue eyes, whose eyes are these?

Doctor Magandanz stayed with Mary far longer than I expected, and he went into detail reassuring me that she would be okay, but that she had extensive internal damage that would preclude any more children. Explaining the extent of her surgery, a long cut down her abdomen, I was immediately struck with sorrow for her, having just months before become comfortable with showing off her magnificent form that I continually described as perfection, knowing now that she would likely never again think of herself as pretty. And, never again did she wear low cut slacks or a two piece bathing suit.

More days of hospital recovery went by. I went back to work, arriving at the hospital as soon as I could each day. Then Mary and our son were to be discharged into my care. I was so relieved from what I had thought I was facing that I went to the PX and bought the largest box of chocolates available and took it to the nurses as a gift for their care given Mary and Squire. Chocolates was exactly what they did not need, being about twice my size already.

Having bought a small wicker laundry basket, padding, and baby blankets, I was prepared to bring our infant son home. The day came that I placed the basket with Squire behind her seat, then helped Mary into our Alpine and drove carefully to our #8 S. O'Bannon townhouse.

I was deeply concerned; how could I care for them properly and work, too? A solution was already in place; our next door neighbors, the Otwells. Betty was a nurse who took care of Mary and Squire each day for the next month or more while instructing me in what needed to be done. From their arrival, Mary was able to feed Squire who never seemed to get enough of her breasts and steadily gained weight. She gained strength, too, and initially with assistance to and from, she was soon able to attend to her needs on her own. Bloody bandages gradually subsided into cleanliness to avoid infection as healing continued. The day came that Mary saw her scar for the first time. She cried, saying to me through her tears that I would not love her anymore because she was no longer beautiful. Many reassurances thereafter were needed to convince her that my feelings for her had not changed, that I was *Glad All Over,* as one of our favorite songs told, that she was back with me. Her greatest concern was anguish expressed in, "Why couldn't I have had our baby naturally? I almost killed our baby." Years went by before I told her how near death she had come.

We had been repeatedly told that our cat would have to go. So, upon first arrival at our townhouse, I settled Mary in, then brought in the basket. Setting it on the floor, I let Kit-Kit investigate and waited to see what would happen. He raised up on his hind legs, gently placing a front paw on the edge of the basket, he sniffed and looked over Squire for several moments, then concluded that this baby was his. Thereafter, he was so intensely protective of Squire, with hisses and bristled back, claws displayed, that we had to close him in a spare bedroom when anyone came to visit. Mary described our kitty and his new attack mode, writing:

Kit-Kit was a very important part of our lives. We had been married almost four years and we did not have any children. Then, the unexpected happened, I became pregnant. Our friends told us that we were in for problems, that a cat, especially a male cat was going to be very jealous of the new baby.

When the big day came, we took our new son home from the hospital and introduced him to Kit-Kit. We sat him down on the floor in a basket, and Kit walked round and round him and sniffed him, then curled up next to the basket and went to sleep.

However, there were some problems when friends came to see the new baby. Kit-Kit was all teeth and toe nails. We would have to put him on his leash outside in order for our friends to get near the baby.

Kit-Kit was a joy in our lives, and I like to think that he is in Kitty Heaven somewhere.

There is a new big yellow cat in our lives now and a new baby boy but; Ah - that is a another story.

Within a few weeks, the grape vine began telling that Clarksville Base was going to close. The scuttlebutt told that nuclear weapons reduction per the Salt II Treaty was the reason, and my job of maintaining records of all classified material on base, that my license, Authorized to Transport Explosives, meant that I was to accompany all weapons to their point of departure leaving the base as the on-site expert responsible for handing chain of command documentation to the carrier; truck, plane, and train. That also meant late nights doing load-outs, and thanks to Betty, Mary and Squire were looked after. By Mary's birthday that August, she was strong enough to be on her own.

As personnel were assigned elsewhere, Clarksville Base and its housing annex where we lived rapidly became ghost towns. As the summer progressed, all of the pristine features we knew became empty and overgrown with trash blowing in the wind. I was the last warhead guy to leave, and I occasionally drove my US Navy pickup through the Q Area by myself, two having previously been mandated. On this drive, no guards, no communications, no badge transfers, nobody.

My orders were to ship's company on the USS Forrestal aircraft carrier for a Mediterranean cruise, departure from Norfolk expected in November. That gave Mary and me only a month or so to make the move and to make preparations for my long departure. I was assigned another nuclear weapons school while the ship was being readied for departure, and Mary and Squire were able to spend several weeks with me. I checked in at the school during late September to discover that, once again, no married housing was available on Base. We were assigned quarters on the beach, a nice motel with all the amenities. We were among similar military marrieds who had set about partying. Every afternoon and weekend was one clambake or crab boil, one grilling after another, little of it palatable to Mary who was reticent to participate among seafood odors that made her nauseous. She preferred spending as much time with me as she could.

While driving through Norfolk one day, a massive BANG! and a cloud of steam engulfed our Alpine. I quickly turned into an adjacent parking lot suspecting that the engine had come apart, a

157

complete disaster that we could ill afford. Investigating, I discovered that one blade of the fan had broken off, the BANG!, then severed the outlet hose from the radiator, the steam. Rather than a disaster, the repair was hardly a set back because I had driven into an auto parts store parking lot, and they had all the parts I needed. With sufficient cash on hand and the tools I kept in the car, I soon had our Alpine running as before. What a stroke of luck; that fan could have broken anywhere on the long miles from Clarksville to Norfolk, and we would have been stranded miles from anywhere.

I was concerned that Mary remained in a delicate condition and set about securing a place for her and Squire to live. It did not occur to me that her parents might provide their home, so I did not inquire, and Mary did not make such a suggestion. I thought it my responsibility to provide for my family, and when I learned that one of her first cousins was selling a nice two bedroom mobile home, we decided that would be the right thing for us because I planned to exit the Navy after my cruise, and we could move it to our next location; college. With her father's agreement to set the mobile home in his garden spot, we secured a loan and bought it, while arranging with Sammy to pull it with his tractor the mile or two to our location. I set it up on a foundation one weekend while her father hooked up electric power and installed a makeshift septic tank of barrels that worked well. I made arrangements for allotment of most of my income to go to Mary at her home address, and with the day soon coming for me to report aboard ship, I drove her and Squire to our mobile home. Leaving the car with her, I thumbed back to Norfolk. We were set.

Knowing that I was facing nine months or more of sea duty, on the following Wednesday, the 5th day of November, Mary wrote:

Hi Lover Boy,

Well here is your wife with the shattered nerves. Our son got his third set of shots today, he is very sick, feverish and sore. He has cried all afternoon. I feel so sorry for him. It cost $9.00. I had him hold the bill if the government won't pay for it, then I will when I get

158

the money. Dr. Bickley said that you would have to take care of it through the Navy. He said he thought the gov would cover it but he has no forms or anything of that nature, he has never taken care of military dependants before. Will you please see what you can do? Thank You!

I sure hope you get to come home this weekend. I miss you terribly. You know, I really do love you. Do you think you will still love me when you get back; I am getting older you know, maybe I will be old and ugly and you still young and handsome, you may not want me. I guess I have seen so many broken homes and so many quarreling couples it scares me. I want you to be happy. I want you to live with me because you love me and want to, not because you feel that you have to. I love you very much. I just hope the feeling is mutual. I don't want you to think that you have to stay with me because of Squire. I am really backing this all up. I want you to know how much, much I like and love you, and I mess things up. I hope you can come home soon so I can talk to you. I will probably talk your ears off.

We have another tree up, the Asiatic Cypress. That makes three up, 1/3 of them. How about that, some green thumb huh.

I hope to see you soon.

Love, your wife
Mary
Your Son
Squire

We had undertaken growing dwarf trees thinking that such a long term project would be interesting as a growth measure for Squire, that, some day, we could give him a dwarf tree that began life with him. Later that winter, a mouse got in and ate all of them to stubs. None survived.

My exploits during those nine months with my rich uncle's yacht club are covered in detail in my book, *Adventures of an H-Bomb Mechanic*. It contains many references to Mary and our times together and apart. I often wrote to her about my exploits that were more of an extended Mediterranean vacation than difficult, and I always carried in my wallet a photo of her and Squire. Off the ship, I was on one adventure after another, especially historic sites that I had read about and seen in pictures, and there I was in the middle of the real things. My cruise took me to many interesting destinations, but never was there a challenge to my commitment to Mary, even finding myself in the red light district one day as I walked Valetta to see the sights of the old Maltese city. Memory of our moments, of her first butterfly moments were so enduring that there was never a thought of anyone but her in my desires. Being true to her and returning to her was never in doubt.

From my first Mediterranean sunrise to each port-of-call afterward, I was enthused about destinations that my tour of duty provided. My first liberty was Barcelona, Spain, and I had a mission; the son of a family member had married a girl from Barcelona, and no one had met her family. Would I? That proved to be a most interesting and entertaining two days of liberty.

On the 14th of May, 1970 I penned a letter from the USS Forrestal to Squire for his first birthday that June:

Dear Squire,

As father to son, I do sincerely wish you a Happy Birthday, your first in this world. To have watched you grow for less than half a year, and then to wish you a first happy birthday is rather difficult but, sometimes, even the most sincere of fathers are obliged to leave home. Fortunately, my return is near, I hope the better for both of us.

May the kindness of life and the gift of happiness be granted you throughout your life.

With respect as human beings and love as a father.

Daddy

160

On June 18th, I wrote to Mary saying;

Hi Dearest Sweet One,

Well, would you believe the big thing here is "Oldy Goldies." Everyone is buying the albums as fast as the ship gets them. Right now its "Splish-Splash." Even the guys who cut their teeth on this outsville modern stuff are going for it. (It's like a revival of my active high school days.) None of the songs are after 1964 so you get the idea it is.

We've received a change of schedule. This middle-East thing seems to have cooled down so we are back to general "show of force" cruising. The Admiral requested and got permission to go to Naples so we are going there afterall. I'm very pleased about it but I'm afraid I have to put a hold on sending you the $15.00 I promised. Unless you object, I hope to use it for looking over Naples and Mt. Vesuvius....

My love for you is sincere.

Hubby

As my tour of Pompeii and Mt. Vesuvius developed, I was the senior man on the tour and was made Shore Patrol with an arm band signifying my stature. That also meant my tour was no cost, so I used the $15.00 to buy Mary a small cameo that I watched the craftsman carve. When set in a nice gold-silver filigree bow pin, it made a beautiful gift from of my tour, and only cost $15.00.

This item and others were my mementos acquired for Mary during my cruise, some actually surviving shipment to her, that were to remain treasured items as gifts from me. Both of us proved to be pack rats who tended to keep everything that, in time, became our burgeoning stuff of life, most of it stored and never used.

As I spent months cruising the beautiful Mediterranean with liberty in port after port, back home, two personalities were shaping events. Miraculously, our Alpine remained reliable for Mary, in addition to her ability to keep it going, so she had transportation for attending classes at the Community College in Dobson where she extended her post-high school education that had begun in Clarksville

161

at Austin Peay State University. There she reacquainted herself with old friends and family while also returning to her father's life, church functions and such that she attended without comment. She also drove with Squire every week to visit my Mom and Jacob who still lived in the small house that I grew up in.

Some years earlier, Jacob reentered Mom's life to become her second husband. Decades earlier he had been a friend of Dad's, a fellow long haul trucker, and Mary's outgoing personality now included him along with Eula, another life re-entry, this one for Grandpa John. During the 1920s, he had been the school superintendent who hired Eula, a young teacher from Georgia, to teach in the nearby Little Richmond School where my Mom, as a child, and her children attended, myself included. Eula had boarded with Grandpa John and Grandma Alice, then returned a widow to become Grandpa John's second wife following the death of Grandma Alice.

Mary wrote often to tell me of this or that involving Squire and herself, always noting her love for me. I responded in kind. Squire was the second personality who shaped events around him. Our mobile home of two bedrooms was positioned so that the window above his bed faced Garvey and Zell's house a short distance away across the driveway. Squire, if he pulled himself up and stretched to his tiptoes, could just see over the bottom edge of the window, and whenever the noise of the door opening or closing got his attention, he began calling out for Papa or Mema as he watched whoever was in view. Papa responded to the extent that grandpa and grandson formed a life bond that continually grew with pleasant memories. Mary wrote that they were often together, Garvey carrying him as he had done when Mary was a child, then similarly holding hands as Squire began walking. Garvey became the male influence in Squire's life in my absence that was to remain thereafter as many fond memories were made through the years to come, especially during holidays when we regularly returned to Mary's home.

My sailor's income allotted to Mary was just enough to cover basic expenses with a little to spare, and with continual meals in her family home along with a trickle of cash given her by her father and mother and from my Mom and Jacob along with cash that I sent when available, Mary was getting by comfortably, but just getting by month to month. Without an unplanned expense, she was okay. That unplanned expense occurred one day when Charlene came to visit. Afterward, backing her car to leave, she backed into the rider side front fender of our Alpine. With no money for repairs, that crunch remained for the next forty-seven years, until I carefully beat out the bent sheet metal during restoration, returning our roadster of so many memories back to pristine showroom condition. Mary and her brilliant red Alpine became subjects of a local newspaper feature; original owner from fifty years ago, having selected the Alpine off the showroom floor of a Sunbeam dealership on May 6, 1966.

Following that year, roadster production ended, meaning that replacement parts became increasingly harder to find as the years went by, and that required hoarding what parts I came across, eventually to include four Alpines and three Tigers of the same body style that were also out of production. Final count became three, our Alpine and two Tigers as a matched pair, one for Mary and one for me. They were to remain players in Mary's life throughout our later years that totaled almost fifty-five years of marriage, a love affair with my beautiful Mary that never diminished among memories galore that we had gathered in her Alpine.

Raleigh

When Mary and I talked about what we would do after the Navy, my going back to college was my goal that she fully supported. I had the GI Bill for several years of modest income each month, and she was willing to go back to work. I had applied to North Carolina State University in Raleigh to enter as a freshman in Physics, rather than engineering, and was accepted. Our mobile home was paid for, and relocating it to a trailer park in the town of Cary a few miles from campus was completed just prior to beginning classes, fall semester 1970.

Both Mary and Squire were healthy and made the move with me. However, we did not have the funds for tuition. As a veteran, application for a loan secured that need, but it also meant that a $7,500 debt loomed over us. I would have to find income to supplement our needs and did so with a succession of part time jobs through an agency. Mary found a full time job in a cracker bakery/factory in Cary that was to become a curious twist in our progression through that time.

Why physics instead of engineering? Marine Architecture was no longer on my list. My Navy experience with nuclear weapons along with several courses I completed in mathematics and nuclear sciences had reoriented my interests. I had become thoroughly fascinated with modern physics with a deep thirst to delve into its various branches. After reading many books during my Navy time, I had learned that an immense body of learning existed, and rather awestruck by it, I wanted all I could get, especially atomic and molecular physics that I saw as the makeup of everything, and, therefore, important to understand if I was to understand the world I lived in.

Mary had achieved academic excellence throughout her education and expected the same from me. I was more than willing to be a student, but money problems presented continual stumbling

164

blocks. My part time jobs kept me from studies that I had rather have spent my time on, but we continually needed the small income I earned. Traveling was restricted to no more than going home, always a refreshing desire for Mary. A few hour's drive from Raleigh, our families within close driving distances permitted us to visit both during a weekend with overnights in Mary's home where Squire thoroughly enjoyed time on the farm, especially with Papa. The garden spot where our mobile home had sat was garden again, and from it came all sorts of produce, some of it generous gifts to us.

Once again, we were getting by. But along with needing continual attention and associated costs, our Alpine was not what we needed for three. We needed another, much more reliable car with more room. So, with agreement from Grandpa John, I parked our roadster in his barn, there to begin over forty years of waiting for the day when I would revive its purpose; this time as an antique car. Also in that agreement was my Mom answering my request for aid in buying another car, an American car this time, one that I could service, a four year old Chevrolet Camaro that we would keep as primary transportation for years to come, all the way through my completion of graduate school during 1979.

During November of my second year, a doctor visit for Mary returned the startling news that she was four months pregnant. Based on what we had been told by the Fort Campbell medical staff, that was not possible. And, without a hint bolstered by continuing her period as usual, she was not convinced. Her doctor's confirmation became the source of many conversations that sent her downward into gloom. First and foremost was her deep concern that pregnancy was the end of my education. I assured her that was not an issue; we would find our way with another child. As the months passed toward April, 1972, her doctor attended to her needs regularly with close attention to monitoring her progress toward another caesarean section. With her medical history known, preparations were put in place for as gentle a procedure as achievable with the additional incentive that the surgeon's reconstruction would eliminate much of her abdominal scar that she was so ashamed of. Everything went as her doctor prescribed, and during April, Wesley was brought into this world from her womb, another healthy boy, another love child from our union that had remained undiminished from her butterfly moments.

Along the way, her job at the cracker bakery/factory became an unexpected, curious twist of events. My part time jobs through the agency had taken me onto many job sites, one of them the cracker bakery/factory. My job there was to use an ordinary shovel to move peanut butter from where it was produced from cured and flavored peanuts to load into an ordinary wheel borrow by shovels full, roll the wheel barrow to another location, then reverse the process to deposit the peanut butter into a machine that deposited a small dollop between two crackers. Stacks of the peanut butter crackers were then wrapped and packaged for market. I was not impressed with the antiquated factory and immediately saw many ways to improve the process, particularly to improve cleanliness. The shovel and wheel barrow technique had worked just fine for years, so there was no need to improve anything, certainly nothing from a temp.

In her office job, among idle conversation Mary had told her associates about me being a student and about my previous job working part time with the University on a project for the U.S. Department of Agriculture. I had told her about the job and how interesting it was; the USDA was deep into studies of peanut aflatoxin in commercial products, specifically vending machine packages of peanut butter crackers.

Mary's idle conversation went straight to top management who interpreted my presence in their factory as subterfuge by the USDA to reconnoiter the factory's operation and Mary's presence to reconnoiter management. She was fired immediately, and I was terminated, all of it from pure happenstance. But not so for the factory's management; major modernization was soon undertaken to remove production from all human contact, thereafter to be fully automated and computer controlled from raw peanuts to finished products, a thorough and costly renovation.

No adequate explanation for our terminations was given to us, remaining a mystery until revealed the following year. What was especially troublesome was that Mary was progressing in her pregnancy with anticipated medical coverage from her job. That was terminated, too, and we were stuck financially. Recognizing the dilemma we were in, Mary's doctor charged us nothing for her care, a most unexpected and welcomed outcome. Also that spring, I was selected the Hayes Scholar by the Department of Physics with a scholarship that was sorely needed. We were getting by when Wesley arrived, and we continued to do so, largely from my part time jobs while Mary recovered, then soon to find another job.

The mystery of what had happened to us at the cracker bakery/factory was revealed one day when I happened upon one of the managers in a store. He recognized me, and presuming me to be a government spy, he told me proudly, indignantly, in no uncertain terms, that I should see their modernized factory now. I did just that, with an escort into the facility and an escort out. It was so thoroughly upgraded that nothing remained of the old works except the building. Upon leaving, what irony, I thought; all that change because Mary and I were perceived to be government agents due to her telling associates that she could not tell them what I did in the Navy, all secret, then working for the USDA, too? Clearly, we were seen as threats to the peanut butter and cracker business. The up-grade, however, was absolutely necessary in my opinion, if no more than improving sanitation; all of it done purely because of happenstance.

Suddenly without incomes, I had no choice but to get a job. While Mary remained unemployed and taking care of our boys, I drove to work, then to school, then home on a tight routine. Having graduated with a degree in physics, another in mechanical engineering, while working full time I continued my graduate program in the Physics Department. Courses were now more challenging than ever and more intriguing in what I was learning, really interesting physics and mathematics. When offered a position as a teaching assistant in the Department of Physics, I took on additional

167

responsibilities because classes were in the evening. That meant even less time at home.

Our mobile home park was nicely laid out with paved streets that accommodated increasing numbers of homes as new sections were complete. Our location on Peg Drive was convenient to all things we needed in addition to a centrally located clubhouse and swimming pool almost in sight. The clubhouse, however, was rarely used. One day, Mary told me that she and a neighbor lady were discussing use of the clubhouse as a children's day care center. The idea progressed to the owner who saw a plus in additional earnings from rent. I did the drawings that were approved by the city, and once the owner had suitably modified the clubhouse, it was approved and licensed.

Their idea proved a good one. So many families in the park with young children took such immediate advantage of the new facility that the two of them were soon in need of assistants. Sisters of the neighbor lady were brought on staff along with other mothers in the park looking for employment. This enterprise quickly flourished into a significant source of responsibility and income for everyone involved, but when Mary's accounting began showing discrepancies, she was accused of robbing the till. Within months of its establishment, she found herself against an array of sisters, each suspected to be pocketing cash payments for childcare rather than turning it in for accounting as was done with checks. Dissolution of their partnership resulted in Mary leaving to become Director of Children's World, a Montessori school for pre-kindergarten through third grade. Thoroughly professional, this position proved ideal for her interests and lasted for years, toward the end of the 1970s. One aspect that made Children's World such a welcomed position for Mary was that Squire and Wesley went to school with her.

Parenting was not without its terrifying moments as shown one day when we could not find Wesley. We thoroughly searched our mobile home, even inside our boys' toy chest where we had found him asleep on a previous search. Mary was near frantic; she checked outside and with our neighbors if they had seen him. No one had seen him. Wesley was lost, and when Mary curled in my arms amid her tears asking if I thought he had been abducted, we faced the most terrifying moment that any parent could face. We sat in our mobile home looking at each other, about to call the police, when Wesley came walking in, rubbing sleep from his eyes. Relieved beyond description, we asked where had been. He had crawled under the pillow of his bed and went to sleep. He was so small that the pillow and covers had remained undisturbed, and we had repeatedly overlooked him.

Signing on with the Environmental Protection Agency research center located in the Research Triangle Park put me in a satisfying position of basic research studying the hottest topic of the time; degradation of earth's protective ozone layer by manmade freon gases used in refrigeration. My boss was the Congressional Special Investigator on the issue, a chemist of high renown, who led a team of researchers that produced new information resulting in the ban on use of the culprit freons. I was doing fundamental research on atmospheric and stratospheric physics that led to adding another minor in that area to my graduate program.

Becoming quite proficient in Fast Fourier Transform Spectroscopy and use of high precision optics for analysis of the chemistry of earth's atmosphere, my research led to fulfilling that portion of my graduate studies, determining infra-red absorption coefficients of the atmosphere. My identification of five wavelengths at which the atmosphere was transparent led to unexpected applications; lasers of those wavelengths became "Star Wars" defense studies presumed to be the answer to how to knock out a missile attack with high power lasers of those frequencies. The long path cell, its optics, computer and associated equipment was given to the University of California-Riverside, and trucking it out to the west coast was a multi-day excursion that became another travel story.

My job with EPA was on track to expire, so I sought other employment to land a position as an engineer with Aerotron, a

169

manufacturer of professional quality radio communications equipment with facilities across town. With both of us requiring transportation, Mary and I went into debt for another car. I was driving an hour or more each way while Mary drove to her school with our boys about thirty minutes each way. With two incomes, we were in the best financial position that we had seen in years.

How Mary became friends with a real estate agent is, perhaps, due to a child under her care. We began discussing buying a house, a huge step up in debt that caused both of us to blink. However, in further discussions with the agent, she mapped out our finances saying that rent bought nothing and that as our incomes progressed during years to come, we would see ourselves in an increasingly better position. We could afford payments for buying a home, and that would pin our expenses unchanged through coming years making payments increasingly easier toward eventual paying off the purchase. When paid off, our cost of living would drop drastically with no mortgage. Not only would we own our home, it would have value that we could use as collateral for such things as college education for our boys. She was convincing, and we began looking at homes.

In the nearby town of Apex, a home builder had cleared a forest into a housing project with spacious lots. His method to keep initial selling prices low was to complete portions of a home necessary for living while leaving unfinished portions that a buyer with handyman skills could finish over time. We looked at such a home on Boxwood Lane on the back fringe of the development, one that had remained unsold for months, and it appealed to both of us. During 1974, it became our first home, and while Mary fretted about having so much debt, I was enthused with prospects of finishing a third of the tri-level myself. Doing so, our living space increased while also enhancing the value of our home, and, it was done to our taste. Completion took years that was a carpentry learning experience for me while also fulfilling for Mary, a new home of her own in which she employed her interior design interests. She was thirty when we moved in.

170

The following years were among the best of our lives. Her surgery with Wesley had made the scar on her abdomen much less disappointing, and her natural good looks had progressed from pretty to beautiful. She had stayed trim and shapely with gorgeous hair, attributes that she enjoyed culturing with fashions, made or bought, that enhanced her presentation. Showing no signs of aging, she could easily pass for twenty. And, we danced and danced.

Mary was pleased with herself and our situation, although by far the deepest in debt that we had ever been. She endeavored to assist financially by submitting writings to magazines. Such as the following written during 1974:

Mrs. And Proud Of It;

Lately when I read articles in many of the most popular young women's magazines, I really get irked. The articles always seem to be written by someone with a beef against someone. Either she is wanting to sign her name Ms. instead of Mrs. or they are griping about whose job it is, hers or his. His job to carry out the garbage, hers to do the cooking.

Why is there a his and hers in a marriage? To me a marriage is a partnership, no his and hers but whoever sees something that needs to be done, and has the time does it.

I am not speaking off the top of my head but from experience. I have been married for nine years and have two little boys ages 5 years and 2 years. And believe me, we know the struggles of today's world, but I still am proud to sign my name Mrs.

My husband and I were married in 1965. After one year of marriage Uncle Sam beckoned and my husband answered the call. We spent four years in the Navy. We both continued our college education wherever we were stationed. Then after four years of marriage we were finally expecting our first child. I had a perfect pregnancy, but when I got to the hospital everything went haywire. I did not dialate; the baby could not be born....

... as told in the foregoing. She continued to end in summary:

... So you see, it has not been easy, but we are a happy family. We are still struggling, my husband is still a student, and I will go to work again this fall to help him to obtain a long waited goal. We work together, we are partners. We have problems, we are two individual people, but we sit down and talk them out. We have a lot of faith and trust in each other, and... I will always be proud to sign my name <u>Mrs</u>.

Like previous submissions, this one also did not get into print.

Two new aspects of our past re-emerged, dancing and cars. Many functions at Children's World involved dressing up, exactly what Mary liked doing best, and she was often in an eye-catching outfit. We joined a square dance group where we progressed to become exhibition dancers. With three other couples, another set of four, perhaps a third, we put on exhibitions at shopping malls among other sites that drew crowds. Being rock 'n' rollers, we also attended street dances where we polished our moves once again, doing our twirls, spins, dips, and '50s sock hop moves that also drew crowds of spectators. Mary had kept her poodle skirt outfit and put it to good use again. These were mostly good times, but the gasoline crisis that emerged during that time caused considerable worry; without gas, getting to our jobs was questionable. Without incomes, keeping our house was questionable. Mary worried about things like that.

While I was both full time employed and a graduate student, my Navy time came to an advantage with another part time job; with my security clearance from those years, I landed an afternoon assignment as bank courier that involved a little over two hours of driving to branch banks after hours to pick up the day's receipts, then returning to the home bank with the cases. Before becoming a courier, bank management needed to verify my credentials. Since I had my official military records, one of the managers went with me one day to see my records. Upon arriving at our Apex home, Mary was outside talking with a friend. The manager was instantly taken by her good

172

looks and remarked without thinking, "Oh my aching bacon...", then abruptly apologized for the outburst. When I told Mary, she was pleased that I got the job and to have such a compliment said of her. Arriving home about seven-thirty each evening. Mary and our boys arrived before me, and she prepared our evening meal that was regularly served as a sit down family occasion.

Then, our lives turned serious one spring when Wesley was diagnosed with spinal meningitis. His decline was worrisome and quite apart from anything that we, as parents, could do. Mary was especially heart struck because he was her "miracle child", the description that she had often said of him since being told that she could have no more children after Squire. A long recovery resulted in fragile health that led to recurrence of meningitis the following two springs, three successive bouts. With the third, our family doctor became absorbed with resolving Wesley's condition, largely driven by his own young daughter having died from a similar affliction. His attention to our boys was such an influence that both decided at their young ages to become medical doctors, and did.

Spending our evening meal and family time together brought a fatherly challenge to me; Wesley's stubborn streak emerged. He would stub up and not talk, worrisome to us as we wondered what was wrong that he would not talk about. Father and son had some issues, a test of my fathering that did not go well on occasion. I bought more books to help me, but they proved ineffective due to that aspect of Wesley's behavior remaining unreachable.

Mary's position as Director of Children's World brought many opportunities for involvement of the school, its teachers, and students. One was the parade that a municipal organization planned and phoned to inquire if Children's World would like to participate with a float among other activities. Mary and her staff seized the occasion and developed a range of ideas. One was to promote foreign languages taught at the school. Wesley was in the French class, about four years old, and to prevent potential over-exertion, he was selected to ride a float and represent France. Among other students dressed in costumes of the country they represented, Mary sewed a knickers outfit for Wesley that was topped with a beret suitably cocked to one side of his head. The teachers used parade preparations as learning tools for the children who participated in all aspects of the undertaking. The students and staff had a beautiful and enjoyable day for the parade.

Another opportunity was a phone call one spring from the local Cracker Jacks people who were looking for two children to participate in a television commercial. Mary offered our boys, Squire at seven and Wesley at four. Perfect! The filming showed our boys running gleefully with open boxes of Cracker Jacks in hand, their contents bouncing out all around them, a delightful commercial that brought lots of compliments.

Cultural activities at the school involved regular dress up days in which the teachers and staff dressed a particular theme, such as pirate day, western day, Spanish day, and similar themes, much to Mary's delight. Students were encouraged to participate, if they wanted to, and many did. Each year's Halloween season included a masquerade, another of Mary's delights and a photo of her in her Zorro outfit has survived.

For the graduating class that year, 1977 - '78, the staff prepared for the annual ceremonies with the theme, Discovery, in which students participated with songs and dances as tools for developing bodily coordination and rhythmic awareness, along with exploring foreign languages and culture, ending with achievement awards. The program flyer cited Mary saying in acknowledgments:

And to our Director, Mary Alice Gabbard, in appreciation for her cooperative efforts and assistance in maintaining and helping to implement our high level of education.

Mary was immensely proud of her school, staff and students, and their activities, a satisfying time in her life that also kept her boys nearby during those years. From Children's World, our boys graduated to become students of the A. V. Baucom Elementary School near our

174

housing community. During this time, I discovered an A. C. Cobra that could be bought for $8,000. With a loan lined up, Mary did not arrive at the bank during the prescribed time, a school function required her attention, and further discussion led to our only stand of opposites. I wanted the Cobra, and I had a plan in place to pay for it, but her comment, "Eight thousand dollars for a 1964 car that doesn't run? We can buy a new car for less than that" was correct, and another debt at that time was a looming concern, but.... I did not buy the Cobra, a roadster worth more than a million dollars today that has since then become a topic of discussion from time to time; a fortune lost due to a difference of opinion.

Later, I discovered a rarer Sunbeam Tiger that I bought for $2,500. Mary went with me to look at it, a check in hand, and did not quibble with its purchase. That roadster was a good looking, running car, after some attention, that I often drove to work while first giving our boys a ride to school at A. V. Baucom. In addition to Mary's Sunbeam Alpine, the Tiger led to our lifetime of being Sunbeamers. Later, several more of the roadsters were acquired, three to remain with us as of this writing, each beautifully restored, among them her Alpine that was returned to showroom condition with the plan to retrace our Route 66 drive; same car, same couple, fifty years later. Events did not permit the outing.

Along the way, I became aware that my photos needed upgrading to a good 35mm camera. So, I bought the multi-volume set, *Kodak Encyclopedia of Photography*, that led to a top of the line Canon with assorted lenses and equipment. Learning methods of professional quality photography produced the results I was looking for. Those techniques grew into a second profession with thousands of publishable quality images. Most importantly, many family photos were acquired, especially images of Mary, so photogenic, that are now treasured moments.

Capturing her presence and beauty on film has filled many albums, photos that became additions to her collections prior to me entering her life. This equipment also expanded her interest in

175

photography begun in her 9th grade science class where she learned basic photo and dark room techniques. Later, taking a college course resulted in excellent images with a submission winning a photography contest. Both of our boys also became excellent photographers, and as her portfolio grew, these photos led to renewing fashion modeling, an aspiration recalling the opportunity presented to her during our time in Chicago.

Our lifetime of avid participation in car activities revived with earnest during our early Apex time. When I learned that the Shelby American Automobile Club included Sunbeam Tigers among Shelby cars, having built the first prototype that led to production of the roadsters, I joined, then complained about not seeing any Tiger features in the club magazine. The editor wrote back saying that if I wanted to see Tiger features, write them. That admonishment began my writing career that has remained a steady source of adventures resulting in hundreds of auto magazine features with my photos, including cover stories, along with dozens of books, three of them receiving Book-of-the-Year awards in international competition. Book fairs, signings, speaking engagements, racing, and all sorts of car functions in which Mary and our boys participated are recollections that we often reflected upon during later years. Being associated with many of the world's premier racing personalities among some of the most historic cars has given us a lifetime of memories, all from an admonishment to get busy.

Branching into travel stories for magazines and newspapers added another facet to our lives that involved lots of travels throughout the United States and Europe, stories that harkened back to our Navy time in our Alpine, especially driving Route 66 and New Mexico. All of it has been a family enterprise with Mary the General Manager of our business. Along the way, hundreds of photos of her have become the source for my compilations of MP4 Mary's Movies, each one a fabulous walk down memory lane for me, especially seeing my beautiful Mary in so many settings; wonderful, wonderful memories.

176

After recovering from another surgery during the summer of 1974 to resolve gastric problems due to adhesions grown from her previous abdominal incisions, Mary's health received another boost when she went through procedures to identify allergies. Suitably treated, she was largely free of their influences giving her several years without such encumbrances nearly as limiting they had been. Another health benefit came from her surgeons who reduced her abdominal scar to much less obvious, but it was still there, and she remained concerned that my expressions of admiration for her beauty would lapse.

I had accepted her reticence to show off for me, knowing that my affection for her was the reason for her scar that so concerned her, and I continually reassured her that she would always be my one and only, that my affection for her was not at all diminished. She, being a worry wart, remained continually concerned that I was unhappy about this or that aspect of her. Then, as happenstance would have it, one day I saw a small plaque humorously displaying a lackadaisical frog with the admonishment, "Thought for Today: It is better to get laugh wrinkles than worry warts." That so perfectly fit what I wanted for Mary that I bought it, to remain displayed in our bathroom ever since.

Humor, however, was simply not part of her being, and I was never able to instill lightheartedness in her outlook. Mary had good reasons to worry, an entanglement of her deep desire for carefree happiness that she had known as a child along with the sobering secret from her childhood that she kept to herself; she had learned that her physiology was not quite right, and she continually had to be careful not to exert herself to avoid fainting. Adding a mother's worry for her children, especially her concern for Wesley's tenuous condition, the same that had taken the life of his doctor's young daughter, was ever-present and led to parent talk with serious overtones.

As the years advanced through the 1970s, Mary's well-being steadily improved, although she remained concerned that I thought less of her because her surgeries had left her unable to conceive another child. I assured her that Squire and Wesley were enough, and

177

as a family, I could not have been happier. Wesley's recovery from meningitis led to sustained good health as he grew; Squire's health remained strong; my health also, and Mary was beautiful. We were a model American family who lived in a nice home; our income sustained us with jobs that were fulfilling; I was advancing toward completion of graduate school leading to a professional career; and, we could often "go home" for visits and holidays that occasionally included Sunday church services. To "go home" was a continual source of rejuvenation for her while attending church had largely become looking upon the cemetery with remembrance of those she had known.

We were busy living the good years, and Mary rarely asked for anything more. She was comfortable with herself with attention to always looking good, her gift to herself and to me that often came with a smile, a kiss, and a hug. Her up-beat manner with everyone she met was a life habit that drew compliments, beginning with her delightfully spoken, "Hi". She liked being positive and pretty, and I never missed a chance to express my admiration because I knew that hidden within her were worries that bound her from the free spirit feeling she recalled from her youth. And, I captured many of her best moments on film. In our private moments, she tended toward melancholy, especially if an irate parent had yelled at her, a source of worry if she had handled the situation correctly. She quietly endured such pricks without argument, but they were hurtful. And, her students coming from widely varied backgrounds were continual sources of how she saw life to be so unfair, especially unfair to children of parents who seemed more committed to their careers than their children, mothers who brought their children to school unwashed, unfed, in dirty clothes, and left unconcerned.

I look back upon those years through photographs that show our model American family captured in a instant on film and remember that not shown in the photos are the circumstances of the moment; Mary was not developing laugh wrinkles. Serious concerns kept coming across the horizons of our lives.

During the spring of 1978, Mary showed me a discharge from one of her nipples and cried. The specter of breast cancer suddenly loomed large, and diagnosis of a lump resulted in another surgeon slicing into her beautiful form. Thereafter, that breast remained misshapen, and Mary's concern that I was unhappy with her reached a new level. This beginning was to take her down a long and disquieting road that she was compelled to go, a road of great concern to her when looking upon changes to her feminine form. What began with the scar on her abdomen, her now imperfect breast would also remain hidden from me. One lumpectomy after another during years to come left her in despair. She endured but was further saddened with each occurence.

Being a student at N. C. State, I was an avid Wolfpack fan and thoroughly enjoyed the university life. Including Mary and our boys in frequent events, such as stage performances put on in The Theater In The Park, a Raleigh city function involving students of the performing arts. While full time employed, my research with high power lasers brought Squire and me to the lab during numerous evenings and weekends toward fulfilling my research requirements.

Family life continued to present its challenges. Mary wrote:

Growing Pains

The children of today do not just have problems due to growing pains, puberty, and pimples. They have to face drugs, alcohol, sex, and peer pressure. Believe me I know; when I was in school my biggest worry was whether or not I would get a pimple before my next date or what to wear to the ball game. Not so with today's children.

What would you do if your 8 year old joins in the dinner conversation with, "Mom, how do you have sex?" Would you do like we wanted to do, scream and bury your head somewhere, or try to give a calm answer?

It seems that an 8 year old neighbor boy took some of his dad's Play Boy magazines and was educating most of the other children in the neighborhood in the fine arts of sex. (It seems that) he

179

was also using some very choice four letter words to describe the pictures.

My husband and I handled the situation in what we hope was, if not the correct way, at least the rational way. No - we did not bury our heads in the sand - even though I wanted to.

We had what we called a pow-wow with the boys; we tried to make them feel comfortable and not like they were being lectured to or scolded.

My husband and I tried to explain sex to them using simple but yet explicit terms, medical and also the beauty of sex between a man and a woman who love each other.

We then let them ask any question that they wanted to and use any of the words that they had heard. We tried to explain the words and answer their questions.

My husband and I feel that this approach has worked for our children. They were satisfied. The subject very seldom comes up anymore, however as they get older, we know that it will, but we hope that by being open with our boys that they will feel confident and comfortable enough with us to come to us in the future if any situation should come up that they have trouble with or don't understand.

This was another magazine submission that did not make it into print.

Finally graduating during the spring of 1979, attending the ceremonies was a dress-up family affair with photos taken to document the occasion. I had become so enamored with the intricacies of modern physics and supporting mathematics that I could have become a lifetime student, and opportunities for further studies were abundant, but employment remained necessary. Setting further education aside, a job and its income was required, and when the Michelin Tire Corporation in Spartanburg, South Carolina expressed interest in hiring me to develop non-destructive testing of tires using laser holography, Mary and I talked about the prospects. A career of making tires?

What I wanted was to do Fusion Physics at a National Laboratory, and both of us recalled our Albuquerque time with such satisfaction that I repeatedly sought a position at Sandia Labs. Each enquiry resulted in being told that the lab was not hiring.

Mary was supportive of whatever decision I made, and when an offer for an interview at the Los Alamos National Laboratory was received, we were enthused, until we went there. Squire and Wesley stayed with Mary's parents for us to fly to Albuquerque, then we were driven to Los Alamos. The long drive itself was a demerit, and once there, the isolation was another demerit, meaning that near nothing supported families other than the great outdoors, and there was plenty of that. Mary was not outdoorsy. And, housing was far more expensive than anticipated, another demerit. What Mary's real estate lady showed her, small homes on tiny lots on the market in White Rock, the bedroom community of Los Alamos at the base of the mesa, resulted in the list of demerits growing longer. Significant among them was the cost of water that had to be pumped up from where it was available, then the cost of sewage that doubled that cost. Even though the salary was thirty percent higher than my engineer's income, the cost to live in or near Los Alamos far exceeded our anticipation. That offer; thanks, but no thanks.

One memorable aspect of our interview was meeting Doctor Strangelove. While we sat in the waiting room, who should walk in but Edward Teller. Credited with being the father of the H-Bomb, I was immediately struck with the very human aspects of this infamous Hungarian physicist who led the development and production of warheads that I had trained on. The man himself. With introduction, our brief conversation has remained a memory of contrasts; this grandfatherly looking man with a heavy accent was instrumental in shaping the Cold War, when the USA and USSR stood nose-to-nose for decades bristling with nuclear weapons, weapons that he promoted sufficiently for him to be placed at the top of his own laboratory charged with designing and producing progressively smaller, lighter,

181

more easily utilized warheads designed for no other purpose than massive destruction.

Following other leads, the same outcome resulted from my pursuit of a position at the Lawrence Livermore National Laboratory in California. Costs of living were staggeringly high, while the location of the Lab surrounded by bustling city was not appealing to either of us.

Given our disposition against city life, neither Batavia in Chicago nor Brookhaven in New York made it onto our list that had been reduced to a single location; Oak Ridge National Laboratory in eastern Tennessee. We had visited Oak Ridge a decade before during our jaunts to and from Clarksville, and both of us liked the location that was remarkably similar to where we had grown up; Appalachian mountain terrain. I had answered postings for positions available that were applications through the Lab's hiring network with no results. I tried another plan. I wanted to do controlled thermonuclear fusion research, and the Lab had a Fusion Energy Division. So, I wrote directly to the Director of that Division. I knew about uncontrolled thermonuclear fusion in detail from my DASA H-Bomb time, weapons of enormous explosive power utilizing the physics that Teller has been mistakenly given credit. I wanted to get involved in civilian applications of nuclear energy, controlled thermonuclear fusion as the source of electric power production.

A letter extending an invitation to interview for a position was received during the spring of 1980. And, once again, our boys visited with their grandparents while Mary and I drove to Oak Ridge during the Easter Holiday weekend. When we arrived, I was told that three interviews were set up for me. The first was at Y-12, a huge complex also dating to the Manhattan Project of World War Two. Being well informed with the history of that A-Bomb project, I was interviewing in the very heart of that undertaking, the location being the site of fuel production for "Little Boy" that destroyed Hiroshima. Two Y-12 interviewers were particularly interested in my weapons experience and with my Top Secret Q-Cryto clearance. I did not realize why they

182

were interested until I learned that Y-12's function was bomb making. With that realization, my response that I did not want to do bombs anymore resulted in my immediate dismissal.

The second interview was with the director of the Instrumentation and Controls Division of ORNL, also known as X-10, its code from its secret WW-2 origins. That Division Director was looking for an engineer, but funding for the position was not yet in place. Expressing my interests in physics rather than engineering resulted in dismissal from that interview.

The third interview was with two researchers in the Fusion Energy Division. One was looking for a new hire with strong electronics experience, not my field, although my laser background was of interest. The second interviewer presented a problem; he was British and the NOFORN (Not Releasable to Foreign Nationals) part of my clearance meant that I could not discuss my military experience with him other than saying I was a Gunner's Mate in the US Navy, my old cover. The person he was looking for was to replace a Fusion Energy veteran who was retiring in a few months. The position was middle management for operation of the Division's highly complex fusion research facility, exactly what I was looking for. The match was made, and I was his new hire. A few months were required to make arrangements, and during November of 1980, Mary and I once again packed our belongings, our boys this time, and we watched movers clear out our house, then move into another one.

Our beautiful blond pure bred cocker spaniel did not make the transition with us. Buffy was stolen just days prior to our departure.

Oak Ridge

We liked our Apex house, and we liked our lives in it, but my working toward a career in physics had materialized. Our move to Tennessee to the Lab was exactly what I wanted, but it soon proved near disastrous for Mary and our boys. Our house quickly sold giving us some cash reserve, but once in the Oak Ridge area, prices for a comparable home were considerably higher, and worst of all, our move was during the time of mortgage interest rates nearing 14%, almost double the rate for our Apex home. My primary family attraction to Oak Ridge was its school system, one of the best in America, but we could not afford to buy in the town.

The Oak Ridge National Laboratory reservation was only part of the huge expanse of land sequestered from farmers for the Manhattan Project of World War Two. Beyond Oak Ridge was housing in the western reaches of Knoxville and Knox County, but that required a lengthy drive both ways. Roane County to the west, Loudon County southward were other directions outside the reservation.

The Lab gave us three days to find a place to settle, and when our real estate lady showed us a Loudon County home vacant for months, a fixer upper that I saw within my capability to upgrade and within six miles of rural driving to the lab, I was interested, especially that the property adjoined a TVA hydroelectric dam reservation with out-doorsy recreation available to us. Its road a lengthy drive through the park became our driveway, a pretty place to live where we as a family enjoyed swimming, picnics, basketball, and walking. With its varied backgrounds, it proved to be a great location for photographing cars.

Our first months, however, set an uncomfortable trend; Mary was not able to find employment comparable to Director of a Montessori school, and she worked a succession of part time assignments in hopes of finding a position she liked. My income was reduced by 21% from my engineer's salary in industry that began our financial difficulties. Both Squire and Wesley were enrolled in an out of Oak Ridge school system that proved to be less than expected. Continuing and compounding difficulties were made steadily worse because I chose to put most of our financial reserve into purchase of the house to reduce our monthly payments; reserve we kept was soon exhausted. That set us on a worrisome course. Our troubles were just beginning. Mary never complained, but I soon recognized that I had made an enormous mistake with the move.

During the following months, that conclusion was made solidly evident when Squire's growth required larger shoes, and we did not have the money to buy new shoes for him. I was able to find a heavily discounted pair of zippered dress style boots for him, but they were too big and were not at all what he liked. I watched him walk uncomfortably in them and thought, what have I done to my family? Worse, they became the subject of ridicule among his classmates.

When Wesley came home from school distressed day after day, I soon learned that student taunting was new to him, and he had no experience with such behavior. Both Squire and Wesley had proven to be excellent students, where such behavior was unknown, and we, as parents new to the area, wanted to help where we could. At our first PTA meeting, Mary introduced herself to the Principle with a brief statement including being past Director of a Montessori school. His response was telling; we stood there disbelieving when he told Mary in no uncertain terms that he was not interested in her in his school in any capacity, and he did not want her even talking with his teachers. We were dismissed cold. At that moment, I realized that my mistake was a more than serious setback to our boy's education than I had ever imagined.

That stuck in my being and was amplified as the year passed; not once was there any assessment of our boys' education, except for Wesley's teacher who recognized his distress and sought to resolve his despair brought on by his being accustomed to close association with his teachers, especially for having his mother nearby during previous

185

years. Attention to him produced significant results: Wesley formed a lifelong admiration and affection for his teacher, and his transition to so different an educational environment was eased toward returning him to excellent performance. Mary and I remained ever grateful to his teacher who turned out to be a neighbor.

That first year was distressing for numerous reasons, largely driven by our much reduced income and my growing dissatisfaction with our boys' education. I thoroughly enjoyed my position at the Lab and could not wait to get to work each day, but Mary was often sick. That October, our 16th anniversary month, she was diagnosed in need of a hysterectomy to remove her right ovary that was showing signs cancer. That completed, just seven months later, a similar diagnosis about her left ovary resulted in a repeat surgery. Mary was not well for extended periods of time, and that bore heavily on her, that she was not doing her part, that she was a burden to me, and her trend toward melancholy was augmented by being alone each day. I often had to work late, and once home, assurances that things would get better, my ever-positive outlook, was ill placed; she handled our finances and saw their steady decline. I had to do something, perhaps a part time job, but that would keep me from home longer, exactly what neither of us wanted.

Having received good reviews for my performance at the Lab, I set about to fulfill my initial notion that permitted entry with that 21% decline in income a target to increase. I believed that I had joined a prestigious institution of world renown, the highest concentration of Ph.Ds on the globe, and I was deeply proud to be included. I believed that I was due for an increase in salary, desperately needed at the time, so I arranged a meeting with my Division Director to discuss the matter. I laid out our financial need that was near bankruptcy and augmented our need with good reviews of performance. I had shown interest in advancing my career with a succession of courses and believed justified in asking that my entry at 20% below median for my pay grade be brought up to median, not an actual raise, just median, a reasonable request, I thought.

The Director listened without comment, then asked pointedly, "Do you have a rich uncle?"

That question took me by surprise, and I stumbled for an answer, saying something akin to each of us live with hope that we might have a rich uncle somewhere.

He was serious. "Ask for your inheritance early," the Director told me bluntly.

I left his office with an entirely different perspective of the Lab and my position; mine was just a job, and I was just an employee. When I arrived home that afternoon, I had formulated a plan; I could not expect anything more from the Lab, I would continue to be a good employee, but I was on my own. That evening, I sat down at our dining room table with Mary's Underwood typewriter and composed another car story, this time for a recent newsstand auto magazine I had on hand. Prior to our move, we had attended a number of auto races, and I had a selection of good photos for the story. I knew what to do from my experience composing features for car club magazines that paid nothing, and once photos were captioned and integrated, I put everything in an envelope addressed to the editor and put the package in the mail the next day. In less than a month, a check for $400 came to me. I saw a way out of our financial hole.

That first feature led to a succession of features that grew into a second career. A year later, many magazines had bought features and photography to the extent that my earnings exceeded my Lab income. Mary and I were more than out of the financial woods and began traveling to get the stories and photos required... going to races, and that led to extensive weekend travel, 3-day, or 4-day excursions. Going places led to branching into compiling travel features and photography. Each succeeding month, newsstand magazines and newspapers continually contained my features. During succeeding years, so many of my features had been published that acclaim began coming to me. That acclaim led to more assignments and an evaluation of my Lab performance as, "...does not appear to be dedicated to the laboratory."

I enjoyed working at the Lab, always looking forward to a new day of adventures among its cadre of premier scientists and staff, but I was not dedicated to the Lab, it was just a job to do to the best of my ability, the same outlook that I applied to everything I did. Later I rose to senior research staff, was technical lead on a number of projects and topped at Group Leader with millions in funding to design, build, and operate a seriously complex facility to test and evaluate highly radioactive nuclear fuels, a first for the Lab and the world. My group achieved that goal, and we received commendations from the Division Director that our facility worked perfectly.

Among a career of other assignments due to my demonstrated ability to get things done, with each of my projects brought to end on schedule and within budget, I had the satisfaction of completing each objective in addition to inventing and demonstrating new concepts in the Lab. Along the way, my acclaim as a widely published writer was not lost on Lab management, being told once that, "If you'd put the effort into the Lab that you put into writing, you'd really be something around here."

My answer, "What something would I be more than I am already? Writing rewards me, the Lab doesn't."

That comment was to remain the measure of my twenty-five year career with the Lab, retiring at 20% below median of my pay grade, exactly where I began, never having received a raise regardless of good reviews, well managed projects, and continual contributions to lab missions.

At home, Mary's quiet time provided opportunities to record her thoughts. The following is another attempt to get published in a women's magazine, another attempt that did not materialize. She wrote:

There have been many articles lately concerning the pros and cons of the working mother, articles concerning day care centers versus private home care. Some of the articles really are opposed to women leaving their children for any reason.

188

I, as a mother who had to work, would like to pose this question: Which is better, the quantity of love that you give your child or the quality of that love?

I was one of the few lucky working mothers. I was the director of a day care center, therefore, my two boys were able to be with me. I did not work in the room with the boys, but I was nearby, and I could pop into their room from time to time.

Since I was the director of a very large day care center, I had the opportunity to observe many children over a span of about five years. I found, through my observation in almost every case, that the children benefitted from their experience at the center. The center offered kindergarten from 3 year old up to third grade. We offered French lessons starting at age four, ballet and tap lessons, swimming lessons ages three and up.

The children learned to share, to trust other people, to be comfortable around grown ups other than their parents. Their academic record was great; we had some three year olds that could read. From my experience I think I can honestly say that a mother can work outside the home and still give her child the best of both worlds; a lot of love at home and a rewarding experience found in a good day care center.

I had the good fortune to take my observations a step further. After I left the day care center I worked in a public school system for almost two years. I worked with the five year kindergarten program.

The children that came to us from day care centers or play school programs were easy to adjust and within a week were settled down to a classroom routine. However, the children who had never been away from their mothers many times cried for two or even three weeks, or were selfish and sometimes destructive.

Again, weigh your own situation and if you decide to go to work, do it without feeling guilty. Just follow some simple advice; check out the center you are considering carefully, visit the center two or three times, talk with other mothers who have their children there. Three points that are very easy to spot are; if the center itself is clean,

189

the children are happy, and the center's license and health rating should be posted for you to see. If these things are obvious, then you can feel safe to leave your child there.

I hope that this will help you feel better about your decision to go to work. You can have a career and be a good mother, too.

Meanwhile, Mary's medical concerns became tormenting. She wrote:

OH NO! Not Again

As I listened to the doctor's diagnosis, I thought I was going to faint. Fear squeezed my heart, and anger and panic swept over me like a splash of cold water. How could this happen again? More surgery! The last operation was supposed to be the last one.

Surgery is certainly nothing new to me. Eight was more than enough, this would make number nine, and I dreaded each more than the one before.

The worst of my anguish is fear of being put to sleep. I always have the terrible feeling that I won't wake up. It seems instead of getting easier, each time I face surgery I am more afraid than the time before, and the things I read did not help at all. There are so many negative reports in books, magazines, and in the media that any type of female surgery seems to have lots of doubt connected with it. Surgery as simple as a D&C has consequences blown out of proportion in some articles I've read. ("Do You Really Need That D&C?", Woman's Day, 8/2/83). It is hard to find literature that is informative and does not cause doubts about what needs or does not need to be done.

The surgeries I have had in the past were the type that did not require any soul searching. They either had to be done, or I would die. It was as simple as that. I had both of our sons by C-section. Later I had a huge ovarian cyst removed, then three breast operations to remove tumors. These were surgeries that helped me, and did not

190

take anything away from me. My body was still complete, I was still a whole person.

Then in October of three years ago, I was told I would have to have a hysterectomy. I could not believe it. Me! I was still in my 30s, and certainly not ready for that much of a change in my life.

Before I agreed to the surgery, I tried everything else I could first, including every type of medication the doctors prescribed. I took nerve medicine, pain medicine, one medicine after another to try to correct my problem.

I read articles like "Hysterectomy: What Every Woman Should Know," Ladies Home Journal, 8/83. I talked to everyone I could think of, hoping they could give me some insight into such a major step. What I got was more confused and depressed than ever.

In hopes of getting a different diagnosis, I chose to have a small incision made in my navel so the doctor could take a look with a light and let me know what he found. The verdict was the same; to stop the bleeding and increasing pain, I would have to have a hysterectomy.

Soon the realization struck me; I was becoming dependent on my medication, and the pain was getting no better. Even though scared and afraid of not waking up, I knew I could not spend the rest of my life in pain or on pain pills.

I felt almost forced into surgery and lamented, "Why me?" I consented although I wanted the doctor to, if possible, leave one of my ovaries so I would not have to take hormones.

The surgery was lengthy and very difficult because of adhesions all over everything. The surgeon remarked that my insides looked like they were stuck together with glue. My right ovary was so badly damaged it had to be removed, but I was able to keep my left ovary. Heavy loss of blood required transfusions two days in a row, but the worst was over, or so I thought. My left ovary was in good shape, and I would not have to take hormones.

I was relieved and thankful that at least everything was taken care of. I hoped I was finally going to feel good again, it had been

191

three years. However, such was not to be. Much to my horror, about six weeks later I had a huge knot in my left side, and walking became increasingly more painful. Then back to the hospital I went for more tests that showed a growth on my left ovary. I tried again to correct the problem without surgery.

Within six months I knew, deep down inside, I knew I needed to have surgery again. I would have to be put to sleep again, and the thought scared me more than ever. It seemed as though I was being punished for something, but what? I was afraid of dying and terribly confused. How could this happen again?

The night before the surgery was awful. I kept thinking, "How will I feel? Will I be able to tell that I am empty inside, that I cannot produce hormones? How will this affect my sex life, my mental wellbeing. How will my husband react? How will he feel? Will he think of me as only part of a woman? Will he no longer enjoy our sex life? Will he leave me like some of the stories I had been told?"

When I woke up after the operation, I was surprised that I did not feel any different than I had after any other operation. The surgeon told me of removing a growth the size of a grapefruit along with my left ovary. He consoled me saying that if I had not had the operation, it would have gotten worse until the surgery would have become an emergency operation.

I was still worried about my relationship with my husband and wondered if I would grow a mustache. I was told it might happen, and everyone said I would get fat. I feared the worst and told my doctor about my fears. He explained, that if he could have removed my ovaries and uterus by magic without me knowing that they were gone, and I started taking hormones, neither my husband nor I would be able to tell the difference.

My recovery was faster this time, and after three years, I am taking hormones daily and feeling great. Hormones are the only medication I am taking on a regular basis, and my husband and I have a very normal and enjoyable life together.

192

We feel that the surgery saved my life, and neither of us feels that I am less of a woman from having had a hysterectomy. Instead, I have regained my health, and my husband now has a happier wife. We are both looking eagerly toward a long, productive and happy life together.

During January, 1984, Mary submitted her story to *Redbook* Magazine for consideration to be published in the "Young Woman's Story" section. We never saw it in print. Later, she submitted it as a college paper and received an A+. In her journal Mary recorded private thoughts and reflections, including:

Stress:
1. My father has been an invalid for over a year now. He has Parkinson's Disease and Alzheimer's. Mother is trying to take care of him at home. We live about 5 hours away and cannot help out as much as needed. I also injured my neck and shoulder trying to work with my father.

2. One of my brothers cannot deal with our Dad's illness and he won't come around any of the family. He says, to him, Daddy died a year ago.

3. We are also trying to get a writing business going, and when things don't go right I feel at fault.

4. Both of our sons are in college; Squire is an M-2, second year medical student in Memphis, TN. Wesley has one more year at UT, then he plans to go to medical school. There never seems to be enough money to go around.

Mary and I talked often about our growing up years, and I encouraged her to continue writing her stories. She dusted one off

193

from her Hope Chest, a childhood remembrance composed in her teens for high school.

Princess Rose

The night Princess Rose died was a blue norther. The gigantic moon hovered strangely on the distant horizon. Its light shimmered through the trees making shadows dance to their own mischief, shadows that wavered and moved giving me an eerie feeling. The frozen air was charged with a crackle that magnified sound; the brittle brown grass of winter with its crests of hoars frost crunched underfoot as I walked. Every step sounded as if I was walking on glass. In my young mind, I sensed that the spirits were restless. As I made my way through the trees, fragile, leafless limbs snapped and crackled, adding to my feeling of expectancy, my feeling that something was about to happen.

I wondered what death's door would look like. Muted talk had spoken of Princess Rose at death's door for several days. Would the door be open or closed? Could I look into what was beyond it? What would I see? I held Daddy's hand tighter as prickles danced on the back of my neck. Chills crept up my spine to meet the cold wind that blew in around my collar. Shivers ran to the very tips of my fingers. I quivered inside. I was full of flutters as I wondered what the Angel of Death everyone talked about would look like. I wondered if she would be looking at me from beyond the door.

I was certain that everyone had it all wrong. The Angel of Death wasn't waiting for Princess Rose, it was the Great Spirit that had come for her and charged the night with his presence. The white man's Angel at the door to the beyond would be disappointed. Princess Rose was a real Indian Princess, I was sure of that, because Uncle Levi had called her his Indian Princess for as long as I could remember. I knew that her long wait to go back to her people was over. The Great Spirit was there to take her back. I felt him in the prickles that raced each other up and down my neck, and in the cold wind that licked at my cheeks and made my eyes water. She had

194

wanted to return to her people for many years, the promise that Uncle Levi had not been able to fulfill. I knew that the Great Spirit had come for her. Death's song murmured in the trees with the wind and moaned in the night for Princess Rose.

The front room of the small house I was so familiar with displayed strange shadows in the dim light. Everyone talked in hushed voices and moved so slowly that I was certain that the world had slowed down. I knew that Princess Rose was dead, and I knew that I should not hop on the feather mattress of her high bed as I had so often done. I stepped up on the small stool at her bedside, but this time as I stretched up on the tips of my toes to see her, I kept very quiet. She seemed so small, so very small. I wanted her to look at me, but she didn't. There would not be a story this time, and I knew I would never see Princess Rose again.

She had been sick for a very long time, and everyone talked about how she was wasting away. I expected that nothing would be left of her as I peeked over the bed. I was sure that her baggy, wrinkled skin and boney features had somehow disappeared with her last breath. To my surprise she was still there, though so shrunken that she barely made a lump under the covers.

Princess Rose was the first dead person that I had ever seen. I am not sure of what I expected to see, but I am sure that neither the Angel of Death nor the Great Spirit were as surprised as I was. What I saw that night attacked my senses. There she lay with a white handkerchief wrapped under her chin and pulled up to a knot on the top of her head like she had a toothache. Gold coins lay on her eye lids. I wondered if that was right because I knew, if everyone else didn't, that she did not need money. What was even more strange was that people did not spend gold any more. Paper money was used now, maybe coins other than gold, but not gold. Nobody used gold.

I knew that Uncle Levi had performed this strange ritual, and I heard him say it was the least he could do for her. He kept rubbing his chin, his worry habit, saying that if he had taken her back to her home in the West that her tribe would perform her burial in the

195

manner befitting a real Indian Princess. I was sure that Uncle Levi knew nothing about how a real Indian burial was performed and that he had made this up as he went along.

I also did not understand why everyone was walking around so quietly shushing the children and talking in whispers. They just did not understand that Princess Rose could not hear them. The more I looked around, the more nervous I became. I felt a fit of giggles welling up from deep inside me, giggles at how silly everyone was acting. I certainly was not glad that Aunt Rose had died, it was just that all the whispers around me gave me an uncontrollable urge to do something silly, or maybe just plain stupid. I needed to do something to make things feel normal again. I knew if something didn't happen soon that I was going to be sick. The room was so quiet that I could hear my heart beating. Each pulse pounded louder and louder until I thought my heart would pound itself right out of me. A lump welled up in my throat, and I felt my body pulsing as if keeping time with the loud ticks and tocks of the old clock on the dresser beside her bed.

Each moment, the sounds got louder and louder. Everything in the room was so loud, the ticks and tocks, the moaning of the wind outside, and everyone kept whispering, except now I was seeing their mouths move but no sound was coming out, just weird facial gestures. Everything seemed to move in slow motion. I looked at Princess Rose in her bed. I knew she was dead, but everything about her looked like she was asleep, except for that big white handkerchief tied around her head so that the points stood up like the ears of my white rabbit at home in his pen and the gold coins that winked and glittered on her eye lids.

My ears began to buzz, and I felt Daddy pick me up. The world was so very slow. Someone put a wet cloth on my face. It was so cold, but I could not talk. Daddy carried me home. I did not feel the cold, bitter wind on the way home. I was safe and secure in the warmth of Daddy's arms. Daddy put me to bed, and that night I dreamed once again about Princess Rose and Uncle Levi. The stories that they had told me swirled through my dreams.

I cannot be certain if their stories were true or just made up to entertain a young girl on long, rainy afternoons. That night in my dreams those stories came to life just as they had many times before. Combined with my imagination and fueled with the events of that day, I can still vividly recall their fascinating tales of the old West, about gold, saloons, whiskey, gambling, cowboys, Indians and working ladies of the night.

I keep watch for the Great Spirit. I knew he was there, I could feel him there on the edge of my dreams.

While I was regularly sending features for publication, Mary rarely saw her compositions in print, an aspiration of hers that went largely unfulfilled. We were active in area writing clubs and regional book fairs that featured my work, and she was always with me, promoting me to anyone whose attention she could gather.

Those times were postponed from time to time due to another surgery. Mary's recovery from each of her surgeries was lengthy and led to continual concerns that I was less than pleased with her, concerns that waned as time went by as her outlook became brighter, especially when she completed a regimen of allergy tests and treatments that freed her of many discouraging symptoms. Our hugs and kisses were heartfelt, often with repeated assurances that she had been and would always be my one and only, but my comments were less than fulfilling due to her concerns over the circumstances of our lives, especially her being repeatedly sick. My regard for her never changed, but her comments that I was around other women all day told me her thoughts. And, once she sufficiently recovered, our travels grew more frequent and more extensive with each venture resulting in one or more magazine features along with a growing library of photography as resource material for additional features.

Not only was I able to significantly augment our income, we were soon in another good position similar to when we lived in Apex. Further financial growth came with the first book contract that arrived with an advance of thousands of dollars, and we were soon doing a sequence of books with a major publisher, three books on contract that sold over 53,000 copies to far surpass a million dollars in new commerce. That first book received Book-of-the-Year accolades in international competition, as did my second book two years later, and thereafter, almost everything I produced was published somewhere, even in Japan in that country's native language.

While spending more weekends and late hours writing, occasionally an all-nighter to meet a schedule, we returned to dancing for exercise. Mary's outlook continued to improve, and to give her something to do, I encouraged her to go back to college. She was not so sure about that and began with a single course where she met Ginger, an instructor who was so physically similar to Mary that they could pass for sisters. That beginning led to a long and enduring friendship

Upgraded to an electric typewriter, I had the annoying habit of leaving out a word within a sentence, requiring retyping with more care. At the Lab, personal computers were becoming significant time savers for the staff, and I learned word processing that easily and quickly solved my peculiar habit. One evening, that electric went sailing off the deck; I resolved to acquire a personal computer, word processor and photo image processing software, and a laser printer. With $8,600 spent on the acquisitions, I was in business big time, and compositions flowed from my fingertips sufficiently to pay for the new equipment in a matter of months.

Now more productive than ever, more late hours were spent at the keyboard, and Mary knew what to do to get my attention. After our boys were asleep, she often slipped quietly to me, gathering my immediate attention by sitting in my lap. With her beautiful eyes, light fragrance, engaging smile, if not a bit naughty, her soft lips and tempting gestures... I was captured again and again... just what she intended. Lap sitting, hugs, and kisses had long been our affair, just touching her a delight to me, my hand caressing her cheek while fondling her earlobe between finger and thumb, and this late night addition soon became a welcomed expectation for ending another long session at the keyboard. Save. My computer kept everything for my return another time.

Those years were the early 1980s leading to completion of our first two decades together. Along the way, Mary progressed from pretty to beautiful to gorgeous, but never pretentious, with her attention to both fashions and beauty secrets that retained her youthful good looks. With her slight frame of five feet, six inches in height at around one hundred ten pounds, she was the very picture of radiant good health, glowing with feminine virtues that she had cultured all her life. No one suspected that her health was anything other than vibrant. That was demonstrated at a race one day in the paddock of Road Atlanta when a participant approached me asking, "What are you doing here?"

With camera in hand photographing a car for a feature, we were beyond Mary hearing our conversation when I answered what seemed to me to be obvious, "I'm working."

He gestured toward Mary. "You ought to be in a motel room somewhere hosing that."

Surprised at such a comment, I answered, "THAT is my wife."

Thereafter, Mary being my wife became generally known to the extent that she received enumerable requests by car owners to be photographed with their cars, each one suspecting that catering to her improved the prospects of getting their car featured in a national magazine. It worked on occasion. By then, she was savvy to what kind of car was magazine worthy, especially those that were historically significant, and she led me to several features while also getting rides in many cars.

Beautiful women and beautiful cars definitely go together, and I collected many photos of her with cars that most people never see beyond photos in magazines and books. I look at those photos and MP4 compilations that I have composed featuring her and wistfully return to those really good times with my beautiful Mary.

That message, family ties, also extended to our boys who were equally adept photographers who got an assortment of rides in famous race cars on tracks wherever assignments took me.

During late 1983, I schemed to bring together the next year the 25th reunion of the 1959 World Sports Car Champions, Aston Martin team cars, team manager John Wyer and his wife, Tottie, lead engineer John Horsman, and drivers Roy Salvadori and Carroll Shelby. Phone calls and letter writing brought my scheme together during 1984 when everyone gathered at Road Atlanta along with five of the seven DBR teams cars and a host of other Astons among a grand gathering of racing cars of their time. Wesley spent so much time with Carroll and Roy that it was circulated that Carroll was there with his grandson. The occasion was a huge success resulting in many photos and features, the long enduring highlight of that year.

During the following year, Mary wrote a brief update of her situation for a college class, in part saying:

Exercise and Good Nutrition
I can speak from personal experience, a regular exercise routine and good nutrition can be a must for a healthy body and mind. I have had major surgeries 10 times in the past 16 years. However, I have recovered very fast after each one.

Her notes also include those written during the time around our 20th anniversary, 1985. Anniversaries were always times that Mary went to extra lengths to emphasize love and feelings. That year she was studying those very topics involving Interpersonal Relationships in marriages noting, "How powerful would you be if you could love without restrictions." And, "Unrestricted love. Love even though you get hurt you bounce right back. Continue to love." And double underlined, "You have to want it to move forward" and followed with, "Be positive."

All of these study topics were already fixtures in our relationship, largely because of our focus on each other from the very beginning, and being reinforced through classroom studies confirmed Mary's deepest desire, to love and to be loved, her innermost core guidance that she had come to recognize on her own.

Earlier, when she told me of her interest in karate classes, including our boys, I encouraged involvement as both family outings and a regular exercise routine. Our family time was busy time; working, traveling, writing, dancing, college, and now karate. Four years of regular classes later, she completed her goal of achieving Black Belt in full contact karate as did Squire and Wesley.

She was active and busy while having to endure a succession of lumpectomies that further disfigured her. Continual worries about breast cancer led to quiet moments of despair and conversations with me that were always laden with concern about my regard for her. Both of us remembered her near perfect physical form that became seriously challenged during July, 1986 when a double mastectomy was deemed medically necessary to prevent onset of cancer.

That diagnosis shook Mary to her very core, but her succession of lumpectomies had prepared her for the ultimate decision that was dramatically demonstrated when an associate at the Lab told that his young wife was similarly diagnosed. She was a staunch Bible believer saying that God would protect her, she did not need surgery. She died eighteen months later leaving two small children. Mary chose surgery with implants that did not return her to her previous form, but she remained free of cancer thereafter. She chose life, that episode to remain her guidance thereafter. She was, however, continually beset with worry about what was to happen to her next.

Recovery time required acclimating to her new life that she regarded herself to be... less than the woman she had been while I remained with a healthy appetite for her attention, although forestalled as needed when she was recovering. The latter was a continual source of worry for her, that I would seek female attention elsewhere regardless of my assurances to the contrary. Adjusting our time together to bolstering her wellbeing was not entirely successful as demonstrated one day when Squire ran excitedly to me saying with considerable concern, "Mom's going to kill herself!"

Quickly by her side with more reassurances while keeping her pistol from her reach, I was not entirely unprepared; I knew Mary's tendency toward melancholy, but now I recognized that tendency to have sunk into serious depression. For this I was unprepared; what to do? All I could do was talk with her, listen to what she said, and try to help her sort through her anguish.

"Am I a bad person?" she lamented.

"No. Not at all," I assured her.

"I've never hurt anyone... that I know of.... If I hurt you, I didn't mean to."

"You've never hurt me, Mary. Never! I think you are a genuinely good person. You want good for everyone. That means you are a good person."

"Then... why does all this keep happening to me? All these surgeries? Sick all the time... What have I done to deserve all this?"

Being careful to remain supportive rather than dictatorial, to listen rather than tell, I recognized that I was on thin ice with how to handle the situation while my tendency to protect Mary remained foremost in my thoughts, but with wonder at what she might do when I was not there. So, we talked and talked, and when I resorted to my tried and true; "There'll never be anyone else for me but you..." She smiled. With deep breaths, despair on her face, she looked at me.

"I love you with all my heart. I just don't want to be a burden to you," she said with tears in her eyes.

"Mary, you are not a burden. You are the most special person in our lives, our boys and me. Please don't ruin that. Promise me... you won't ruin it, okay? I want you to promise that you will take care of you for me."

Mary sighed. "I can see... I know I'm a burden... I just don't know if I can keep going... I'm so tired of all this. I just don't feel good."

"I'll help any way I can," I assured her. "We'll get through it, we always have. That's all. We'll get through it. Okay? But you've got to promise me. I'll keep my promise to you... you've got to keep your promise to me. Okay?"

Mary promised, and we got through it, although having to venture down the depression road occasionally thereafter.

As her health returned, during autumn of that year, 1986, a degree of vigor came with it, and she expanded her classes. This time, she set her goal to finish a Business Administration degree and set to it with the academic excellence that had always been her normal. Her health remained stable, and Mary went to college each day dressed as if she had stepped out of a fashion magazine. With her flowing hair, trim figure, her natural features and her charming manner, my beautiful Mary had returned. Having her regular schedule of classes and homework, her goal was reinforced with Squire starting his college there as well, both of them having achieved their Black Belts.

While Wesley finished his high school year with an "A" average and attended Governor's School during summers, both Mary and Squire completed their academics that year also with "A" averages, and I bragged about my A-Team.

During 1987, Mary's superlative performance resulted in receiving the Market & Finance Award, a President's award at the college, and I thought she deserved a reward, a new car, a new, brilliant yellow sports car that she enjoyed driving; a beautiful car for a beautiful lady. Upon receipt of the car, a secret purchase, I drove it to her karate class, then invited her outside with some fanfare that drew her entire karate class out to see the car. She was pleasantly surprised, but her immediate worry was... how will we pay for it? I handled that.

For a sociology class, Mary composed the following Field Project #2 entitled:

Pre-1940 Adults:

I discussed what it was like to be a child and an adolescent during the twenties and the thirties with my parents.

Mother's adjustment to life was made even more difficult due to the fact that she was born out of wedlock. During the twenties, there was no such thing as a love child, an illegitimate child was a disgrace. Mother was sent to a distant cousin in the country where she was raised in a small cabin as a foster child with eight other children. She grew with no electricity, no running water, and no indoor plumbing. My mother was a teenager before they got a battery operated radio; even then they could only listen to it on Saturday nights so they would not use up the battery.

They grew almost everything that they ate. They raised pigs, and chickens for both eggs and to eat. In the family garden, they grew their own vegetables and had a cow for milk and butter. Their water was drawn from a well and their bathroom was an outdoor toilet. Bathing was done in a wash tub in the kitchen with water heated on a wood burning stove.

Mother said that she had to walk two miles each way to school, and it had only ten grades. Before she could leave for school in the mornings, the chores had to be done. Drawing water from the well to wash clothes, carrying wood for the cook stove and fireplaces, feeding the pigs and chickens, and milking the cow.

My father lived on a larger farm with his parents, a brother and a sister. They also did not have power until he was a young man. They were one of the first families in the area to have a radio. Several members of the family played musical instruments for evening entertainment and on Sunday. They formed a small band and played for barn dances, hay rides, and community functions.

My dad also had to work hard before and after school. They raised a lot of cattle and pigs, as well as tobacco, so everyone had his share of the work.

I asked them what they thought about doing when they grew up; how they looked at the future. Dad said that most young men just

204

expected to be farmers like their fathers and most girls to become mothers and housewives. He said that they did not have the free time that young people have today to think about things like that. He said that almost everyone around there was in the same boat, therefore no one thought anything about being poor.

Mother and Daddy both felt that learning how to work and how to be self-sufficient made life easier for them when they were adults. They felt that their experiences made them better able to cope with life, and they felt that if a child is not taught to work and how to cope with some of life's problems as he grows up, when he gets out into the real world, he is going to have a tough time making his own way in the world.

I am over 25, but I will say that my parents taught my brothers and me how to take care of ourselves at a very young age. We grew up with hard work, milking cows, canning and freezing fruits and vegetables along with raising many acres of corn and tobacco, and other farm chores filled our days before and after school.

My adolescence was not very different from my parents although I benefitted from their hard work and earnings. I learned a lot from those lessons, and I now appreciate the knowledge of how to run and maintain a household. I also learned that I would do almost anything in life rather than farm tobacco.

There were a lot of similarities between my childhood and my parents in that we both had to work hard. There were also a lot of differences. I grew up with electricity, indoor plumbing, radio and television. We also had a farm truck and tractor. A car came along when I was about 8 years old.

Since I have experience in life with a lot less than the norm today, I wonder how today's kids would cope without all their electronic wizardry and its noise making, cars and the freedom to travel, telephones and fast food.

Cars and freedom to travel were the hallmarks of our time. Were it not for cars, Mary and I would never have met. During our parents' time, boy-girl pairings were most often within local community functions, mainly school and church. Freedom brought by cars in post-war America also brought a sexual revolution involving night time dating, the very thing that Mary's father forbid her to do when she was in high school and afterward. During the 1960s when topics of cars and girls were hit song and movie themes, she was restricted... until I came along and her determination to be with me skirted his dominion over her, causing her to resort to secrecy.

For one of her classes, Mary composed the following:

Managing a Writer and a Hard Headed Husband

If there was one word that I could use to sum up all of our efforts, that word would be perseverance. Many times I was ready to give up, throw in the proverbial towel. But not Alex, he was always determined, he just does not know the word quit or can't. Over the first 10 years of our efforts we received enough rejection slips to wall paper a room. Our efforts and hard work has paid off, and after we got the first article in print, the next ones were easier.

The first step to getting your ideas in print is to familiarize yourself with the magazines that print articles on subjects you are interested in doing. In our case automotive magazines and general interest magazines, such as airlines magazines. Magazines have a list of their departments, addresses, and phone numbers on the mast head. There are magazines that tell you which publishers and magazines will accept unsolicited articles, some even tell you how much each magazine pays per word and how much they pay for each photograph.

There are several ways you can go about getting your articles into the hands of the editor: 1) A query letter with a sample of your work, and an outline of what you can provide for their magazine. 2) A phone call to the editor. This method works better after you have been published a few times and your name is known. 3) Send your finished article to the magazine with a cover letter to the editor. 4) Magazine articles are more readily accepted when they are accompanied by photography. (Slides preferably)

After you have been published a few times and your work is well received by the readers, your reasons for calling editors will change. Now your calls will be to make verbal commitments, and many times they will be calling you to ask if you have time to do an article for their magazine. Since we have graduated and are now doing books as well as magazine articles, some of our objectives have changed from placing materials to selling them.

The same scenario goes; make as many contacts as possible. 1) Book stores. 2) Magazines that sell books. 3) People and organizations that critique books. 4) The media; T.V., radio, and newspapers.

Our second book just came out, and book stores and media personnel are calling us to set up autograph sessions. Alex's hard headedness has cost us a lot of money in many instances, as in expensive equipment, however it has always paid off in the long range scope of our business.

What I am saying is don't give in to emotions as I am inclined to do; spend the extra money to buy good equipment when you need it. Example: an instamatic camera will not get your work into print. You will also have to send your manuscripts in letter quality format; a good typewriter or a computer that will give you a good quality print out.

I will close with a story about Alex. He had been making noises for some time about buying a computer but I had continued to talk him out of it; I thought that they were just too expensive. Alex kept saying his fingers were too fast, that he made too many mistakes on the typewriter, and he could make more money and save time if he had a computer. You guessed it; I still said no. I thought that the typewriter just needed some repair work. The typewriter was cleaned and overhauled, and Alex was hard at work at our kitchen table when, about 10:00pm, I heard our deck door open and a crash. I ran to see what had happened and there, two stories down was the typewriter. Alex calmly turned around and said it is broken, I need a computer.

The next day we bought our first IBM.

Being much more productive with professional quality computing and photographic equipment, my writing soon provided our most significant need; more income. Rather quickly rising to a national caliber byline, my published work brought a contract from a major publisher to produce a book, my first, a lavishly illustrated coffee table hardback. Needing more photos to fill in gaps along the timeline of automotive evolution, using my advance I arranged an extended trip to California as a family outing. We flew into Los Angeles, then I rented a vehicle for traveling to a museum for another photo session, then we traveled northward to attend races at Leguna Seca and the concours d'elegance at Pebble Beach for more photos.

Traveling along coastal highway #1 was memorable for being so visually spectacular. Photos gathered, we returned to Tennessee, and I set to completing my contract. The book, released during 1986, was beautiful and was a huge market success while also being awarded Book-of-the-Year honors for both text and photography. It also received the Moto Award granted by the National Automotive Journalism Association. And, that brought another contract. My second book was another Book-of-the-Year recipient.

Throughout our California adventures, particularly when we were in Monterey and Cannery Row, I captured Mary and our boys in many photos that now illustrate my MP4 compilations. Mary was gorgeous.

Another of her compositions also had a personal theme:

Marriage and Communications

There is no doubt that communication affects everything we do throughout our lives. We use some form of communication in everything, either verbal or non-verbal. I think there are many different kinds of communication. There is the kind you would have with a friend, your boss, or a relative. Then there is the deep sharing communication that you experience with your spouse. However, if the divorce rate is any gauge as to how well couples communicate, then it would seem that we fall very short of the goal.

I have read several articles and case histories written by marriage counselors that report that in more than 95% of the cases studied, lack of communication was the primary reason that the marriage was in trouble. There was usually some other reason given for the break-up, but when the counselor was able to get all of the facts together, it was almost always a lack of communication that was the real problem.

While reading the different cases, there were some that had money problems, some with in-law problems, even some where one or the other of the two was having an affair. In almost every incidence, the husband or wife was failing to express themselves, or they were not listening to what the other person was saying. In most cases, they were failing to understand the message that was being given. I think that having patience, listening and understanding what the other person wants or expects is as important as being able to talk about what is bothering you.

After 21 years of marriage, I still believe that it takes a combination of many things to make a marriage work. A marriage cannot be built on love alone or even money; sure, it takes love and money but it also takes a lot of communication. Looking back at my own marriage experiences, I can see that communication has been a big factor in making my marriage work. There have been many times when my husband and I needed a lot of verbal as well as non-verbal communication. Many times we have talked more than half of the night. For example, when the children were sick, or when we just needed to reassure each other, or when money got tight and we had to make plans as to how we were going to make ends meet. Then there was the time that my husband was leaving for the Navy and we talked about all night.

My marriage has been strong, but that does not mean it has been free from conflicts. Far from it. My husband and I are two different individuals, therefore, we have different interests and ideas. By trial and error we learned early in our marriage that everything was not all take or all give, but some of both. At times we would not

209

agree about who would do the giving or the taking, but we were able to work things out by communicating. We also learned that it was just as important to listen as it was to talk, and sometimes it was harder to listen, especially when some truths were being said that we preferred not to hear.

Looking back at our marriage, I can see that there were times when a failure to communicate our differences to each other could have resulted in our marriage becoming a case history such as those I have read about. Over the years, I came to realize that I was spoiled and headstrong when we were first married. But, I also knew that I really loved this guy, and if I wanted our relationship to last, I had better start listening and stop complaining so much. So, you see I know that it is a lot easier sometimes to talk than to listen.

In notes for her speech classes, Mary jotted admonishments; *Be positive. A person has to be free. Everyone can be strong - attitude. Faith - hope - love* were topics discussed for insights into male-female involvement, concluding that *the greatest power we have is the power of choice.* Mary had arrived at that conclusion on her own years earlier, an arduous emotional path for her now confirmed in a college classroom. Love had been her guidance that opened the door to free will. To love and to be loved was also confirmed as the core of her existence. Her grades in four speeches were 95 - 98 - 98 - 100.

Prior to graduation, Mary's Black Belt in karate returned her to teaching; this time girl's self-defense classes, driving her new car to the college campus each day, and I bragged about my team of karate experts guarding my body.

A phone call to me one day brought a sudden turn of events. I had gone on an errand, so Mary answered the call. Our friend's message was that he was on another phone with a neighbor friend of ours who was in the process of ending his life. The call was in hopes that I could prevent that from happening, but I was not there. Mary took immediate action; Squire was studying for a calculus test and was inducted into the rescue. The two of them quickly drove to the neighbor's house. Mary wrote:

...somewhere between the call and getting to the house, I saw a watch; it read 7:45pm. When I arrived, we heard loud music, a motor running, getting louder as something was pressing on it harder. I ran to the door & told Squire to check the garage doors, see if they would open. We banged on the doors and I rang the door bell; no response; we had to act quickly. I unlocked house, ran through to the garage. I saw him very white and slumped in his truck; house and garage were thick with fumes. Told Squire to call an ambulance. I went to victim, shut off car & music, pulled his feet off the pedals and started calling his name some more, rubbed hands & face to try to get some blood circulation back. Got him under the arms, pulled him from the truck. When instructed to do so he would kind of shuffle his feet. With that & dragging I got him outside.

The two of them saved a life, a man of almost twice Mary's weight. Being very much a macho kind of man, saved by a petit beauty, to my knowledge he never thanked Mary and Squire or acknowledged their life-saving in any way.

Mary thoroughly enjoyed college and often told of her exploits on campus. One particular occasion became a lasting memory. A sequence in the film *Top Gun* where a beautiful female character is sung to by admiring guys, "You've lost that lovin' feeling..." played out in the student lounge one day with Mary being the beauty. The playful episode was both embarrassing and exhilarating. We had seen the movie together, and she played her role to perfection, to receive compliments from the guys who had some fun at her expense, all of them knowing not to mess with Mary. And there was that son of hers, another Black Belt.

Life was good. I was working and writing, we were traveling, our boys were on track with academic superiority toward becoming medical doctors, and Mary was pleased with herself, but recurring minor surgeries to remove nodules here and there in her body remained worrisome. Reassuringly, none were malignant, but what was causing them remained unknown. However, none prevented her from continuing a full time student.

Then, during the spring of 1988, she graduated Summa Cum Laude with a 4.0 average, once again achieving her level of academic excellence begun during childhood. Afterward, the college hired her to administer student grants, a position that she held through coming years.

These were, generally, good years for Mary. She had remained trim with gorgeous hair, and with attention to retaining her natural beauty, no more than light eye shadow and pink lipstick, she could easily pass for twenty years younger. That was demonstrated one day when we went to a restaurant for a late lunch. When our young waitress commented, "That's nice", she gathered our immediate attention. Asking what she was referring to, she said, "Father and daughter having lunch together... that's nice." We just smiled at each other, particularly Mary, who would definitely not set the record straight. She turned fifty that year.

Whatever hair style Mary chose, she always looked good, from Dutch Boy to "big hair". She had always been attentive to her beauty, and as a regular reader of several women's magazines, she repeatedly attempted participation, such as during 1988 when she responded to an ad:

I have camera potential because of my 44 years' experience of keeping myself attractive and fit. My management skills learned from working with people, my black belt in karate, and my recent "late bloomer student" college graduation with a 4.0 average gives me confidence that I can represent Dove in a professional manner.
Name: Mary Alice Gabbard
Date of Birth/Present Age: 8/9/44 (44)
Height: 5'6"
Weight: 128lbs.

Eyes: Hazel
Hair Color: Blond (frosted)
Have you entered this contest before? Yes
Region: Southeast

And the following:

Dear McCall's Editor,

This letter is to introduce the Gabbard family. I am Mary Alice Gabbard. My husband, Alex, and I have been married for 23 years. We have two sons, Squire (age 19) and Wesley (age 16). We also have a cat, Ninja. I think our family would make an excellent selection for the honor of Reader of the Year on the basis that we have weathered the lows together and enjoyed the highs together. We have, of course, had difficulties from time to time, but when an issue was important, whether ours or our children's, we have been able to come to terms because of our goals of good health, dedication to purpose, and belief in a bright future have led us to work hard toward achieving our goals.

To recall some memories, we were married while Alex was in college, but shortly afterward he was drafted and spent four years in the Navy during the Viet Nam era. We had our first son during that time, a troubled delivery that produced doubts whether I would survive. During the next nine years, Alex and I did our best while he attended North Carolina State University where he completed a Master of Science degree in Physics. We actually bought a home! But shortly after it was finally finished, Alex accepted a position with the Fusion Energy Division of the Oak Ridge National Laboratory where he pursues scientific research.

Also during that time, we as a family pursued my husband's interest in vintage and historic cars as a hobby. Alex has now written two books that are in print, and he regularly contributes to several magazines. He is not only a good author but is also a fantastic photographer. His photography was used to illustrate his books. His

213

first book was selected as Book of the Year in 1986 and received the Moto Award granted by the National Automotive Journalism Assn. Alex plans to continue writing and is working on several more books. Someday, he hopes to write "the great American novel".

Squire, our oldest son is in his second year of college as a pre-med major. He won an academic scholarship and has maintained a 4.0 GPA so far. An interest of his has been Isshinryu Karate in which he has attained the rank of Black Belt. Following in his father's footsteps, his writing and photography have also been published in national magazines. His goal is to become an immunologist specializing in allergy. As an extracurricular interest, he currently assists one of his professors in research in chemistry.

Wesley, our youngest son, is a junior in high school. He completed his sophomore year with all A's and has been an excellent student throughout his entire school tenure. He is a member of the National Honor Society, works on the school's newspaper and is a photographer. His work in 4-H has resulted in several photography awards. Although karate is not one of his strong interests, Wesley has achieved the rank of Blue Belt. His plans are also a career in immunology and allergy beginning with his hoped for scholarship to Duke University.

As for me, I am wife and mother of a wonderful family. I also stay very busy. Following several surgeries including a double mastectomy and a hysterectomy, I went back to school a few years ago and graduated from college on June 4, 1988 with a degree in Business. I graduated with a 4.0 GPA which I am very proud of. My successes include the honor of being selected as recipient of the Marketing and Finance Award as the top student in that curriculum, then the unexpected honor of becoming a finalist for the President's Award granted by the college president.

I am currently self-employed and try to handle all of the business end of our little writing business. This includes cataloging the thousands of color slides of automobiles that we have, working with book publishers, magazine editors and publishers, a toy

214

manufacturer, learning computer techniques for desk top publishing, all the time trying to keep our home together AND keep my sanity. In between, I squeeze in fashion modeling for a local boutique. And I also have a Black Belt in Isshinryu Karate. My son and I are probably one of very few mother and son Karate teams around.

As you can see, we value staying active and a good education very highly. Alex and I believe that the youth of today is our hope for tomorrow, and a better educated youth will make a better tomorrow. We are deeply pleased that our boys have significant goals and work so hard to achieve them, especially in today's world of many shallow pursuits and diversions.

If we had time, the boys would like to learn to play the piano, and Alex hopes to master the classical guitar someday, but some things have to be left undone in our lives. Even the remodeling I had hoped for has had to wait. Somewhere along the way, between photo sessions, heaps of books, hours of study, the laundry, computer frustration, (our home most of the time looks like a battle zone of the paper war), we manage to be a family. It's tough, sometimes overwhelming, but never dull.

Along with helping our boys, we plan to produce five books in five years, remodel our house, add a dark room so we can do more photo work at home, modernize our office with real file cabinets instead of cardboard boxes, and get ORGANIZED!

Through all this, Alex plans to stay with ORNL. He regards his fusion energy research work at the lab, along with his associates, as important to the future of mankind. He enjoys what he does, including his hobby which involves all of us in many interesting automobiles and the fascinating people surrounding them. Ours is not a boring lifestyle.
Sincerely,
Mary Alice Cheek Gabbard

Even with photos showing her little impish smile, her natural and youthful photogenic qualities, nothing came of her submissions.

Those years brought enumerable experiences from activities that had become our family's normal. The Cold War was winding down as the Soviet Union was experiencing political turmoil among its citizens who demanded more liberties. The American model of life had become sufficiently known through dissemination of information brought by worldwide advances in technology that Soviet communist underpinnings soon collapsed. Scientific interests became more freely exchanged such that the U.S. State Department and the Lab arranged for a dozen or so Soviet fusion physicists from Moscow's Kurchatov Institute to visit Oak Ridge and ORNL facilities as a cultural and scientific exchange. My position brought marginal interaction, but when requests for invitations were made for the Russians to visit in our homes after hours, I signed on. The day came that Kovrignik, about 65, and Mukavotov, about 45, were our visitors for a leisure evening and dinner. The elder of the two was director of his lab's theoretical efforts while the younger was director of experimentation.

At the lab, they were amazed at the quantity and variety of nuts, bolts, wiring, machinery, electrical equipment, and assorted hardware kept on hand and readily accessible. At their institute, such material of considerable value was tightly controlled by officials of the state, and I learned that they thought my similar position meant that I had to be CIA, and that all of Oak Ridge was a CIA front similar to Soviet political strategies that show only special towns to the world.

On the drive from the lab to our home that afternoon, I drove by the TVA hydroelectric dam complex as usual, and Kovrignik's attention was piqued. He asked, "Where are guards?" I explained that the complex did not have guards, that the dam was remotely controlled by another much larger dam complex a few miles away and staff was for upkeep and maintenance. No need for guards.

Upon arriving at home, he stood for a moment on our sidewalk, breathed deeply, then said in his heavy accent, "You have good air." Once in our home and introduced to Mary and our boys, our cultural exchange was largely dominated by Mukavatov who was fascinated with Mary's preparation of various Christmas treats of

216

candies and cakes to give as gifts. She, being a coffee drinker, offered them fresh brew and a selection of treats, to which he took with gusto. Mary's collection of spices were of particular interest to him, having never heard of most of them, and the cream and sugar so freely offered resulted in him depositing far more sugar in his coffee than seemed reasonable for taste, cup after cup. She was nearing completion of another dance fashion, and she showed it to them. Being trim, fashionably dressed, and friendly while completing her kitchen interests in a meal for them, he told that what Russians knew of American wives was that they laid on the couch all day watching TV and eating bon-bons. Kovrignik sat quietly on our couch, and when they talked, I understood only one phrase, C-I-A.

Having interests in cars, I wanted to learn about their car culture, to which Mukavatov replied, "We have cars." That was all I could get; neither of them had ever had a car of their own, not needed, it was said, due to public transit in Moscow. When talking with Kovrignik about typical homes in Russia, he replied that four families would live in construction as large my home, further convincing him that I was CIA to have both cars and a home of my own, being so well treated by the state. When I explained that everyone in America owned cars and owning a home was part of the American dream that everyone aspired to, he remained in disbelief. KGB influences, apparently, were still in effect.

That evening of friendly exchange, a sumptuous meal prepared by Mary, to which Mukavotov complemented her and Kovrignik did not, has remained a highlight of our Oak Ridge experiences. When I learned that the Russians planned among themselves to have ORNL staffers take them further than Oak Ridge, particularly to distant supermarkets and shopping malls, thinking that Oak Ridge was a CIA model community built to impress visitors, I presumed that they returned to Russia taking starkly different perspectives of American life than they had been led to believe.

During 1991, the Soviet Union collapsed; the Cold War was over because the largest military on earth could not compete with stealth technology that very likely could place a 340 kiloton B61 thermonuclear bomb that I had once serviced in the center of Moscow regardless of Soviet military preparedness.

In my Oak Ridge Institute of Continued Learning presentation composed years later, "Cold War Weapons", I cited:

March 26, 1992: Russian presidential advisor Anatoly Rakitov stated:
    "Over the last six decades, 80 to 90 percent of our national resources – raw materials, technical, financial, and intellectual – have been used to create the military-industrial complex."

It failed. During our Navy time, Mary and I had been operatives in that failure. The entire Soviet culture based on unsustainable precepts of governance driven by central planning and paranoia, fear of American aggression toward Russian society that did not exist, fear that their government fostered and taught to generations to suppress the masses, all thoroughly false, led to collapse. One super-power remained; America.

After a decade with the Fusion Energy Division, Department of Energy funding was cut so deeply that only a few staff members survived. I transferred to another Division to become a Group Leader on a project that began with nothing with requirements of designing, building, and operating a new facility. My new location about six miles from home was close enough to have lunch with Mary when she was home. Beginning during 1990, that worked well through retiring from the Lab fifteen years later.

Since I was an early riser and regularly at the Lab before 7 am, there was no issue of time away, and since Mary was a late riser on her days off, our schedules meshed well. Then, home between 4:30 and 5pm on work day afternoons gave me time to confer with magazine editors and book people to gather assignments, especially those in California, and off we would go on another adventure during the time when Mary was able; almost every weekend beginning with Daytona in February, then Sebring in March, good places to be during

218

Tennessee winters. We then traveled northward as warmer weather progressed in that direction, our normal routine for years.

In time, Mary became so adept with editor and publisher dealings that she developed congenial relationships with several who seemed to prefer calling her for whatever they were looking for. Again, she led me to assignments. All of our exploits during those years included her and our boys, if they were available. Then, college followed by medical school took so much of their time that Mary and I often traveled on our own.

From time to time, Mary put pen to paper to record her thoughts, such as the following:

5-26-90 Saturday - Wesley graduated from Farragut High School. For me it was a bittersweet experience. I was sad knowing he will be leaving home for college but very proud of him and all he has achieved.

5-27-90 Sunday - Alex and Squire went to Bristol to the drags. Wesley and I spent a quiet day at home.

5-28-90 Monday - Alex was at home. We went out to breakfast and to see Back to the Future III. Alex spent some time working on the Mustang book.

Three books released that year, 1990, brought my total to five, and all of them had been family efforts. The fifth was co-authored with Squire who received half of its proceeds that helped fund his way through college as an adjunct to scholarships he was awarded. They were well placed; he graduated with top honors. Wesley enrolled in college with sufficient classroom courses to begin as a sophomore with a full scholarship that also led to another top honors graduate. He earned two Bachelor of Science degrees in his four years.

Back home, Mary's father was experiencing serious mental degradation that tended to bring memories of his war in Europe to

219

dominating his thoughts, often warning that Nazi soldiers were in the basement. As his detachment from reality grew, so did instability on his feet, and while visiting one day, Mary attempted to catch his fall that ruptured a disk in her neck and damaged a shoulder.

During July, 1992, she underwent surgery to repair the damage in her neck using a graft of bone taken from her hip. Although the surgeon attempted to hide the incision into the side of her neck, that scar remained visible. All previous scars she could hide with selections of clothing, but this one.... "I just wanted to help Daddy," she lamented. "He's done so much for me...."

His decline continued through coming years that led to continual anguish for Mary. She wrote:

Merry Christmas, Daddy

Daddy will spend Christmas in a nursing home this year. It breaks my heart to think that he won't know it is Christmas, or even recognize me when I visit him. Whatever good cheer the season may bring for other people, there is none for him. As I remember Christmas from my childhood, when he was Daddy and everything was good, I am saddened to see what has become of him. It's been quite a while since he recognized me, and that breaks my heart, too. I am his war-time child, born during the time he fought the Nazis. He is still fighting them. You see, Daddy isn't with us anymore. His mind has become locked in the past, the past he alone can see, and he is fearful of the Nazis hiding in the basement, or simply in the shadows of his memories.

Daddy carried a rifle through France and Germany with the 69th Infantry Division. From his copy of the "69th Infantry Pictorial History", I've learned that he and his fellow GIs slogged through wintertime Montenau passed many German graves. They crossed the Siegfried Line. They took the high ground between Honningen and Gescheid and ran the Nazis out of six towns. Then they freed thirty-six more towns from Hitler's clutches. They won Schmidtheim, then took the Ludendorff Bridge at Remagen. They crossed the Rhine. They took

220

the famous fortress, Ehrenbreitstein, on 27 March 1945 and raised the American flag over the fortress for the first time since the Germans lowered it on 23 April 1923. German and American soldiers lay dead along the way to Leipzig; still he marched on with the 69th, passed an earlier edifice to insanity - Napoleon's Monument. The allies made rubble of Eilenburg. Then, on 24 April 1945, they met the Russians at Torgau on the Elbe, and the war was soon over. Four hundred and three of his fellow GIs did not make it back.

Daddy fought the Nazis all the way. He was a young man then, and the war changed him. He hasn't forgotten, but he has been forgotten. This is a man that gave almost five years of his life for his country. His tour of duty during the war was so traumatic that he has never been able to talk very much about it. As children we were never allowed to watch war movies on TV or to see a war movie at a theater. For many years after his return from Europe, loud noises such as a car back-firing or a sudden "bang" of any kind caused him to react in fright. Little-by-little I learned that Daddy was pinned down in a fox hole for several days and that most of his friends were killed. Their bodies over him kept him alive in the freezing cold, but his legs and feet were frozen in several inches of water in the bottom of the fox hole. He suffered frost bitten toes. I do not know how long he was hospitalized after this ordeal. To this day, his toenails are very thick and have to be trimmed by a doctor.

The trauma that Daddy endured and lived through left him permanently shaken. He had bypass surgery in 1987 and had a stroke in 1991. While he was in the hospital he was diagnosed to have Alzheimer's and Parkinson's diseases. One night in the hospital he became confused and started fighting the Nazis again. He ripped a piece off a nearby water fountain and used it as a weapon for killing Germans. His language was terrible. This was a man that I had never heard use profanity before.

Like all the GIs who kept the torch of freedom burning, he was promised veterans benefits. His benefits have expired this Christmas. It's that "Contract With America". We've been told over

221

and over that the government has to cut expenses, and I now know that the "Contract" is to break promises made over fifty years ago. There was no mention of expiration dates when promises were made, but on December 7th the Veterans Administration said they would no longer provide care for Daddy. Odd, isn't it? The VA chose the day Pearl Harbor was bombed, the day that the war for America began, the day that changed Daddy's life forever, to kick him out.

What happened to the promises that were made to Daddy and all the other veterans of World War-II? This is what happened. He helped win the war, then became the Daddy I knew. He was always big and strong, with a willing hand to help anyone at any time. Daddy was the deacon of our church. He was also active in politics, and for many years he helped manage the local polls in Wilkes County, North Carolina. He worked for the highway Department of the State of North Carolina and retired in good faith. Now he is in a nursing home, and both the VA and State retirement health benefits have been revoked.

Most of the time Daddy doesn't recognize anyone, his wife or his children. He requires medication and skilled medical attention. Mother is seventy-three and frail, but she has been told that that she must tend to his care or pay several thousand dollars every month.

I want to tell you about my Daddy. His care at ---------- in North Wilkesboro is being terminated, unless Mother pays. It makes no difference that he gave five years of his life to fight a war that scarred him so deeply that he still fights the war. It makes no difference that he gave almost thirty years of his life to help keep highways of North Carolina safe and clean. It makes no difference at all that he has been a faithful American, reverent of the land he loved and worked for and a staunch supporter of the American way of life. It makes no difference that Mother is being forced to pay for his care, the same care that was promised by his country and state but now refused. And when she can no longer pay, she has been told that she will have to sign over all the family property and belongings to the nursing home if they are to continue to provide his care.

222

Daddy taught me to always be honest and fair to everyone. Who is being honest and fair when he needs it? He has paid for his care, and he accepted promises made by his America.

Is this the America my Daddy fought for? Is this the America my Daddy worked for and believed in? Is this the America my Daddy helped keep free and strong? This is the America that forgets its promises and steals from those who have little to give. This America has forgotten my Daddy. If a "Contract With America" really exists, then what it has done to my Daddy is the real America which is neither honest nor fair.

The Veterans Administration and the State of North Carolina have refused to honor their commitment for lifetime commitments Daddy gave them. The VA has refused to honor its wartime debt to him, and Mother has been forced to pay over $3,000.00 for about three weeks care, care ended on December 31, unless several thousand more is paid to the nursing home for another month of care. Then more money month after month.

When the government called, he did not hesitate to do his duty. Now, when he calls out in need, America refuses to honor its duty. He believed that the Veterans Administration would always be there for him. And he believed that the State of North Carolina would stand by him. He paid his insurance premiums for all those years, and to the best of my information, he was hospitalized for about four days during the time he worked for the State.

Daddy is now in diapers. He has to be fed. He has to be given medicine at regular intervals. He has to be bathed and dressed. He can no longer relieve himself without help. He doesn't speak unless spoken to, and to get his attention you have to be very close to his face. When he opens his eyes, they are hollow and expressionless. Sometimes he sings wistfully; sometimes for hours, mostly old hymns from his church.

The State says that Daddy is not sick enough to get coverage under his medical insurance. Pray tell me, how sick does the man have to be? He has permanent heart arrhythmia combined with effects

223

of Alzheimer's and Parkinson's diseases. He can't tend to himself and rarely knows anyone, and he is completely dependent on care from others. He is never alert, and could not be roused from coma-like sleep on occasion. He has not shown normal functions for several years.

I truly think it is a sad state of affairs that Daddy's state and government has turned its back on him when he can no longer care for himself. He has no say in what happens. The life savings that he and Mother struggled for will soon be gone. At that point, we are told that Social Services will take the deed to their small farm, and Medicare will provide coverage leaving nothing for Mother's care in the future. Only by making paupers of Mother and Daddy will government care come into effect. Mother can live in the house until her death, but our home and everything that they spent their lives building will be gone.

This is the real "Contract With America". Meet my Daddy, Garvey Reece Cheek, World War-II veteran, forgotten American. Merry Christmas, Daddy.

During this time, the 1990s, Mary's own striving for return to good health was interrupted. She wrote:

I have had headaches since I started having my period at age 14. About the last day of my cycle I would get a bad headache. Usually I could lie down in a dark room and take an aspirin and it would go away. After our first son was born in 1969 until I had a hysterectomy in 1981 - 82, my headaches were less frequent. After hysterectomy the headaches got worse. A doctor started me on the estraderm patch. I used the patch for about six years, and at some time I stopped absorbing the patch. The doctor started me on an estrogen dose, then doubled it, then back to single dose. During this time my thyroid and cholesterol went crazy. Since about the middle of Nov. 1992 I have started throwing up with the headaches. I throw up

224

until I throw up blood. The hospital usually has to start IVs and give me enough medication to knock me out.

In addition to health issues, during the first months of 2001, her left jaw inexplicably became painful. When her jaw locked, she had to have TMJ surgery to reshape the bone for smooth motion. That surgery solved this problem, but others were not so successful. Complications continued requiring more surgeries. In her log she noted:

October 1992 - Laser surgery to free movement of left shoulder
August 1994 - Abdominal to remove adhesions & partial blockage
October 16 1996 - Left elbow to reroute compressed nerve
June 1997 - Admitted to CCU for chest pains, angioplasty unsuccessful
December 18 1997 - Esophagus, hiatal hernia
March 3 1998 - Admitted to CCU for chest pains, cardiac rehab 23 weeks
April 17 1998 - Double mastectomy, removed 2 ruptured implants w/saline reconstruction
July 7 1998 - Hemorrhoids, bleeding fissures
August 1999 - removal of bone spurs, left shoulder
November 8 1999 - Torn rotator cuff, left shoulder

From 1969 into the latter half of the 1900s, Mary endured twenty serious surgeries, and after each one her efforts for quick recovery were motivated by our activities that she insisted on being part of, even if she was not entirely recovered or up to the challenge. We were, however, always protective of her recoveries, letting her go at what was a comfortable pace for her. When I look at many of my photos of her and recall that she was pushing herself to be there, I am constantly reminded how she so wanted to live, to be active, to go places and do things with me, and whatever physical condition she was in, she never lost her friendly smile or her outgoing personality

225

that won many friends, none aware of her physical condition at the moment.

In her journal of the decade, she wrote:

5/24/96 New truck delivered from Ford Motor Co. & Road & Track. Keep two weeks for drivers test & article. Right arm numb / Left two fingers numb. Hot pain in side of head (left).

5/25/96 Went on off road driving tour of Duck Town/Copper Hill. Photographed yellow truck for Road & Track.

5/26/96 Hands shake after taking--------. I feel good - no problems. Rained most all day. Went to Sam's shopping.

5/28/96 B.P. 126/82 Cereal/skim milk/coffee. Not as shaky as before, seem to be tolerating---------- better. Emily Block came for a visit. We are invited to her house Friday for dinner.

5/29/96 My neck & arm hurt and I have a burning pain in the side of my head. Used some relaxation tapes, did not take any medication for pain. Had some blood when I had a B.M. Squire and I went shopping, after a friend cancelled a shopping trip because her mother was ill. Teresa and I will go next week.

5/30/96 B.P. 124/93   Took books to Dollywood. Went to Apple Barn for dinner. Squire joined us for dinner. Feel fine, still some sinus drainage & sinus headache.

5/31/96 B.P. 125/88 Someone tried to steal my car. I called the sheriff to report it. A deputy sheriff came out to investigate. A lot of paint was broken or scratched on moon roof and hood. I have a bad headache across my brow and side of my nose. Still taking -----------. Slight temp 100.1. Alex & I went to Emily Block's for a dinner party. It was fun to see a lot of our old friends from previous wine & cheese parties.

6/1/96   B.P. 147/70   Alex has gone to Atlanta. Squire has gone camping with a few friends for several days. I have a day to myself. It is nice to get caught up on letters and phone calls. I can just relax and do whatever I want. I feel good.

6/2/96   B.P. 126/68   I feel fine. A bit stopped up with allergies. We went out to eat. Went to West Town. Talked with Wesley in Memphis. He is getting ready for Medical Boards. Wesley will be home 6/14. Had some more blood when I had a B.M.

6/3/96   B.P. 157/72   Monday - I woke up feeling fine. I got a headache and left arm numb after I braided my hair. My arms were up for 7-8 minutes. I have noticed this happening before.

6/4/96   Went to lunch with Teresa. Alex could not sleep, ear infection, temp 100.9.

6/5/96   B.P. 122/80   Alex saw doctor. 2 medicines for two weeks. Re-check June 18th. Alex could not sleep nor could anyone else.

6/6/96   B.P. 118/90   Alex still home, pain was bad last night. He feels much better today. I feel a little tired from two sleepless nights.

6/7/96 B.P. 142/80   Friday   Alex was able to go back to work. I am still having some neck & arm pain. Have some blood in my stools again this morning. Generally I feel OK.

6/8/96   B.P. 140/90   Went to Georgia to some old gold mines. Toured several museums. Ate lunch at an old re-modeled 1800s house. I had the salad bar (1 corn muffin).

6/9/96 B.P. 147/78 Sunday Squire is off from UT Hospital today. We got to see his new car, bright red Eclipse. He is proud of it, since it was his first major purchase since Medical School. I have a lot of pain in my neck & arm today.

6/10/96 B.P. 140/87 Monday I feel fine, some pain in my neck & arms. Everyone back to work. I have several orders to fill. Raspberries to fix pies & jam. Doctor's app 3:30. Ask about lymphs in right side of neck. Sandy stools, could it be a result of --------?

6/11/96 Alex and I went out to lunch. Appt Dr. Vargas. Will have therapy on elbow/ulner nerve - If surgery? Not until we get back from Europe.

6/12/96 B.P. 138/88 Today is Squire's birthday. 27 years old, hard to believe. Squire and I went to breakfast, then shopping. Dinner plans - Squire & Stephanie Jernigan - Alex and I at the Blue Hound. Wesley is taking the final portion of Boards Part 1 today.

6/13/96 B.P. 141/79 Beautiful day out - I would rather be outside than inside doing laundry. I feel fine except for persistent neck pain. I have noticed when pain level is up my B.P. is up. We are going to N.C. for the weekend. Both boys are going with us. Father's Day is 6/16.

6/14 - 6/15 North Carolina - My neck really hurt going down. Did not hurt as much coming back. Dad is a lot worse. Mom is having left arm pain. After two nitroglycerine tablets under her tongue, pain went away. Doctor ordered heart workup.

6/18/96 B.P. 148/90 Making final plans for trip to Europe.

6/25/96 B.P. 120/70 I feel fine. Very hot and humid. Daddy is worse. Mother insisted he be taken to the emergency room. It won't do any

228

good to drag him around. I wish she could come to grip with the fact that he will not be getting better. I may seem mean to her but in some ways I think it will be a relief to let him go. That is what he wants.

6/29/96 B.P. 130/76 Stock club meeting. Our Coke stock split. We bought Viacom stock today. All of our stocks are doing well averaging about 30% gain.

7/2/96 B.P. 141/85 My arm has hurt all morning.

7/4/96 B.P. 149/85 I have been very nervous, did not sleep well. Woke up at 4:30am with a splitting headache. Arm and fingers tingling. Tingling around my lips. It is now 12:55pm. My head still aches. My hands shake. I feel lousy.

7/6/96 The nursing home nurses let Daddy fall out of bed head first. He has several stitches in his head - bruised ribs and black & blue all over.

7/7/96 Daddy is very sore, his eyes are swelled shut. Mom is an emotional basket case. So far I have remained calm.

7/10/96 B.P. 137/77 I feel fine except for my neck & arm. I guess that is something I will just have to learn to live with.

7/11/96 I woke up today with leg cramps. Yesterday after our walk my legs felt extremely heavy and my big toe on left foot was numb.

7/12/96 I feel fine. We are going to N.C. tomorrow. It is Communion Day at our church and I wanted to attend with Mother and also to see how Dad is doing.

7/13 7/14 7/15/96 We were in N.C. for a few days. Daddy looks like he has been in a car wreck. He is black & blue all over. The stitches

229

were removed from his head Saturday. They left the ones in his arm. He frowns when he coughs. I think he is in pain.

7/19 7/20/96 Saturday Beautiful day. I did some shopping. We have everything we need for our trip now.

7/21/96 Sunday Storms this afternoon. I was not able to get my walk in.

7/22/96 B.P. 139/69 Monday Did not sleep well. Dreamed a lot. It is almost 8:30am and I am still in my robe. Beds are made, dishes done but I feel slow. It is raining again today

7/23/96 Tuesday Therapy at 9:00am. Discharged from therapy. Therapist feels it will take surgery to correct my problems.

7/25/96 Thursday Went to lunch with my friend Teresa. She told me that she and Jim are getting a divorce after more than 30 years of marriage. I feel very sad for them.

7/28/96 B.P. 140/100 Sunday It is raining. My BP is up but I have a lot of pain in my neck. I bent over to turn off the switch on my computer and pain shot down my neck and back and down my arm. It looks like I am going to have to take something for pain.

7/29/96 B.P. 138/90 better Typical Monday - laundry, cleaning house after a long weekend. Rained most of Sunday - everyone was inside for most of the day.

7/30/96 Tuesday Still raining this morning. It is supposed to rain off and on all day. I just found out we will have company this weekend. My brother and his family. My 14 year old niece, Mary, plans to spend a week with us before school starts back the middle of August.

7/31/96 Wednesday Rain again. Our yard looks like a rain forest. Too wet & soggy to mow. Squire is doing well in Radiology. He is also looking at joining the Air Force Reserves for doctors. Watched Grumpier Old Men on Pay Per View. Very funny.

8/1/96 B.P. 138/80 Thursday Sunshine - The world is very green for now. Grass is in need of mowing. I am waking up several times each night with pain in my arms (both) and neck pain. I turn & turn to try to find a comfortable position. I am more tired today than usual.

8/5/96 Monday Squire wrecked his new car. It is torn up pretty bad. We are all very lucky that he was only shaken up and not killed or seriously injured. I have had real bad heart burn or indigestion, pain in my neck and under my chin.

8/6/96 I saw Dr. Vargas today. He said I will have to have surgery on my arm. Therapy has not helped. Dr. Vargas says I can wait until we get back from Europe unless my hand & arm starts getting worse.

8/9/96 Friday Today is my birthday. My brothers called. Mother called - she sent me a card & a check for $30.00. Wesley called from Memphis. Alex and Squire took me to dinner. The guys gave me a pair of emerald ear-rings to match my bracelet & ring.

8/10 8/11/96 Sat. & Sun. Was mostly a wash out. Rained both days. I caught up on paper work and computer work.

8/12/96 The guys are back at work. I am pretty much stuck. Squire is using my car since his wreck.

8/ 13/96 I had to wait until Alex got home to do grocery shopping & get my allergy shots. Mom called, she said that Dad is still losing weight. He is down to about 130 pounds.

231

8/14/96 Wednesday I am starting to feel house bound. You forget how much you depend on having transportation until you have to do without.

8/15/96 Thursday Nice, beautiful, even cool for August. We have had about a week of really nice weather. The house is clean, laundry done, and bills paid. Now I can work on my book some. In about 3 weeks we will leave for Europe. I am excited but a bit scared about flying that far.

8/16/96 Friday Cleaned house, did laundry. Ho hum day.

8/18/96 Alex and I went to McGuffy's for brunch. Went to West Town bought a Pinky & the Brain tie for Wesley.

8/19/96 B.P. 135/81 Monday Our trip is getting closer and I am on the verge of a major panic attack. I am a big baby about flying, it scares me something terrible. Dr. Sharp removed two moles from my right shoulder. He said he is sure they are OK but one was under my bra strap and kept getting sore.

8/21/96 Tuesday Did basic household chores. I have a sore throat. I sure hope I am not getting sick two weeks before our trip.

8/23/96 B.P. 132/90 Thursday Appt with Dr. Bennett at 9:45am. Finished last minute shopping for trip.

8/25/96 Saw Dr. Overholt. I have an ear infection, sore throat, almost pneumonia. Tight chest. He added to my meds.

8/27/96 I have a dentist appt. I have a cracked filling that has to be replaced.

8/28/96 Wed - Thursday Spent most of time finishing our packing for our trip. Two of my neighbor friends, Betty and Sandy, took me to Aubrey's for lunch. Kind of a bon voyage gift for our trip. Most everything is done except picking up some traveler's checks tomorrow.

8/30/96 Friday Everything is usual except more anxious.

8/31/96 Squire took us out to lunch at Cozumel's. We had a lovely time. Squire bought a new BMW.

9/1/96 B.P. 157/90 Sunday Alex & I did our final packing for our trip to Europe. I am still having some arm and neck pain.

9/2/96 B.P. 160/92 Monday - Labor Day It is rainy. Our trip is day after tomorrow. I am very anxious, almost scared. My arm and hand are numb and tingly. Everything is ready for our trip. Passports - luggage - money - traveler's checks - maps. Alex and I updated our will - We will sign it tomorrow and give both boys copies.

9/3/96 Tuesday The day before we leave for Europe. Man do I have butterflies.

The reason for our trip: My work at the Lab brought a request during 1996 to give a scientific paper at a conference to be held in Prague, and that brought about many memorable events that we added to our adventures; extensive travel by automobile in Europe.

By then I had become sufficiently established in the auto magazine world to request and receive a new vehicle on loan from a manufacturer; this request became the focus of another feature on automotive related travel. Having also become well known among officials of Ford Motor Company due to my many magazine features and books, my request for a Ford of Germany vehicle was granted.

Arrangements were made for almost a month long excursion that would take us by air to Germany to receive the vehicle, then we were free to drive it wherever we chose. I had a firm itinerary centered around the conference with a week or more before and after, each day a relatively short drive to take us to overnight in a historic site among those available with "Romantic Hotels & Restaurants" credentials. That gave afternoon and evenings to wander.

The Lab would not grant my travel request, so I took vacation and paid for our trip, knowing that a feature was to result with another check from the publisher. My feature became a Silver Medal winner in the Olympics of automotive journalism that year, awarded by the International Automotive Media Association.

When planning, Mary was not so sure. She wrote:

Europe? Oh no!

I had many fears about an extended trip to Europe. I was anxious, downright scared, to be honest. Up to the day of departure, I had many dreams that fueled my mounting doubts. Among my worst fears was the flight itself. Coming on the heels of several well publicized plane crashes, panic continually ebbed at my consciousness. And what about connections? Would our luggage arrive on time and safe?

What about the unknown once we get there? Germany: its language and currency barriers fueled my worst nightmares. And what about the other countries and their currency, all different? How much to tip was the least of my fears.

What if we got lost? Horrors! We would be driving through 8 countries, about 2,000 miles in 21 days, and each country posed similar problems. How would people react to Americans? I had heard that many Europeans do not like us at all. Was that right? If so, I imagined that we were walking in to one very real nightmare after another.

I agonized about one of us becoming ill or injured on this extended trip and got little relief to learn that our insurance would cover the cost. How would we handle an emergency while we were in Europe, an emergency either there or back home?

234

The unknown; everything was unknown, and I was anxious. So, I busied myself with planning and organizing the trip and found that it was both a pleasure and a fantastic learning experience.

Finally, the day came, and we left Knoxville for Charlotte, then England by British Airways. Forty-two minutes later we were in Charlotte and Fran - the hurricane - awaited our passage across - EGAD! - the Atlantic Ocean. Fear piled on fear! The layover for an hour gave me pause to invent some more fears, then at 3:15 on a sunny, tranquil afternoon, we boarded for the big crossing. The take-off was a bit bumpy, and my stomach leaped into my throat. My ears started to ring, then closed completely for a few seconds, and my cloistered fears came tumbling through my consciousness. Then, at an altitude of several miles, we were sailing over clouds so white they looked like a giant, fluffy white blanket - Fran.

Since we would be flying all night, British Air crew provided each of us with blanket and a flight package containing toothbrush, toothpaste, slipper socks, a sleep mask for our eyes, and head phones to listen to our selection of in-flight radio entertainment or the movie. The Movie! Twister - well I certainly would not be thinking of my own fears with such visual drama. The second was Mission Impossible, and there was no time for my fears during that show, either.

Seven hours in flight across six time zones put us arriving in Gatwick about 7:00am. The flight was smooth, but our connections loomed as an enormous challenge. We were heading for Cologne, Germany, and we had to go from one terminal to another, then run to catch our flight across the Channel. When we arrived, you guessed it, our luggage had not made the flight. Despite being told that, for security reasons, passengers and luggage fly on the same plane, we had gotten separated. It was 11:20 local time, and the next plane from Gatwick was due about 4:00pm, and there was no guarantee that our luggage would be on it. We were supposed to drive a couple of hours south to Heilbronn to meet friends, so we had to exchange US for German currency. My fears come true!

A fellow traveler, Guido Pitzen from Dahlem, Germany, was also without luggage, and in his auto racing T-shirt, as the beginning of conversation, we learned that he was a racing fan returning from attending the Southern 500. Guido helped us with an exchange window, so we had Marks, and he became our guide on the bus ride into the city where we got on the subway under the imposing Cathedral of Cologne.

It was the first time in my life I had ever been on a subway, and I was in a foreign country during rush hour. I couldn't read the language, and I had no idea if we were going where we should to pick up the vehicle we were to drive during our tour of Europe. Oh yes; we. I was with my husband who had made all the arrangements. I was just about certain that he was lost, too! Panic was my companion.

Then we were in the vehicle, a nice and comfortable German version of Ford's 4-wheel drive Explorer. That part worked out OK after all, largely thanks to Guido. With my husband at the wheel, we drove back to the airport to wait. Then another pleasant surprise; British Airways gave us a voucher for 100 Marks (about $65) to have dinner in the airport. We were assured that our luggage would be on the next flight... maybe.

Compliments of the airlines, we ate well, very well. I selected an excellent Riesling, not suspecting that it would lead to another fright, and we passed the warm, sunny afternoon quietly watching the occasional airplane arrive and take off. Our luggage arrived on the next plane, and at 5 o'clock we set out on our trip.

The unknown quickly asserted itself. The AUTOBAHN! Exiting the airport toward Bonn, we were able to get onto the Autobahn without any problem, but the first time we got off we found out that German motor ways are not like US interstate highways; where there's a get-off, there's a get-on. Not so on our very first exit. To make matters worse, signs were of no help, even if we could read them. Somehow we ended up on the west side of the Rhine River, not the east side as planned, but we were heading in the right direction. Soon we were in Remagen where my father helped fight for the

236

"Bridge Too Far" during WW-2. Then that Riesling sent me a message about a nap. I asked the driver, my confidant husband, if he needed a navigator. "No", he said. "we're doing just fine." So, I dozed off.

The sunshine coming through the windshield was warm when I awoke in a small town in who-knows-where. One turn led to another, and we came to the end of the road in a resort. We were lost! Really lost! Helplessly lost! Well, almost. We stopped along a narrow road by a small river and asked directions of two elderly women. They spoke no English, but one of them went for her husband who directed us to the Autobahn.

Finally, on a magnificent 2-lane highway through increasingly beautiful farm and timber country, my Riesling was speaking to me again, and my confidant husband assured me that we were "doing just fine." So, with eyelids I could hardly keep open, I dozed off again

When I awoke again, the sun's shadows were long, and my confident husband was saying something about the sign to Saarbrucken saying we were headed in the wrong direction. France was not far away, and we were supposed to be going to Heilbronn in the central part of Germany. Yes! We were lost big time!

At an intersection with an east-west highway about the same size as the north-south highway we were on, my confidant husband rolled the dice and turned east. No towns were in sight, so I couldn't even find us on the map.

With the setting sun and my fears looming ahead in the coming darkness, we were still in who-knows-where. Finally we came to a town, and finally we were on the map - just two hours west of where we were supposed to be. Thanks, driver!

On a winding road in a tiny burg buttoned up for the night, we found a pizza shop just closing. My husband finally stopped for directions and came back with a surprise; one of the workers was an American girl who gave clear directions over the hills and through the valleys to the Autobahn. By then it was 10 o'clock, and my Riesling was demanding a comfortable bed for the night. But nooo! My

237

confident husband drove on and on, by this time of night I was ready to call him anything but confident, perhaps Pig Headed! We were supposed to be in Heilbronn.

One thing about Autobahns; drivers go really fast, and my confident husband mashed the accelerator down in a vain attempt to keep up with passing traffic. By then I was numb to the thought of a horrific crash, but to my delight we were soon in Mannheim and my confident husband was looking for a place to spend the night. After 6 hours of what should have taken two, we spent our first night in Germany. I didn't know that we had driven through a portion of the Black Forest. I was asleep.

With the morning sun we had a new strategy; highlight every town along the route we were driving, and should we get lost, stop and ask directions. Almost everyone spoke at least a little English. A sign with the town's name upon entering, and a similar sign with a line diagonally across the name upon exiting is the measure of progress.

We didn't get lost again, and one by one my fears subsided, including my question about how Europeans would treat Americans. Everyone we met was more than willing to help. Even with a language barrier, a genuine and courteous smile was a valuable asset.

Medical questions? Our insurance company told us how to handle emergencies while out of the US, and we took all of our medicines - and enough of them along with precautionary medicines - with us to last until we got home. I also called the airlines to make sure that we could change our flight back to the US if there was an emergency that required our presence. So, I had earned some peace of mind.

...Once we got on track, our trip was fun. My new thesis is; when in need, remain calm, smile, and be polite. After about 2,400 miles and three weeks through Germany, the Czech Republic, Austria, Liechtenstein, Switzerland, France, Luxembourg, and flights to England; everywhere we traveled people were willing to help and

238

usually responded with a smile. Had I known how easily that most problems can be solved, my fears would have been much less stressful.

And when fog kept us on the ground missing our return flight to the U S, I was a seasoned traveler with a smile, though not quite as confident as my husband. British Airways provided us with vouchers for three meals apiece and a nice room for the night. We spent an extra day in England and browsed the shops followed by much needed rest before our flight back to the States.

My itinerary for the first leg of our tour did not include my navigator getting soused on Riesling. During our first, a really tasty German meal, Mary drank the entire bottle. So, my driving was navigator-less, a most interesting drive for me to see so much while Mary slept. My itinerary did include visiting with Klaus and Margret Scheer whom we had become acquainted with through a cousin who had befriended them years earlier while stationed nearby on an Army base. They were wonderful hosts who invited us into their wine country home with hospitality and attention to our interests that included visiting the towns of my ancestors who left their homes and lives in the region during 1731 for new lives in America. Those towns were Forchtenberg in the fabled Hohenlohe and Schwaigern in the Lein valley. Both being very old compared to us American newbies, I was deeply interested in their histories and spent several years tracing my genealogy back to 1575, generation by generation, by names and dates to these towns.

The second leg of my itinerary also included driving the Burgenstrasse, Germany's Castle Road that took us from one picture perfect town to another, each pristine and colorful, yet unique in character. Many travel features with photos came of this tour including three books, *Blood of the Roses* about Forchtenberg during the Nazi era; *I Am Gisele, Empress* that tells the story of a local princess who rose to become Empress of the Holy Roman Empire, with Mary photographed on the cover; and *Schwaigern* that was the location of a ferocious battle during World War Two. Drawing everything from historical records proved to be a most interesting learning experience for me. Being there enhanced visualizing the stories I wrote.

In her journal, Mary wrote beginning 9-4-96, then followed with:

9-6-96 Friday Klaus took us to several small villages in Germany where the first Gabbards were thought to come from. We purchased some kind of delicious pastry and a kind of almond & sugar pretzel, a typical sweet snack in Germany. We went back to Klaus and Margret's and Margret had a lovely meal, a meat pie in a pastry crust with ground beef, spinach, carrots, onion, peas, potatoes wrapped in pastry and baked. Wine and apple strudel. All of it was delicious.

9-7-96 Saturday Klaus and Margret went with us to some old castle ruins dating back to 1050. At an old church in a Medieval town [Schwaibish-Hall] we had green potato soup, coffee and apple dumplings. We watched a real wedding with honor guard and band. We went back to Margret and Klaus' and had Wienerschnitzel & German potato salad, Green Beans with parsley, Bread and Chocolate moose, wine cheese and bread. Beer always.

9-8-96 Sunday We left Klaus & Margret's headed for Prague. We drove through several rain storms. We stopped for diesel fuel in Weinberg. We reached the Czech border at about 12:00am. We had to go through two check points, I was very nervous, but we were waved through. We drove into Prague without any problems. We arrived at the Gordon Conference at around 3:00pm. The weather here is quite cold and damp. Our room at the Park Hotel is a bit unusual. You enter to a bath on the left, a living area in front, and the bed is in a loft.

Driving through Germany was a thrilling experience for me. My father had spent almost five years [actually about one year] *in Germany and France during WWII. He told us a little bit about the*

240

terrible destruction that he had seen almost all over Germany. Now for the most part Germany has healed herself. You can see the pride of these hardy people everywhere. The homes, farms, both large and small are beautifully well kept. There was little, if any, litter anywhere, even the road sides were cared for.

Oh! The vineyards. They are a marvel - green grape vines as far as the eye can see. The groves were criss-crossed with small paved roads. Paved roads also bordered the vineyards. The rows of grapes were planted vertically up and down the hillsides instead of horizontally like most vineyards that I have seen in the USA.

We traveled on Highway E-50 our last leg of journey across Germany and into the Czech Republic where we had to show our passports twice to get across the border.

Immediately after crossing the border we were struck by extreme change. The Czech Republic was very unkept. The roads in great disrepair. Many of the homes were falling down. Everything, even the tree trunks looked dirty. The people tired and sad somehow. We saw old women wearing long cotton skirts, woolen jackets, a scarf tied around the head and knotted under the chin, many with no or few teeth. Further into the Czech Republic we started seeing signs of recovery, new roads are being built. New construction is underway and many of the old castles are being restored into resorts or museums. I think the economic and visual recovery of the Czech Republic will take a long while but it was nice to see that there are major efforts in that direction. [recovering from Soviet communist rule for so long]

I am extremely tired. I didn't sleep much because my neck & arm hurt last night.

9-9-96 Today I have a light day planned. Alex has meetings, so I plan to rest, read, & write. Tomorrow we plan a tour of Prague.

9-10-96 I woke up with a very bad neck ache & head ache today. My left little finger is quite numb. We have a tour of Prague at 1:30pm. I hope to be feeling better. I am going down for a cup of coffee and a roll and then read until lunch at 12:30, the tour.

Sunshine - The world is bright for the first time since we arrived in the Czech Rep. It is nice since we have a tour planned of Prague today. We hope to get some good photographs.

We walked for what seemed like miles - we were walking for 3 to 4 hours. I was in a lot of pain by the time we got back to the room. My little finger especially was almost totally numb. I was having spasms in my neck and throat. I took something for pain and went to bed. At 3:30am I woke to more neck and arm pain. I did not sleep again until after 5:30am.

Last night we met a couple from Raleigh, N.C. who had lived in the same housing development that we lived in during the 1970s. [Their children were friends with our children]

Tuesday - We visited Old City Prague, PRAHA Czech Republic. The city was beautiful and ugly all at once. The beauty of the city could have been breathtaking, but under Communist rule the city had been raped of it pride. The city was a sad and dirty image of her previous self. [Known for generations prior to the Soviets as Europe's "golden city", now blackened by decades of coal smoke.]

However, there are many signs of rebirth. New growth and a lot of reconstruction has begun. The city as well as the country has many years of work to recover its beauty. The people here still seem to be sad or bitter. I am not sure which. They do not smile very much, always so somber. The weather seems to match the mood, rainy, grey, and gloomy.

The food here for the most part tastes good but there is no variety. You get a raw dish - chopped cabbage, chopped peppers, etc. The main course is potatoes with meat usually fried with a crumb coating, some kind of soup. One was curdled looking grey soup - not to my taste. Another was a clear broth with a few bits of chicken and chopped chives.

Breakfast is always the same; cereal, milk, juice, coffee, boiled eggs, meats & cheeses, hard rolls, butter and honey & jams.

The breads are excellent. The lack of water is a problem. I really do not care for bottled water. There is always Coke & Pepsi but everything has caffeine in it.

The statues in Prague were enormous, many Christian. But they were all totally black. They were covered with years and years of coal dust. The only thing that shined was the gold ornamentation [brass plaques] *on each statue. The statues were everywhere, dozens & dozens of them. Everything showed that the country had been very wealthy at one time. - Maybe in time it will recover and the people will get back their pride and even their smile.*

I have enjoyed the conference convention very much except for the food. Tonight we had a stew of unknown origin with canned cherries. Every meal either has steamed rice or potatoes. At lunch today we had a potato. It actually tasted better than it looked.

We visited the castle and church on the grounds of the university gardens [in Pruhonice south of Prague]. *I think we got some wonderful pictures. There were a lot of ducks and swans on the lake. The gardens are still beautiful. I can imagine that they are breathtaking in the springtime.*

9-11-96 Wednesday We did not walk as much today - still a lot more than at home. I don't know if it is a strange bed or exercise but I am tired. I only sleep to about 3:30am. I wake up and am in a lot of pain. I have taken a lot of Aleve.

9-12-96 Thursday I feel fine today. Rain again. We are scheduled to do a Castle tour today at 1:30. I hope we will not have a lot of outside walking or maybe it will clear off for a while. I am drinking lots of bottled water. Some of the fizzies are awful, like drinking an alka seltzer.

It has been unusually cold here for this time of year. Germany and the Czech Republic had frost this year in August, that the locals say is unusual even for this area. Tomorrow we leave Prague and head for Vienna, Austria. Friends we met here are going to travel with us, Ray and Gerry from Raleigh N.C.

Last night I washed my hair and with an attempt to turn on my hair dryer I blew a fuse that plunged our whole hall into darkness. As many times as our power has gone out I think a lot of people have had the same problem. Other cultures make me more proud and appreciative of what we have in the USA. Prague is embracing the western culture more and more. We can get CNN in English 24 hours a day in our hotel room at the Park Hotel at the conference.

Last night Alex and I walked out of our hotel going to dinner and a police car was across the street with country music coming from the radio or a tape. Randy Travis - Country music in the Czech Republic. For a second I could close my eyes, and I could be anywhere in the USA.

9-13-96   Friday   I am feeling good. We are leaving the Czech Republic for Vienna, Austria. Ray and Gerry traveled with us, and we arrived in Vienna about 12:00pm [noon] and found a gigantic street festival going on. We checked into the Hotel Capri and took the subway U-1 straight to the VIC or IAEA [for a meeting I was scheduled to attend]. We had lunch with Roger Seitz at the VIC. We had a lovely salad bar; it was great to have fresh vegetables. We also had apple strudel. The VIC was impressive, very large and with a lot of security. An aspect that I don't care for.

[After the meeting] Vienna sure seems to have a love affair with the west. There are street performers everywhere and about 90% of them doing songs from the USA. There is one man with a great backup band doing all of Elvis' old songs, another group doing Peter, Paul & Mary, and still more doing The Beatles, and country. There are a few OomPa bands. There are street vendors everywhere selling everything you can think of.

The streets here in Vienna are very narrow, a car can hardly squeeze through between other cars with a few inches to spare. I guess that is why the cars are so much smaller here. The crowds are *crushing but everyone here seems to be having a great time, unlike the frowning people in the Czech Republic.*

The food here is also fabulous. We had some pastries that were almost sinful; a maple topping, some kind of heavy cream center. It was heavenly after the food in Prague. Ray also bought us an éclair that had a rich chocolate filling. We ate dinner at Handy's [in our hotel]. *We both had pork; delicious.*

9-14-96 Saturday I have had a touch of diarrhea today. I feel OK, just a bit of a touchy stomach. Shopping in Vienna is interesting; the shops close at 6:00pm Monday thru Friday. Some shops open on Saturday morning at 7:00am but all shops close at 12:00 noon on Saturday. None of the shops are open on Sunday or at night. Everyone has to plan ahead and shop wisely to have food and necessary items on hand because there is no running to Wal-Mart or K-Mart on Sunday or late at night to pick up a bar of soap or toilet tissue. This is a big adjustment for people that come here to work or school from the USA.

We had breakfast here in the Hotel Capri this morning. It was very good; cereal, rolls, margarine & real butter, jam, jellies, honey. Scrambled eggs with bits of ham, boiled eggs, yogurt, peaches, several other kinds of bread - Meat platter, 3 kinds of meat, 3 kinds of cheese - Coffee which you could have with cream, hot or cold milk. Coffee here is very good but it is very rich and thick almost like espresso but it does not seem to have a lot of <u>acid.</u> So far it has not hurt my stomach.

We spent most of today in Old Vienna with Ray and Gerry. We visited many beautiful old buildings and churches. We also visited two Roman ruins that have been partially excavated and dated back to 2-4 AD. We had lunch in Vienna, then went back to Hotel Capri to rest and get ready for dinner tonight with Turf Martin and his wife and friends. They are Sunbeam people. We are going to take a taxi since we do not know the area. We are told that the cost will be around $30.00 round trip. Everything is extremely expensive here. I

245

looked at a wool sweater that might sell for $100.00 at home; it was $275.00 here. Leather boots ran $250.00 to $600.00 a pair. We saw Rolex watches ranging from about $1,200.00 to over $20,000.00 - for a watch. Silk blouses that were over $200.00. Beer is about the only thing that does not cost an arm and a leg.

Saturday night. We met with Turf Martin & his wife and friends. They took us to the Vienna Forest and to the mountains to see the lights of Vienna. They took us out to eat in an Austrian restaurant run by a local family. I had pit roasted chicken, salad & sunflower seed bread and white wine. Alex had a pork joint, salad, bread & white wine. After our drive we went back to the Collins' home, lovely old furniture. We sampled several wines - met their two teen aged boys. One played his guitar for me.

9-15-96 Sunday We left Vienna for Salzburg about 10:00am. The sun was shining and everything looked beautiful. The farther we got up into the mountains toward Salzburg the darker the clouds became. By the time we were about 60K out of Salzburg it started raining and it poured on us all the way into Anif which is on the outskirts of Salzburg. We checked into our room, then went for a drive around Anif and Salzburg. There are castles and ruins of castles everywhere. There is one castle that is about the most beautiful thing I have ever seen and it is huge, more than huge, it is tremendous. We ate in a restaurant that is part of Hotel Schlosswirt in Anif bei Salzburg. The menu was very Austrian. There was deer steaks, roast duck, rabbit, chicken, Austrian Potato Salad, Black Pudding, fish - mostly smoked salmon. Strudels and pudding for dessert.

I have had a real upset stomach today.

At dinner we met 3 old gentlemen who were touring Europe. They were 80, 80, and 83. They were funny and two of them spoke fairly good English. We made pictures. I was amazed at the amount of food they ate. They had a venison, or deer meat, plate, then a chicken plate while drinking wine, beer, later schnapps of which they ordered Alex and me a glass, then they finished with brandied coffee. One of

246

the gentlemen owned a glass factory, one was a veterinarian, one was a retired Swedish Air Force Colonel [who thought Mary was Swedish and sent the treats to our table]. *So far I have been mistaken for German and Swedish.*

9-16-96 Monday So far everyone has been very friendly and most helpful. At our Hotel today we met a young couple from Florida. We have tickets for the Sound of Music Tour that we will have tomorrow afternoon. Today we visited Old Town Salzburg. We saw the house where Mozart was born. We saw St. Peter's Church and St. Peter's Stiftskellar which is a restaurant that was licensed in the year 803AD. It has been a restaurant ever since. We had dinner there. Alex had Wienerschnitzel with potatoes, we shared, it was large. I had cheese strudel with vanilla ice cream which we shared.

There was a family in the pub that were arranging a wedding. The father and daughter (the bride) got into a fight about where to have the wedding. The father wanted to have it in Venezuela. The bride wanted to have it in New York where she and the groom met. She was Italian, the groom was Austrian. They were arguing in three languages, English, Italian, and Austrian. The bride was in tears.

Many times in the exchange Dad was paying so he wanted it his way, the daughter wanted it her way, and the poor groom sat there looking between his fiancé and his future father-in-law. I would not have blamed him if he ran and did not look back.

We did some shopping today in Salzburg, mostly window shopping. I could not believe the cost of some of the items, sweaters from $250.00 up to over $1,000.00. Alex looked at a handmade Austrian dress, it was $1,650.00. I could hardly believe it. I did get lucky. I found a very small shop that had reduced some 100% wool sweaters - virgin wool. I purchased a tan & brown heather with toggles that looked very Austrian. As it turned out it was made in Salzburg. It was 1/2-price. I got it for $149.00. I feel like I got a good price in it.

I really have not made very many purchases. Everything costs about 3 to 5 times or more what it would cost in the USA. We actually ate at McDonalds in Salzburg. Two pies, 2 Cokes, and a McFish sandwich cost 89 shillings or $8.90, more than double what it would have cost in the USA.

We parked under a mountain in an underground garage. We did not know how to operate the machine to get out, a man came along and showed us you have to pay first, then the machine checks your car off. You put the card in the box and the gate raises up so you can drive through. Many things have been a bit intimidating but there was always someone there to help

The mountains have even more snow on them; it is strange to be in early September and see snow. One of the passes across the Alps in Austria was closed for over 24 hours due to a snow storm.

9-17-96 Tuesday I feel better with my stomach but my arm hurts and my little finger in numb. We went on the Sound of Music tour this morning with three other couples from the USA. Our guide's name was Alex. We left Anif at 8:45am and got back from the tour at 1:30. We saw the pagoda that Lisel and the soldier danced and sang "Sixteen going on Seventeen". We saw the lake where the canoe turned over and the tree where the children were playing from dressed in the clothes made from drapes. We saw the castle from the beginning scenes [Our overnights and the meal with the three gentlemen were in that castle's annex, Anif castle] *and we saw the balcony scene. The whole area was beautiful. We wound up at an outdoor cafe where we had apple strudel.*

We drove from Anif to Innsbruck that afternoon. We went to a live performance that was typical folk dances of the area, the Jealousy Dance, the Maypole Dance, the Wood Choppers Dance, and a Wedding Dance. The group played several instruments that were local instruments. Beer was served free with the ticket to get in. The beer was called Adambrau.

9-18-96 Wednesday Waked up about 3:30am. Nose stopped up and a smashing headache. My neck and arm are spasming. Sure hope things settle out for the rest of the trip. Alex and I drove to Italy. It was a beautiful drive, there were more castles than you could count. It seemed everywhere we looked there were more castles, some with rock wall fortresses all the way around them. Alex photographed the Ford in the Brenner Pass in Italy. We were back in Innsbruck by about 1:30pm. We left our hotel and went for a walking tour of the old city. I purchased a silver pin of the state flower, Edelweiss. We bought six T-shirts and two beer mugs for the boys. I hope they don't get broken before we get home. All of the buildings here are very old, most of them much older than the USA. We will be leaving Innsbruck tomorrow. We will go to a town near Switzerland.

9-19-96 Thursday I had a terrible night. I woke up at 3:30am with a spasm in my neck, this turned into a migraine headache. We stayed in Schwarzenberg, Austria, a very small town with cows right down the street. There was a lovely little church across from our Hotel. The grave yard was interesting; there were whole families in each grave, from 2 to as many as 8 in one grave.

9-20-96 Friday My head hurt all day - I felt lousy, my neck and arm were in a spasm. We left Austria headed for Liechtenstein, then on to Switzerland. We crossed the Swiss Alps on a road so narrow that in many places one car had to pull off for the other car coming in the other direction to pass. We were well into the snow line; there was a foot or more of snow. We arrived in Grindelwald, Switzerland about 4:30pm.

Mary left a lot out of her travel notes, such as visiting the Bavarian castles of "mad King Ludwig", especially Neuschwanstein, his mountaintop fairy tale construction that is the most photographed castle in the world and the inspiration for Disney's replication. Her worries are also not expressed in her notes, especially worrying about the mounting cost of our tour and how frightening some of our adventures were. So, the following is added:

In the Hall of the Mountain King

Roused from slumber, Mary forecast, "Storm ahead."

"Look again," I said.

"Oh...," she stammered. "Oh!"

She looked beyond the empty stretch of 1-lane road ahead into craggy peaks far above the trees that rose into dark slopes and dense fog; this Swiss mountain terrain was like nothing we had seen before. Where were we going? Into what? It was up there, somewhere way up there. Klausenpass, our map told us.

As we drove slowly along, I had no suspicions as to why we met no traffic, no traffic at all. I missed that point as Mary dozed and I wandered along with wonder at every turn. Winding our way through the valley, we drove to well above the tree line in Switzerland's back country of long winters, short summers, and lots of time to make cheese and carve briar pipes. The fog and rain accompanied our climb and soon engulfed us.

I had routed us along back roads and managed to get onto this path less traveled for no other reason than to traverse passes in the high Alps. We were driving a Ford-Germany produced Maverick, a 4-wheel drive, turbo-charged diesel SUV, and I wanted impressions of Alpine passes, never mind the weather.

Puttering along was good for seeing glacial sights, rather like the setting for a James Bond thriller; Alpine cliffs jutting skyward, rock faces that spent their time from eons past shedding boulder size bits of themselves that littered the meadow's edges below. Mist shrouded tops seemed to soar on forever above them.

This high valley, a narrow glen of few people, had infrequent house-barn-stable combines nestled into the earth with portions on top of the ground. This region had been home to a tough breed of mountain herders from time beyond memory. I was certain that the 5,000-year old "Ice Man" found frozen in the Italian side of these

250

mountains had passed this way, and when slowly rounding a turn, we came upon his progeny.

There seems to be a highland law that says, "whatever gets there first has right-of-way", and the cows sauntering along, their over-sized brass bells strapped to their necks clanging with each step, had the road and seemed to be churning their over-size utters that swung from side-to-side. This was open range as evidenced by no fences anywhere, and wherever pasture invited them, that's the way they went. We came to a stop for the herd and looked upon a world of another time whose clock was set by late sunrises and early sunsets dictated by the jagged cliffs above and clouds that hung on them. We were making a summertime advance into the Alps where we found the warming sun and always-available snowmelt the makings for succulent grass during short growing seasons that was so attractive to the small herd in front of us, surely the same that produced the creamy milk of Swiss chocolate and cheese fame.

And there, standing just above us on a knoll watching his herd was a picture-perfect example of an Alpine herdsman. I didn't ask to photograph him because of a sense of intruding, but I marveled when thinking of the days of his life. His long, heavily carved pipe arched downward from his lips and curled upward again at about his waist, then expanded upward into a large, fist-size bowl with a silver ring around its lip. My first thought was, "Why is this man standing out in the middle of nowhere playing a saxophone?" Then a puff of smoke emanated slowly from his lips that told me the answer.

His Alpine hat inspired me to buy one in the next town we came to, but his was authentic far beyond my tourist copy. Made of grey felt, bigger than tourist models, it was adorned with a double loop of woven green hat-band cord. From the left side of the band emerged a decorative silver, funnel-shaped attachment with a glorious plume of white rising upward to a brush of stylistic flourish perhaps a foot long. I have since wondered what the history of this typically Swiss adornment signifies.

One hand held an elaborately carved herdsman's staff of dark wood while the other held his pipe. Wide leather bands surrounded the cuffs of his woolen jacket that was finished with similar leather lapels and collar. Decorative silver adornments on each lapel told of another Alpine tradition; just what, I've never learned. Two smaller breast pockets of leather with silver buttons matched much larger waist pockets with their flaps. He stood in the day's warmth, not yet sunny, seemingly basking in the tepid weather, so much so that his jacket, also with silver adornments, lay open to reveal the bib of his leather lederhosen belted at the waist. The bib displayed what appeared to be stitchings of colorful Alpine flowers.

His wide belt with a broad silver buckle revealed a trim man, easily of six feet in height, a man likely to be past his prime but very distinguished in presentation. I imagined him to be a powerfully built man accustomed to a regular routine of manual labor. Out here in the pasture, he seemed to enjoy the solitude, for he was quite alone and far from any human except those of us on the road, just Mary and me at this moment.

Woolen knickers of dark grey stopped just below the knee where leather bands met stockinged legs. The bands tended to blouse the knee portion just above them, and on their outsides, another silver adornment held a downward pointing plume of white, a smaller brush than on his hat but still a noticeable flourish. The tops of ribbed stockings emerged from the tops of calf-height leather boots, and Alpine scenes engraved along the sides of the heavy, dark brown boot tops told of long winter hours of handwork tooling the leather, probably hand tanned as well, along with stitching of each adornment around the top. Laced to form-fit his legs below the knees with boot strings that were tied into a bow at the top, each boot was crowned with colorful red and gold piping that accented the plume on each leg.

This is the picture of a Swiss Alpine herdsman that remains fixed in my memory. We looked at him; he looked at us, and puffed another slow puff. We waived, he nodded, and onward into the Alps we went.

Somewhere up there was Klausenpass; our map said so. But Mary wasn't so sure as we made one hairpin switchback after another, zigging after another zag, slowly making our way up the mountain toward whatever lay above the clouds that would soon engulf us. Along the way the narrow pavement had its own elements of treachery; no safety barrier whatever. In places, a delicate hand-rail sort of construction marked the edge of the world, and it was on her side. The sight down into the distant valley beyond the boulders was eye-opening. At intervals where room permitted, a small pull-off was paved for the purpose of allowing vehicles to pass. As we climbed upward, her fright index steadily moved nervously into "Oh my God!" as it became increasingly apparent that a wheel misplaced led to off-road ventures that our 4x4 was not designed for. Would the herdsman we passed come to our aid when seeing our red Ford Maverick tumble thousands of feet down the mountain crags?

By the time we reached the fog, rain came with it, and not only did our vision diminish to only a few car lengths ahead, wet road insured that Mary's fright meter was pegged from there on. The eastern facing slopes around us seemed to be in perpetual fog, dark, dreary, and drizzly, thoroughly soaked, cold and slippery with little sign of growing things. The higher we went, the more barren the terrain; boulders in infinite disarray gave evidence of rock slides, hopefully ancient, and all grey-to-black in color, and ominous. I concluded that the peaks we climbed toward were what German operas mean when singing about the Hall of the Mountain King. Who would possibly want to travel this road; some tourist wanting to experience passes across the top of the world? How foolish!

Then, snow....

By now, Mary had resorted to closing her eyes and breathing slow measured breaths, the ostrich defense. And higher we went. Snow, rain, ice and fog... Treacherous 1-lane... Threatening rock slides... What more could anybody want when doing a road test of an SUV? Darkness....

Even though our drive was planned to top the Alps by two o'clock in the afternoon, the warmest part of this September day, the nearer we got to the pass, the gloomier our surroundings became. The fog was so dense that the filtered grey light gave impressions of darkness rapidly closing in. Even though I was confident that we had hours of daylight ahead of us, Mary's comment about it getting dark gave me pause to wonder if we might have driven through a time warp back into the stone age. At that moment, I would not have been startled to see the fur clad Ice Man, spear at the ready, around the next turn.

Only the paved road ahead illuminated by our headlights gave reassurance that we were still in the modern age. The pulsating beat of the wipers clearing the windshield added to the drama. No signs along the way was disconcerting. Just a little one telling where we were or how far to somewhere would have been a relief. Nothing. We were on our own, seemingly lost in time.

And on we went, slowly climbing the mountain, back and forth, hairpin after hairpin. Then, from out of the fog, the road ahead seemed to flatten a bit. We were reaching the summit, Klausenpass, at last.

This strange mountain top world shrouded in mist seemed to be the setting of a stone age movie, and we arrived the only travelers. Three items told that we were still in the modern world; first, a sign displaying Klausenpass; second, a manned - with a real human being - memento stand offering trophies reading "I braved Klausenpass" and similar one-liners that no one would understand who had not been there, done that; third, a small, stone, open-air church with a cross on its roof silhouetted faintly against the day's grey shroud. Here, the brave could give thanks, knowing that either way was down, a long, long way down.

We stopped, stretched our legs, breathed the cold mist, took some of the gloomiest photos ever, and prepared to go on.

"Sustenpass is next," I said to Mary. "It's only a thousand feet higher."

254

A few of her firmly spoken comments changed our course, and Sustenpass was no longer next. We were headed into the valleys, not the peaks, and not more than a few miles down the western slope, the day took on an entirely opposite demeanor; sunlight... bright, glorious, sunlight. We left the snow, cloudy mists, and fog behind as we wound our way slowly downward, past the occasional brightly painted and flowered Alpine chalet. People actually lived here, though widely separated requiring large measures of independence. When I pulled off to do some photography, I soon recognized why real people made this terrain home. Unshrouded by fog, these highlands were magnificent; deep, deep valleys of green below, each with a meandering river, high peaks of patchwork grey up abrupt, rocky slopes topped with the white of snow and ice silhouetted against a rich blue sky. All around were truly stunning panoramas that inspired awe at the natural beauty, very different than the eastern side we had driven up.

When we arrived at our destination, Grindelwald, a rustic ski lodge across the valley from 13,000 foot Eiger, the young woman at the desk made pleasantries by asking if we had just flown in to Switzerland.

"No," I said. "We drove over from Austria."

"Oh, how do you like our highways?" she continued as she filled out the register.

"We came over Klausenpass," Mary said.

The young woman paused and looked up at us. "You came Klausenpass?"

"Yes."

"I have lived here all my life," she said seriously, "and I have come that way only once, when I young. I shall never do that again."

Mary wrote:

This is the very end of the world, really. The road ends and there is nowhere else to go, except up the chair lift. It is not snowing

255

here but it is very cold. The hotel is gorgeous - really beautiful. From our balcony we can see a snow capped peak called Eiger over 13,000 feet high. When the sun is out it feels good outside. When the sun goes down it gets cold very quick.

9-21-96 Saturday I was unable to sleep but about 4 hours last night. My back, neck, and head throbbed. I finally slept a little sitting up. I woke up at 4:00am with a raging headache. I think my BP is up. My diet has been awful here. I have mostly had fruit and bread for breakfast, cereal when it was available. The European people do not use very much of anything diet. They use whole milk, real butter and sugar. We could not find diet Coke even in supermarkets.

We left Switzerland headed for France. We stopped for 2-3 hours in Mulhouse, France in order to go through an Auto Museum. There were more old cars than I had ever seen in one place in my life. There must have been acres of them, all European, all in almost perfect restoration. We left Mulhouse and drove to Strasbourg. We will be here for two nights. The old city here is surrounded by a canal with boats that go right up to the back doors of homes. There are water buses that take people around the old city on sightseeing tours. There was also a dinner tour at night. We walked around the old city; there were little beer gardens everywhere.

One of the walking streets had several such gardens. I saw a father pushing a carriage with his young child of less than two years old. He met some friends and stopped for a beer. The child got fussy; the father poured some beer in the baby's bottle and added some water. He gave this to his child and within a few minutes, the child was asleep and the father was having a wonderful time visiting with his friends.

We ate dinner at an old restaurant, St. Martin's. The building was built in the 1600s. I had a pork dish with wonderful potatoes. Alex had sauerkraut with several kinds of sausage and meats.

From my notes I added;

256

Mary and I saw beautiful surroundings in all directions as we drove the Wine Route after exiting Switzerland to the city of Mulhouse where we visited the extraordinary Sclumpf collection at the Musée National de l'Automobile, one of the world's foremost automotive museums and a prized location of Tourisme Alsace. With my interests in automotive history, this vast collection includes the finest assembly of Bugatti automobiles on the planet along with many historic cars in excellent presentation for photography that could consume months of visits, but just one day was all we had.

More excellent weather greeted us each day as we rolled along the Wine Route that now includes every village, town, and city lying in the foothills, eastern slopes, and valleys of the Vosges Mountains. This modern Wine Route is the sort of magical journey that could become a wine lover's lifetime beckoning, and to visit each of the towns on the Wine Route and learn their histories, some back to before the Roman Empire, would take a lifetime. Our trek was along the traditional route through Colmar on A35 to Strasbourg. Just the drive was worth taking, a good road with light traffic that enabled sauntering along while admiring the Alsacean scenery that, I believe, my ancestors knew well. First mention of my namesake, Gebhard, is recorded in Eguisheim, the source of the Snow White story, perhaps as early as the late 800s, but clearly in the records of the 900s.

My compilation of travel stories outside the USA, *Stories: Travel,* includes the Eguisheim story in much more detail. That book is a companion to my *Stories: Travel USA.* Mary's journal entries continue with:

9-22-96 Sunday I have an upset stomach and still a headache. We checked into the last of the Romanic Hotels on our tour. It has turned really cold and damp since yesterday. Yesterday was warm and sunny. Most everything in Europe is closed on Sunday - only a few pastry shops and souvenir shops. Restaurants and pubs are open. We walked by some pastry shops and the pastry they had on display were a work of art. They use a lot of Marzipan. The fruits look almost real and one shop had little pink pigs made from marzipan. I still find it amazing to see a man or a woman go into a pastry shop and come out with a loaf or two of bread tucked under his or her arm and, perhaps a sausage wrapped in waxed paper. We saw one man with a salami that must have been 10 or 15 pounds wrapped in paper carried on his shoulder. Sanitation requirements are definitely not the same here as they are in the USA.

Sunday. We spent most of today walking around Strasbourg, France. We visited a Cathedral de Notre Dame built in the 12th century. We went inside, it was beautiful. The stained glass windows were breath taking. The outside of the Cathedral had statues of Jesus, the devil, Virgins, and horses as well as the 12 apostles; much more than could ever be described.

The streets were a hive of activity. Tourists from everywhere, street vendors as well as roving street vendors, and on almost every street were beggars. The beggars make me feel most uncomfortable, I would like to help, but we are told that many are quite wealthy, that they do the begging to get rich. We even saw children begging for coins, one little girl playing accordion begging for coins. Alex put some money in the box at the Cathedral, there were just too many beggars to give to all of them.

We will be heading to Germany tomorrow to be in Cologne to catch our flight out at 7:00am on Tuesday.

9-23-96 Monday We traveled from France to Cologne, Germany. It rained most of the way. We spent the night in a Holiday Inn at the airport. It was as nice as any Hyatt that we have in the USA. We had dinner in a German restaurant. Alex had a salad and spaghetti with pork chops. I had a salad with potatoes twice baked. They served a nut bread that was delicious.

9-24-96 Tuesday We were at the airport at 5:30am. By 7:00am we had checked through and were ready to board when the plane was put on a 2 hour hold due to bad weather in London, fog. So we were brought back to the waiting area for our wait. It may actually be longer. The weather here looks awful.

We re-boarded about 8:30am and then sat on the runway another two hours. We arrived in London, England just as our plane was ready to take off. We ran for what seemed to be a mile only to miss our flight. By this time my neck was in a real mess. I blew a migraine, nausea, the whole bit. British Air tried several ways to re-route us but all the USA flights leave before noon. So we were out of luck for a flight Tuesday.

British Air paid for us a room at the Forte Crest at the airport with lunch, dinner, and breakfast provided. The hotel was beautiful in the lobby and outside but the room was only average, about on par with a Days Inn or Holiday Inn in the USA. We had a good meal package. We ate one meal at the Cafe 2 at the Brassiere, buffet. The breakfast buffet was lovely.

I took two pain tablets and two Visteril and finally went to sleep. I slept for about 9 hours.

9-25-96 Wednesday We are supposed to leave for Charlotte, N.C. today at 11:20am London time, 24 hours from when our original flight was due to leave. I just hope and pray everything goes well. The weather is OK for now but is forecast to rain later. I do not know what the weather is like in the USA at this time. London airport is very large, it would be very easy to get lost here. One could really go crazy in the duty free shops. You can buy about anything at lower prices and without paying taxes on it. We got Squire a bottle of X-O Remmy-Martin, about $103.00 American. We found Wesley an ascot, and Alex got 3 T-shirts from London, England.

We have a standby flight out of Charlotte, with a confirmed flight if we miss out on the early flight. Maybe we will get in, in time to make the earlier one.

We left London at 11:00am European time. We arrived in Charlotte about 5:00pm, made our connection to Knoxville. We *arrived in Knoxville at about 6:30pm, and we were home by 8:00pm. I feel very much better.*

9-26-96   Thursday   I saw Dr. Bunick. She was pleased with my outlook on life. I do feel more in control.

9-27-96 Friday I saw Dr. Vargas, he has ordered an MRI to be done at UT Hospital on Tuesday Oct. 1, 1996.
       We left for Nashville at 2:00pm. I am really tired. Jet lag has caught up with me. We went to the SEBA [book convention]. *We went to the cocktail party, we only stayed a couple of hours. Waylon Jennings was going to perform, but I could not stay awake.*

9-28-96 Saturday Spent the day at SEBA at the Opryland Hotel. It takes us 30 min to walk from our room to the convention center which is all under one roof. To my delight I got to meet Dixie Carter from "Designing Women". She is as pretty in person as on TV. She autographed a copy of her book for me. I still cannot stay awake.

9-29-96 Sunday We had breakfast in Nashville, then headed to Knoxville to my friend's parents 50th anniversary. I am still tired but now my head is pounding. After the party I came home, went to sleep on the couch, went to bed at 9:30pm, slept until 7:30am.

9-30-96 Monday I feel much better, but I am still tired. I wonder how long it takes to catch up.

10-1-96 Tuesday I had an MRI done at UT hospital. The bone spur is still there but does not seem to be any larger.

10-2-96 Wednesday Saw Dr. Vargas. I am to have surgery on my elbow on Oct. 16th. I need a few days to get the aspirin out of my system.

10-3-96 Thursday I get a flu shot today and my allergy shots.

10-4-96 Friday I feel fine. No pain from the flu shot. The nurse said my shoulder could get a little stiff, but so far it feels fine.

10-5-96 Saturday Today is Alex and my 31st wedding anniversary . We gave each other cards, and Squire took us out to eat at the Olive Garden. Wesley was in Memphis in medical school. We just had a lovely trip to Europe.

10-6-96 We spent Sunday just relaxing. I feel good, just tired.

10-7-96 I did not do very much today. I felt kind of down. I found out that my cousin's brain cancer was back and she is only expected to have about 3 weeks to live. She and I are the same age, just 6 months apart.

10-8-9-10-96 I have not felt like writing. Mother is trying to worry everyone as much as possible. I know she has a heavy load with Daddy in a nursing home and her niece dying of cancer, but it does not help any of us for her to give up and start threatening suicide. I feel a lot of her problem is for more attention.

10-1-96 Packing again. we are going to Orlando to a car show. Alex is Key Note speaker.

10-12-13-14-96 Orlando, Florida The weather is beautiful. There are about 40-45 Sunbeams here. We have met many old friends that we have not seen in many years. Helen and Wally Swift. Tom and JoAnn Earhart. And we have made many new friends. Dorothy Wood and I seem to have a lot in common. On Saturday Alex and I met Alex's cousin, Bobby Nichols and Annaleise, whom I had never met and Alex had not seen in about 38 years. We also went back on Monday; they made a wonderful dinner for us.

261

10-15-96 Tuesday I had one day to get the laundry caught up and pack a few things for the hospital.

10-16-96 I was at the hospital at 5:25am to check in. They took me back to Pre-Op at about 5:45am and to surgery about 6:30am.

10-17-96 Still don't feel very well, but had some good news. Dr. Vargas said he fixed the problem. I can move my fingers.

10-18-96 I have an infection in my right arm from the I.V., red streaks running all the way to my shoulder. Dr, Vargas put me on K-Flex.

10-19-20-96 Mostly took it easy with both arms out. I feel pretty bad.

10-25-96 Friday Alex is photographing a wedding rehearsal tonight. I am going to go and visit and watch. The wedding is for my Karate instructor's daughter.

10-26-96 Saturday Alex photographed Crisa's & Tony's wedding today. It was a lovely service. I have developed a pain in my elbow and it is swollen. I think I must have used it too much after Dr. Vargas took the stitches out Thursday. He said I could start bending it some, but I think I over did it.

10-27-96 Alex went with me to buy Mother a birthday present. We went in a store and my arm got a small bump and I cried. I guess I am a wimp.

10-28-96 Monday Today is Mom's birthday. I called her and she was in a pretty good mood for a change. My arm is still swollen and very sore. I quit taking any pain medicine. I do not like the way it makes me feel.

262

10-29-96 Tuesday I feel like shit - to be blunt.

10 -30-31-96 I feel some better. My arm only hurts when something touches it. Teresa and I went to lunch.

11-1-96 Alex has gone to Memphis to move Wesley to UT hospital in Knoxville for 4 months.

11-2-96 Squire stayed with me today while his Dad was in Memphis. We made chili and watched some old movies.

11-3-96 Sunday

Her journal entries ended on that date with that entry. Mary's writing returned to life stories such as the last year of the 1990s, the final chapter of her lifelong close relationship with her father. His death remained a continual source of sadness in her quiet moments that she never allowed to interfere with our time together, although hugs, kisses, and reassurances often accompanied our talk about recollections of him. Her world was seriously changing, and she did not like what she saw, the past, especially the passing of her life at home that she so loved, and the future now with only her mother was bittersweet.

Highlights of that last decade include our boys completing medical school, an enormously satisfying achievement for all of us and an enduring legacy of their beautiful mother who participated in every aspect of their lives that she could, celebrations included.

Then... more bittersweet moments and quiet times followed when her boys were no longer at home. With infrequent visits, letting go was tough for her, the same for all loving mothers who are uncomfortable with being sidelined in their children's lives. Passage of time helped soften adjustments, but such moments and their quiet times always tilted Mary toward melancholy with some of those memories leading to more writing, such as the following:

263

I Believe In Angels

About two weeks ago I met an Angel; this angel came to our family with a name, Mr. Felts.

Mr. Felts and my father Garvey Cheek were roommates in a nursing home for the last few days of Daddy's life.

My father had been in poor health for several years. His illness worsened on or about June 4th when he had several strokes that put him in the hospital for several days. After treatment and tests, his doctor told us that they had done all they could for Daddy. He would be sent back to the intensive care sector of the nursing home where he would be kept comfortable and cared for; his life expectancy was a few days to 2 weeks at most.

Mr. Felts was to be Daddy's roommate during his final days. Mr. Felts had suffered an accident several years ago that broke bones and severely burned him from his chest down, during this time he lost his right leg to an infection. He went through numerous surgeries and more skin grafts than he cared to remember. During the time we knew him his mind was clear, his heart was warm and giving, and his smiles and hugs of encouragement were plenty as were his tears, when we would weep so would Mr. Felts.

The last day of Daddy's life mother stayed with him. My brother Eddy, his wife Robbie, my husband Alex and I spent as much time as we could with Daddy and Mother.

But, we had our Angel Mr. Felts. When Mother could not be there, he watched over Daddy. When Mother was there he watched over both of them, making sure Mother got a tray and that she ate to keep her strength up.

Many times over those days I heard Mother say, "You know, God does work in mysterious ways. He knew I could not have gotten through this alone at times, without anyone to talk with. I am so thankful to Mr. Felts, he has been like an Angel to me."

He was an Angel to our whole family. He had a ready smile, or tears when we shed tears, a hug or words of encouragement when we faltered.

264

The night that Daddy died my brother Eddy and his wife Robbie, Mother, my husband Alex, and my cousin Sammy and I were with Dad and of our Angel Mr. Felts.

At one point, when we knew that it was close to the end, the nurses took Mr. Felts out of the room and Mother had to leave, it was more than she could handle. Shortly before Daddy died, I went to check on Mother, and one of the nurses was sitting with an arm around Mother and one around Mr. Felts. They were both sobbing.

My brother and our mates and my cousin stayed with Dad until the end. I held one hand and Eddy the other. When he took his last breath I laid my hand on the pulse in his neck until I felt the last flicker of life leave him.

At this point we had to turn our care to Mother. The nurse said she would take care of Mr. Felts, and we took Mother to the ER to get her stabilized.

After Daddy's funeral my brother went to see Mr. Felts a couple of times. The day before we came back to Tennessee, Mother, Alex and I went to visit him. That Friday, July 16th. We took him tokens of our appreciation, but all he really wanted to know was that Mother was OK and that family was coping. When we were getting ready to leave he hugged and kissed us all on the cheek and told us he loved us all.

I believe that he is now able to meet my father and talk with him, tell him his family, though grieving over our loss, that we are pulling together and that we will be OK.

So, our Angel and Dad went home two weeks apart. I believe that everything has a purpose and that God has arranged to have Angels among us to help and guide us through our toughest times.

Goodbye Daddy and Goodbye to our Angel Mr. Felts. We have a hope in God that we will see you and be with you again.

With love from your daughter, Daddy. And from your friend, Mr. Felts.

Concerns about her father's death ran deep. She wrote:

My oldest brother is angry, he blames me. Our father is dying, paralyzed from a stroke that left him with no brain activity. Mother, my younger brother and I made the decision not to start life support. My older brother accuses me for, in his words, "letting his father die." He has forgotten that he has not spoken to Daddy in over 3 years. After the funeral he came to me and apologized for his angry words.

It is hard to do what I know is right - forgive him, but as I look into his hurt, sad eyes, my heart opens, then my arms. We hugged as only a brother & sister can, a hug to heal so many hurts.

Mary began the new millennia with deep concerns that life was unfair to her father and mother. Seeing her childhood home in steady decline through her memories of such good feelings there, her sanctuary that was no more, bore heavily on her. Creeping old age was ruining everything, and she did not like any of it.

Adding to her concerns was a sequence of medical issues that began during the previous August and continued through January, 2000 with an over-confident, and therefore, incompetent surgeon. He had performed laser surgery on her left shoulder to relieve pain and to remove bone spurs. Following surgery with physical therapy of several weeks, her pain was worse rather than better, and an MRI revealed a tear and a hole in her left rotator cuff. Her surgeon then performed open surgery, but did not prescribe post-surgery motion therapy resulting in her shoulder not healing properly.

Another cyst had developed in her right forearm that she had noticed to be growing, and during a follow-up office visit, she asked his opinion with intention to consult her surgeon who had successfully removed previous cysts. Dr. Overconfident told that she was already in his system and that he could excise the cyst right then. Accepting his offer proved to be a mistake with serious consequences; he cut an artery requiring hospitalization and emergency surgery that then resulted in a cut nerve. Four months later the same surgeon performed rotator cuff surgery on the shoulder that had not healed properly. That shoulder healed improperly resulting in another surgery later to correct the problem and end shoulder pain. To repair the damaged nerve required further surgery by a competent surgeon that left her right forearm with lengthy scars. Five surgeries by Dr. Overconfident were failures, each repaired by a competent surgeon while Mary was in near constant pain and often cried, lamenting about continually going under the surgical knife.

Advised to get an attorney, we were told by a recommended attorney that Mary had an excellent case. We met a time or two, a letter of suit was sent to the surgeon, and we learned that Dr. Overconfident had been sued five times prior to Mary. Then, our attorney and partner received new Mercedes sedans, and Mary was told that she did not have a case. She was broken-hearted and sobbed; injured with lasting scars and pain with no recourse. We learned later that the surgeon lost his license, and Mary never received the apology that she wanted from him. From time to time during following years, I found her sitting quietly, tearfully rubbing her arm. Years passed before it stopped hurting.

As the new millennium approached, 2000, there was considerable concern in the media that any number of social upheavals would come with the New Year. Mary and I talked about the Mayan calendar showing the end of the world. Computers all around the world would crash because with 1900s programming, they would not read 2000 dates. And... None of them happened. Mary, however, harbored some concern, and she set to composing a newsletter to record the highlights of our lives, just in case.

Happy Holidays 1999
Best Wishes for a Healthy and Prosperous 2000 and beyond!
A newsletter is a new adventure for us. We thought since we were looking back over 25 to 50+ years that it would be best to do a chronological update. We have had many wonderful years and also some sad and painful ones, I suppose to keep us humble.
1964 - Alex lost his father to a heart attack.
1965 - Was a good year for us. We were married October 5th.

1966 - 1970 - Alex was in Uncle Sam's Navy. I traveled with him until he went aboard the USS Forrestal to spend a year in Uncle Sam's yacht club.

1969 - We had the first of our two sons, Squire, "William Alexander" after his father. [The name, Squire, is from Squire Combs, g-g-grandfather, a Kentucky Union soldier in the Civil War who was blinded in the Battle of Chickamauga. His story is compiled in the book, *Devil Bullet.*]

1970 - Alex returned to college, N.C. State University to study physics.

1972 - We were blessed with a second son, Wesley Alan. [The name, Wesley, is from Wesley Alexander Martin, g-g-grandfather, a North Carolina Confederate Civil War orphan whose father was killed in the Wilderness, Northern Virginia. His story is told in the book, *Alec & Flora: The Story of a family.*]

1979 - Alex finished Graduate School at NCSU.

1980 - We moved to the Oak Ridge, TN area. Alex went to work for the Oak Ridge National Laboratory as a nuclear physicist. He is still at ORNL.

1985 - 1988 - I returned to college and completed a degree in Business.

1991 - Squire finished his degree from the University of Tennessee.

1994 - Wesley finished his degree from the University of Tennessee.

1995 - Squire received his medical degree. from U. T. Memphis. Dr. Squire Gabbard sounds great.

1998 - Wesley received his medical degree from U. T. Memphis Medical School, another doctor, Dr. Wesley Gabbard. Wow!

1999 - Squire is Chief Resident and on staff at U. T. Hospital in Knoxville, TN. He plans to leave Knoxville next May to complete a Fellowship in Critical Care in St. Louis at St. John's Mercy Hospital. He will be Internal Medicine boarded with Critical Care.

1999 - After receiving his medical degree, Wesley spent a year at St. Jude's Children's Hospital in Memphis. In June of this year he

268

moved to New Orleans where he works between Charity and Tulane Hospitals. Like his brother he is doing Internal Medicine but with Emergency Room medicine instead of Critical care. [although a fellowship in Critical Care was later completed. Both boys eventually wound up specializing in nephrology.]

1999 - In July of this year I lost my dear father after a long hard fought battle with failing health.

1999 - Over the past 10-12 years, Alex has written and had published ten books and hundreds of magazine articles.

1999 - In June of this year, Alex had the pleasure of publishing his mother's book, "Life Behind the Potted Plant" by Miz M, Doris Gabbard Michael.

1999 - My mother continues to be healthy, though lonely much of the time.

...

I hope to be able to keep good thoughts in my heart now and through the years to come.
Happy! 2000

The new millennia also began with Mary saving my life. That spring while she was at home recovering from another surgery, I came home one Friday after leaving the Lab where I had seen a Physician's Assistant on staff. I did not feel well and had a low grade fever. The PA told me that I most likely had a virus, and he could prescribe meds or not prescribe meds, and it would go away in a few days.

I opted for no meds and went home. My legs were so heavy that I had difficulty walking, and I intended to go to bed. That would have been a fatal mistake. As I described how I felt, Mary immediately diagnosed my symptoms as a bladder infection and that we were going to the ER right then. I had never had such symptoms remotely similar to how I felt, but Mary had. Her recognizing the seriousness of my seemingly unserious condition that was expected to pass in a few days was a pivotal moment in my life. I had never before faced death.

By the time I was receiving ER attention, my temperature had shot up to 105 degrees, and the ER doctor was agitated. Mary called Squire, who was Chief Resident at the UT Hospital in Knoxville, and he immediately came to assist. Mary's diagnosis and my hospitalization permitted his treatment for a raging e-coli infection that would have overtaken me that weekend had I gone to bed.

Several days of in-hospital treatment allowed me to go home for several more days of recovery, then return to work, but it was weeks before soreness in my lower abdomen subsided to normal. Expressing my gratitude to both Mary and Squire time and again always seemed inadequate while I gained a deeper appreciation of just how fragile and easily life can be lost.

During this time as I slept nearby, recovering, Mary composed the following, found in the back pages of one of her notebooks while compiling this story:

What I love About Alex
1. His clear blue eyes.
2. The morning kisses.
3. His moral & physical support.
4. I love his kindness to everyone.
5. I love the fact that he thinks work should be shared, not this is woman's work and this is man's work.
6. I love his response to the inquiry, "How are you?" "Just getting better all the time."
7. I love the fact that he has been by my side through good times as well as bad.
8. I love that he does not see my surgery scars as ugly, but something that had to be done to sustain life.
9. I love the way he smells after a shower.
10. I love that I can lay my head on his shoulder and feel safe.
11. I love the way he hugs me and holds me just right.

12. I love it that he will run an errand without question.

13. He always puts his dirty clothes in the hamper and even helps with the laundry.

14. He is a good cook and does not mind helping out if the need arises.

15. I love the way he makes love to me with gentile caring and concern for my feelings.

16. I really love that he still finds me attractive after 35 years of marriage.

17. I love that he is honest and straight forward.

18. I love that he includes me in as much of his life as possible.

19. I love his intelligence and swift humor.

20. But most of all, I love that he loves me!

In the same notebook, she wrote:

Writing is a release for stress and pent up feelings. I find writing a way to relax and reflect on events of the day or week. Keeping a journal has helped me to accept many health problems and to deal with death. I wrote a short story, I Believe in Angels, the week my father died. It was a way to accept his death.

Mary and I talked a lot, and our daily routine continued in greater togetherness following my gradual decline away from producing magazine and newspaper features. The frequency of our travels also declined, most often to visit family, our mothers in particular, along with class reunions and functions involving our boys. We were fortunate that both of us continued to be able to "go home" late in our lives, back to the farms that were central in our up-bringing.

Instead of business travel, we began leisure travel for our pleasure; two paddlewheel riverboat excursions along the lower Mississippi, two Caribbean cruises with plans for two more. Our mothers did a riverboat cruise on the Delta Queen to New Orleans and flew back home, the first time either had done anything that.

Where we lived? On a sparsely populated and rather isolated rural road of infrequent traffic that had been our walk path since our move to Tennessee; Mary, me, and our boys during their years at home. For several of those years, Mary joined neighbor ladies for walks along the flat portion of the TVA access road to the hydro dam at the base of the mountain we lived on. Beautiful sunrises and equally beautiful sunsets were our norm, as were white tail deer that were plentiful and often in our yard. Their range included grass in our extensive yard while they regularly went to and from a pond across from our forest that adjoined extensive TVA property along the lake.

One of her sad stories involved a little fawn, still showing its spots when first seen upon going out our front door one day. This fawn and other deer were often in our front yard, and Mary began talking to the young deer. As she stopped to talk, the older deer moved further away, but the fawn continued to look at Mary whose soft voice and unthreatening manner captured its attention. Similar such meetings in our yard lasted for years of Mary talking to this deer that grew into an adult buck. He was often in our front yard, a wild deer, not a pet, but not afraid of her, either. One winter day, a neighbor told that a friend, an avid hunter... you guessed it. He bragged about killing the biggest white tail buck he had ever seen.

Deer throughout the huge Oak Ridge reservation caused many vehicle collisions resulting in opening parts of the range seasonally to hunters to thin the population. Mary had such an encounter; on her way into the town of Oak Ridge one morning, a buck leaped in front of the car causing extensive damage, also killing the deer. The most harrowing aspect of this encounter was that, at her speed, the buck's antlers crashed through the windshield; stopped by hanging on the steering wheel prevented her being impaled. She was not injured, although shaken. Passers-by stopped to help.

After seven more surgical procedures between January, 2000 through August, 2002, Mary's health settled giving her four years

272

without another surgery, although sicknesses of various sorts were common. In addition, being a free bleeder required constant care to avoid cuts. A tooth extraction during childhood and another during 1977 requiring special attention to stop the bleeding were frightening memories and ever-present in her cautions.

Those years were complicated, however, with disturbing situations that troubled her for cause. During November, 2002, she wrote:

My temp goes from 97.2° - 101° for no apparent reason. This has been going on for some number of months. If I lay down for very long I wake up with a terrible headache. This has been happening for several weeks. I have had only 2 nights of sleep in over 16 days. The other nights I am up about every hour on the hour. I sleep only a few minutes at a time and then I can't lay still. I have to go to the bathroom, walk around, go back to bed & sleep for a few more minutes. One night I lost 4 pounds going to the bathroom.

11-22-02 About 6:30 I had a twitching in my right temple & right eye, then a hot feeling & a drawing feeling. When I looked across the room I could not focus on anything. I stood up to go to the bathroom and everything was skewed. I held on to the walls in the hall to make it to the bathroom. When I looked in the mirror my face looked like a mask. I looked twisted. I could not focus on my own face. I put a hand on either side of my face and squeezed; I finally got to where I could see.

The right side of my head still feels sore & fuzzy. I am still having trouble focusing my right eye. I still am trembling & and my voice trembles.

Later she added:

My right eyelid has been drooping for a couple of weeks. For over a week now my sense of smell has been elevated by 5 - 10 times. Everything is overwhelming, even deodorant smells bad, bath soap,

273

dish wash detergent. My sense of taste is about non-existent. I can taste sweet, sour, salty & bitter. Most everything else just tastes bland.

Because of Mary's lifelong trend of noting "signs", these episodes were worrisome; stroke? If not, what? Heart attack? Since she recovered without being impaired, her worries were driven by, what's next?

Her old nemesis, fainting, was kept at bay by careful attention to not exerting herself, but on a shopping excursion one day, upon getting out of our car, she collapsed in the parking lot. Immediately drawing on-lookers, I attended to her as she quickly regained consciousness. Enquiries, "Should I call an ambulance?" were dismissed. Mary was angry with herself for such an attention getting spectacle, and once on her feet, determination took hold, and we went shopping.

This episode was another recurrence that she had lived with since high school. She knew well this aspect of her being, but why she had such sudden and unanticipated fainting spells remained a source of consternation that led to cardiac attention. Squire's years at the UT Hospital had enabled him to learn which doctor he thought the best to attend to his mother, and Dr. Cox became her cardiologist from then on, but every attempt to isolate her peculiar problem remained elusive, even with regular EKG scans and wearing long term monitors to record heart function data.

Although I went home for lunch each workday while at the lab and returned each afternoon to spend our evenings together, I was concerned and uncomfortable about Mary being alone for hours each day. So, when an opportunity to retire from the lab presented itself, I opted out with plans for us to travel more that also brought prospects of doing more travel features and photos for publication. With her submissions to magazine editors having been declined so far, we discussed a plan to publish a book, a story that she would write, and she settled on a fiction novel drawn from her father's time in uniform. After compiling an outline, she began with:

The year is 1945, late fall, cold as hell and looking like snow any minute. The sky is that peculiar color of grey, like the barrel of a gun. I shiver and look around at what seems to be a totally dreary world. I could not help thinking of home where things would be bright and colorful for the holiday season; but here I am stuck in Germany for God only knows how long, after all the war was just over and we are still in full uniform.

I shiver again, as a blast of cold air hits me full in the face. Turning up the collar of my heavy coat I spot her for the first time. She is beautiful, it is love at first sight, her coloring is superb, lines classic. To be honest I was captivated. I had to know more about her, but before I could say a word she was gone. The train just pulled out of the station... carrying all her beauty with it. I had to know more, I had to find her, I knew that I would never be happy again until I knew where they were taking her.

That was as far as she got when, one day during 2006, she fainted in the shower and fell onto the edge of the tub, then landing flat on her butt rupturing discs in her lower back. This episode began a long and painful period that included three back surgeries through 2012, all failing to alleviate her pain and included becoming dependent on pain killers. The change from clear minded to foggy was a total setback for Mary.

Her surgeon, another incompetent in my mind, did two major errors that required lying flat. That introduced acid reflux that ruined her vocal capacity from being described as "like warm honey flowing over soft velvet" to gruff while also beginning a litany of esophagus issues. During her second back surgery during 2010, the same surgeon cut her spinal sack again. Two years later while removing the hardware previously installed, he did the same thing again. With similar requirements of lying flat for days, her acid reflux was amplified to the extent that she could never lay flat again, always having to sleep on a wedge pillow beneath her regular pillow. And, her voice never recovered. He prescribed more and more painkillers.

Having to live with heart and esophagus issues dominated Mary's life thereafter while she also was frequently sick, often telling me that she did not feel good. Added to her 20 surgeries through 1999, 29 more invasive medical procedures during the next twenty years weighed heavily upon her. She recorded each episode to tally 54 surgeries from minor to major from her first during 1969. Among them she tallied fourteen procedures for stents to keep normal blood flow into and out of her heart. Angioplasties requiring children's size stents revealed that her vessels had not grown to adult size sufficient to support normal physical activity; that was determined to be the source of her fainting. Having learned early in her life that she had to avoid anything strenuous meant that she lived with a very small margin of endurance; walking was about the most strenuous activity she could do. During our more than fifty-five years together, I never saw her ride a bicycle or run or break a sweat in physical routines, even during her many karate workouts. Mary lived carefully, but whatever limitations that her physiology imposed, she insisted on being active, to live, to go places, and do things. I was more than accommodating, but I recognized early on that I had to constrain my large measures of endurance with consideration for Mary.

She was, however, very uncomfortable with living in the fog of opiates. Determination rose to do something about it. She wrote:

I tried to get the doctor to help me get off. He said no, I would not be able to stand the pain. So, on my own I started shaving a little off. The doctor got mad and sent me to a pain center. When I went in for consultation the doctor asked me how much I was taking. I told him I was off the morphine and taking about 2-1/2 mg of Percocet. He said I was off, to throw that away. He asked if I had brought the tablets I had not taken. I said I had. We poured them out on his desk; there was something over 400 tablets. He yelled to everyone that he had a patient that had gotten off the pain tablets without any help.

We then went to a special commode, and he asked me to pour them in and flush it. I did. He asked how that made me feel. I told him;

276

relieved, that I had been scared with that much meds in the house, that someone could find out and try to break in and get them. I have not had a pain tablet in over 4 years; I haven't wanted one. I think one reason I could get off was that I figured out they were more a physical addiction than really helping the pain.

Getting off opiates was not easy. Her determination rose the day that her scream brought me running to her in our bedroom. She stood frozen, pointing, exclaiming in fright about the giant spiders that had invaded the bedroom. Pointing to them, I placed my hand where she pointed to illustrate that they were not there. Deeply frightened by her imagination that was fueled by opiates, she began her quest to free herself of their effects. Her shaving the pills worked and became a very satisfying return to clarity for her that was amplified by her continued beauty.

Although we were no longer traveling, publishing continued that was centered on compiling stories about my forebear grandfathers who were Civil War connected, one Union and blinded in battle, the other Confederate and killed in battle. Having the time to search for records along with collecting every tidbit of information into a coherent form was a great learning experience for me. Pursuit of Mary's genealogy with the intent to compile her family history into a book proved much less productive; records were few and ran out just a few generations back.

Dated 9-12-07, Mary wrote her last entry in her journal. She wrote:

I pick up my much neglected diary. I felt my life was not of interest but maybe some time to some of my family. Both of our sons are Medical Doctors. My mother & Alex's mother are still alive, Mom 85, Alex's Mom is 89.

We have decided to move back to N.C. so our lives are upside down again. The best thing of all; I love Alex more now than 42 years ago.

The proposed move occurred during an enormous economic downturn, the Great Recession, that ended any prospect of relocating. I spent months reconditioning our home in preparation to sell, and once on the market, it did not receive a single inquiry. That was a blessing. Although I proposed to build an energy efficient retirement home on property that my Mom gave me, part of the family farm, and to teach at a nearby college, we stayed put with our home like new.

During our planning to relocate and my designing our home to be, Mary professed that she really did not want to move; to "go home" for her was not what it had once been because home was no longer there, and relocation being such a huge change, she was concerned that she could not handle the rigors it presented. That was another blessing. We were, after all, comfortable and established in our area. During this time, Mary had entered her "I can't" years. Her physiological limitations had become dominant enough that she gradually became incapable of keeping a routine, as reduced as it had become. Melancholy moments were more frequent.

Our boys steadily progressed in their professions that took them to various parts of the USA in pursuit of additional training, and Mary and I seized upon opportunities to visit them in the hither and yon of their professions. And, during late 2008, Wesley was the first to marry. His chosen, a beauty from the Spanish islands in the Mediterranean, became a part of our family that would, in time, include two grandchildren, Claire and Liam. Four years later, Squire's chosen, a beauty with deep Cajun roots in southern Louisiana, became his bride, but children were not in their future.

As years progressed past 2010, Mary's health became marginally stabilized into a slow and concerning decline that resulted in her frequently saying that she did not feel good. One issue after another slowly ate away at the edges of her confidence resulting in being increasingly receptive to ads presenting Dr. Feelgood and his miracle Fountain of Youth pill, one after another. Driven by her desire to regain her health and a brighter well-being, a sense of desperation grew into seeing homeopathics, chiropractors, and buying health how-

278

to books, reading and trying all sorts of cure-alls, adding dietary supplements, even hypnosis therapy... anything that promised feeling good again. None of it improved anything, largely because she could not benefit from exercise. Low impact exercise equipment purchased for her ended up rarely used, and when she did try to work out, she was quickly exhausted.

One day, Mary came to me and said, "You could be nicer to me." Taken by surprise, my immediate thought was that I had failed as a husband, that Mary needed something I was not providing.

"Wow! Where did that come from?" I asked. "I thought I was a good husband. What can I do to help?"

Looking back, I can see now that her slow descent into feeling poorly more often than feeling good was gradually dominating her outlook to the extent that our relationship, so unchallenged from the beginning, had come into doubt.

"I think we ought to see a marriage counselor," she said one day.

Surprised, I asked, "A marriage counselor, really? What for?"

"You are spending so much money on cars, you're going to ruin us. There's never enough money in the check book to pay our bills."

I had learned over the years that if money was available after paying bills, Mary would spend it on more fashions, boots, shoes, purses, hats, especially jewelry, and with closets already stuffed, overflow was packed in boxes and stored for which we were paying rent, both for storage of my stuff and her stuff.

So, I had adopted the plan of transferring what was needed to pay bills from my account into hers that included paying off her extensive credit card purchases each month. Finances were not an actual issue, but they were a serious concern of hers, that we were going to run out of money. So, her conclusion was that we needed counseling.

My response, "What good is a fat bank account if it's not doing for us what we want? We don't travel anymore, and restoring

279

cars is something for me to do, and it's likely that some or all of the cost can be recovered when a car is sold."

I had infrequently sold a car that provided for the monthly transfers for bill paying, and reminding Mary that we had always paid our bills, never a bounced check, and my compliments for her handling of our finances for those achievements was not entirely satisfying. "What if we need that money?" she often asked.

"I'll sell another car. Meanwhile I want us to go places in them. Do things. Car shows. Drives. Go places like we used to. We've got snazzy cars, why not enjoy them? We don't need a marriage counselor to do that."

Unconvinced by my answers, money concerns continually bothered Mary, but health concerns were now dominating her life.

"I'm so sick... I just can't do that anymore...."

I had often heard this phrase from her and knew that it was real. I had learned to read her eyes, the changes in her eyes that migraines produced for example, and even though she always attempted to tough out such episodes, as time advanced she was less able to cope and was often miserable requiring extended quiet times.

We had often talked heart-to-heart, but my every repeat that I did not know how to help her feel better remained unfulfilling. And, each offering of, "What can I do to help?" was unsuccessful in changing anything. What she wanted more than anything was to feel good again, and she was convinced that she never would. Those quiet times revealed what she wanted from me, to be there with her, and I was often off working on another car, even her own Alpine that I hoped would help her regain her confidence.

While Mary spent most of her time pursuing improving her health, we were comfortable with no mortgage and economically sound such that restoring our cars, now quite old, was within our financial grasp. Our Tigers proved to be in much worse condition than I thought, both requiring major de-rusting, but the result became a matched pair of beautiful, quite rare roadsters, Mary's 1965 and my 1967. Both were rebuilt with inclusion of many options from the

1960s that I had acquired through the years, all of them difficult to find forty years later. I teamed with National Champion street rod builder, Ralph Wright, who masterminded their restorations, but, unfortunately, Mary never drove her Tiger again. It ended up on display in a muscle car museum.

We then took on the challenge of restoring her Alpine. It proved to have survived the decades in much better condition than our Tigers, and Ralph and I had it back to showroom condition and on the road during early 2017. As a valentine story during February that year, our local newspaper did a feature on Mary and her Alpine, a saga of more than fifty years ownership of a snazzy British roadster that held stories galore; being the car that she chose off the showroom floor, then came home from the hospital in with our first child. The car's storied past was our past, Route 66 to Albuquerque included. After half a century, they were together again with memories, memories, memories. Also unfortunately, having driven the car many thousands of miles, Mary never drove her Alpine again.

Her slowly declining health bore increasingly heavy upon her wellbeing that increased her concerns about being a burden, her father's final years the primary source. What she wanted most was return to her cheerful outlook, to feel good again. Through the years, she had become acclimated to feeling less than desirable interspersed in her continuum of good days, but into 2010, the number of days feeling badly surpassed the number that she felt well, even when pushing to go out, to go shopping, to visit friends, or to dine out. And, most troubling was the decline of friends who had once visited or invited her out to lunch. She knew the reason; concerns for her health had grown to dominate her conversation; how sick she was. She was no longer fun to be with. We often talked about the effect that complaining had on other people, driving them away, and although Mary tried different approaches at times, it was too late; almost everyone she knew avoided her because she had little else to talk about.

We did, however, maintain a light schedule of promoting my book, *Return to Thunder Road*, in signings, appearances, and car tours that, in some cases, required significant planning and participation. One such event was the 50th anniversary of the debut of Robert Mitchum's 1958 film, *Thunder Road*, that was first shown in Knoxville's Tennessee Theater during the spring of 1958.

To retrace the route told in his minor juke box hit, *The Ballad of Thunder Road*, our tour began in Harlan, Kentucky to an overnight, then through to another overnight in Cumberland Gap where the entire town turned out in celebration. Photo stops along the way, particularly in Maynardville that is also cited in the Ballad, then on to Knoxville and a gigantic celebration where our 55 car procession was a parade along Gay Street, its curbsides lined with throngs of spectators who had gathered around the theater. Also down Gay Street went our slow speed "chase" of a moonshine car and a federal pursuit car, both '50s recreations. "Captured" at the theater was Jim Mitchum driving the moonshine car. He had starred in his father's film, sixteen at the time and his first film, and he contributed to making the kickoff of Knoxville's Summer Film Festival a huge success.

That event was the second of two 50th anniversary tours, the first being the year before in the Asheville, North Carolina area to each of the film's locations that were still recognizable.

Mary loved these outings, and as our travel exploits for publication in magazines declined, as a result of a couple of missed deadlines due to her being ill at the time we needed to be on the road, our frequency of getting out also declined. Being the cause of missed opportunities was deeply disturbing to her, what she saw as "proof" that she was a burden, but she felt trapped in a no win situation; she wanted to participate but failing health was continually in her way.

Recalling the years of her father's decline, she wrote:

As of 4-3-13

I, Mary Alice Gabbard, do not want to be kept alive on life support due to: accident, heart attack, stroke if there is no chance for a recovery.
Signature as of 4-3-13
Mary Alice Gabbard
Birth date: 8-9-1944

Our lives had become, mostly, just us. Advance of time brought old age, and Mary recognized its presence far earlier than I did. When I reached 70, I described my age as twenty with fifty years experience because that was how I felt; during those fifty years my outlook had not changed, although I wondered who that old guy in the mirror was.

For Mary by then, age 70, old age was ruining her looks, her shape, her ability to go, deepened her melancholy, and most of all, it dragged down her wellbeing that tended to hover along depression road. Many photos show that Mary remained a beauty well beyond her 60th birthday, but the years thereafter showed a steady decline that she recognized, both in how she felt and how she looked, but having learned a harsh lesson about complaining, she resorted to meds when she was in pain that drove not feeling well, and she spent more time in bed.

By then, our mothers had died, and we were the old folks. Neither of us were willing to accept what time had done to us. With all of our forbears gone, especially her father who was so significant in her life, we had difficulty aging gracefully. Although I remained active with our cars that always included her if she wanted to go along, I was often away from her, and that meant she spent more time alone, usually watching TV. The times of her easy going, the world is my oyster manner around cars and car people that brought her lots of attention were over.

Even though I thought my outlook toward her as always supportive, encouraging, and never with a harsh word, my manner must not have been reassuring, as illustrated one afternoon when she approached me with concern on her face. Looking me straight eye-to-eye that was our normal since our first meeting, she said, "You don't love me any more."

I was speechless, overwhelmed with the thought that I had failed my duties as a husband... again. I knew that to love and to be loved was THE most important element of her existence, and clearly, I had failed to show what she needed.

"Wow," I replied. "Where did that come from?"

"I can see. You don't love me any more. I'm sick, and you don't care."

"Mary," I reassured her. "I do care. I do love you. You are my one and only, always have been, nobody else but you, but I don't know what more I can do. I want to be your knight in shining armor coming to your rescue. I support you in everything. I'm your taxi driver to wherever you want to go, and I don't mind. Really. I don't mind at all. I just don't know how to fix being sick."

Hugs and kisses, also our normal, was all I could offer, but I was stumped; I really did not know what more I could do, but something I said or did defused the moment. However, this episode was repeated several times during coming years, and I remained concerned about my inadequate responses. Somehow, I just was not hearing what Mary was telling me.

What both of us wanted more than anything for her was her return to good health, to be active again, to feel good again, and when our talks gravitated in that direction, I learned that such statements simply reinforced her conviction that I was unhappy with her. I was never able to change that conviction other than describing failing health as among the worst aspects of old age. Mary had clear memories, too, and our talks tended to be walks down memory lane, our past adventures, but even those recollections did not change her outlook. She really, really did not like getting old. Everything that had been her was ruined; all she had to do was look in a mirror.

On a Sunday afternoon, April the 3rd, 2016, we were home during another springtime, our 51st together. I was unaware that Mary's depression had reached bottom. Sitting in our office while I tended to flowers outside, the same that regularly produced fresh cut flowers for her, she wrote the following to me:

My Darling Alex,

Please forgive me for what I am about to do. The doctors do not care how I feel and will not do anything to help me.

And now I realize that you are tired of me being sick all the time. I don't blame you. I am sick and I am tired of living like this. I do not know where to turn. I do not want to live like this, a burden to you and in your way. I Love you too much to turn your love into hate.

Please forgive me for being weak and never there for you. I think you will come to realize that I am right in due time. You will not have a weight around your neck always holding you back.

Tell the boys I love them and this was no one's fault but mine. I am weak and after over two years of pain and sickness, I can't take it any longer. You have been the love of my life. I have never been with anyone but you.
All my love - Mary.

Later that afternoon, I happened upon her note signed to me, folded and dated, lying on our office desk. Not sensing anything unusual, I read it and immediately took it to our bedroom where Mary was going through her meds. I was aware from previous conversations that she had, on those previous occasions, counted out sufficient meds to....

"Mary," I asked. "Please don't do this."

She stood in front of me resolute and said, "You don't love me any more."

What to do, even with previous experiences to draw upon, suddenly took on desperation because Mary had demonstrated over and over her fierce determination to achieve a goal.

Our long conversations on previous such occasions ranged from memories of our adventures, memories of her near perfect body that had, over the years become scarred and now so easily bruised that she remained despondent. These "signs" of what was ahead for her were ominous. Her back was continually in pain such that she had bottles and bottles of various remedies, and my frequent rubdowns only temporarily provided relief. Simply put, she had not felt good for so long that there seemed no hope that she would ever feel good again. Most worrisome was that her cardiologist had advised bypass surgery, the very thing that she believed had ruined her father's mind. Even with introducing her to people I knew whose bypass surgeries were successes, all of them saying they wished they had done it sooner, nothing was convincing. Mary really, really did not like getting old, and the thought of another scar, this one a lengthy cut down her chest, was terrifying.

Before each of her previous surgeries, Mary had kissed me goodbye. She forecast our kiss prior to bypass surgery as the kiss of death. Even though she had recovered from every previous surgery, there was no doubt in her mind that her father's fate was her fate. There was nothing more that we could talk about.

"I know this sounds selfish of me, but I don't want you to do this. I know it's unfair to you, but you are me, right from the start... how you took me into your life without hesitation the first time we met. I don't know how to express my feelings for you more than that."

Mary stood quietly looking at me, and after a pause, she said, "Things are different now."

We had crossed that bridge many times, and I knew that her concerns about being sick in addition to getting old had previously taken her to the edge of existence.

"You promised me that you would not end your life. I know it's tough for you, but I expect you to keep your promise."

Mary sat down on the edge of the bed. "You don't know what it's like... being sick... nauseous... hot acid burps that burn my throat... I can't sleep because of it... I can't get over it, either... My voice is shot... Diarrhea... Or constipation... It never ends... Surgery; it scares me to death... I know you are tired of looking at my bruises... tired of...."

I interrupted, "No, I'm not tired of you. I'm not, really... This is just getting old, me and you, getting old together. We are the old folks now." I knew immediately that our getting old was vastly different; I was okay but she was not, and whatever I said changed nothing.

She looked at me and asked, "What do you want with me? You're a famous author, and I'm just in your way."

I tried to be convincing, saying, "None of that matters; it's all just stuff we've done. We are supposed to get old together, and here we are. I don't like getting old, either, but here we are. I remember our times together, too; that was us, we did all that, you and me, and don't forget what you said to me when you wanted to get married, that we would do it together. Well, we did, we have, and it's still - we. Here we are, getting old together, and you are still my sweetie; always have been, always will be."

With a deep sigh, Mary said to no one in particular, "I'm so tired of not feeling good. I just don't feel good."

"What can I do to help?"

Mary thought for a moment. "Pity."

I did not understand. "Pity?" I asked. "What does that do?"

"Make me feel better."

"Pity would make you feel better? I don't know what pity does."

With another heavy sigh, she continued, "It would show that you care. I'm sick, and you don't care... You don't love me any more."

I was confused. "Pity shows that I care? I think talking to you here and now shows that I care, that I love you, my concern for you here and now. I don't want you to end your life... I know, it's selfish of me. I know, but you are important, not just to me but to our boys, and you have grandchildren to think about now."

Mary paused in thought, then mused through her memories; "I saw Daddy suffer for so long, and it just about killed Mother.... Ruined everything. I don't want you to have to go through that."

"Well, sweetie, here we are going through our old age, and what are we to make of it? This is the story of our lives, and I think it's been a really good one. I don't mind taking care of you, never have, not one bit. But, you have to promise me, you won't do this. Okay? Promise?"

Weighted in thought, she added more to no one in particular, "It runs in the family."

"What runs in the family?" I asked.

She named members of her family who had killed themselves.

"No, Mary," I argued. "That's not true. Nothing like that runs in any family. Suicide is an individual act that each person chooses to do for whatever reason. That's not a family trait."

I knew that Mary's determination was a driving force in her life, and I grappled with what to say. "I know that if you are determined to kill yourself, you'll find a way. So, you've got to promise me. Okay?"

As I had done countless times, I placed my hand on her cheek with caresses and fondled her ear lobe, my love touch. And, as always, she placed her hand on mine, pressed lightly, and kissed the heal of my hand. "Your hand is so warm," she said wistfully.

Once again resorting to my tried and true, I repeated, "There'll never be anyone else for me but you."

She sighed again.

"Promise me, Okay?"

Reluctantly she agreed, and when I pulled her to her feet with a tight hug, kisses, too, tears streamed down her face. "I love you with all my heart," she told me again.

I knew that to be true, having never had any occasion to doubt her love, and I hoped that she was reassured that my love for her was also undiminished. "I want to keep it that way, me and you, kiddo. Okay?"

The moment seemed to be resolved as we sat on our couch to watch a movie, *Oh Brother, Where Art Thou*, one of her favorites.

From time to time thereafter, Mary flirted with suicidal thoughts, but she did not get that close again. Holidays, birthdays, and other special occasions were incentives for us to visit with one of our boys, and our drives, with an occasional flight, to wherever they were took us to more memories, but Mary's slow downward spiral had become taking a pill to ease her pain, and they often made her unstable on her feet. More faints, too. And, occasional mishaps further reduced her confidence in her ability to cope. Fortunately, none were serious, but a fall here and there and more bruises had become her norm, and all of them were deeply disappointing, further depressing her confidence.

It was abundantly clear to me that Mary was unhappy, the most unhappy person I had ever known, and I remained unable to significantly brighten her outlook. Our car club activities were our only social outlets, when she felt like going along, and with several nice vintage cars, we were never at a loss for a good looking roadster to drive. Her Alpine was our last addition, and talking about it to wandering spectators while attending a car event was a genuine boost to her outlook, being the original owner with lots of stories about our travels in it. But she was mostly disappointed with lack of interest shown by spectators who, in almost every case, had never heard of a Sunbeam Alpine and were generally uninterested in old British roadsters, however nice or storied. Being very much a people person with an outgoing personality, Mary was thoroughly enthused to be among people, but marginal interest in her car was another disappointment.

Our days were quiet; she had no one to talk to but me, no confidant after heart failure took her last friend... and... there was no one but me day after day... and... there was very little that we had not talked about. So, she spent most of her time watching old television re-runs. Looking back, I recognize that time to have been ideal in

289

compiling this story when she was alive and could contribute and participate is this compilation.

Mary had started a cookbook as a Home Ec project in high school, and with her talents in the kitchen, she had added many recipes over the years along with stories to go with them, but the project languished. I encouraged her to finish it, to write her stories, but she had come to believe that no one was interested.

Even though I began each of our mornings with hugs and kisses in attempts to brighten her day, most often she looked at me with pleading eyes and said, "I just don't feel good." On days that she did feel up to the task, we did gentle things, such as making jams and jellies from berries grown in our yard or bought locally. She no longer walked as a regular routine, and her exercise equipment... I was its only user.

I had resolved that bypass surgery was Mary's next step back to a better lifestyle, but she was terrified at the thought of another surgery and simply could not bring herself to accept that option. Our boys, with increasing concern for their mother, admonished her to do things, to be more active, and helped her through a number of health issues, but they were no longer her little boys that had been the center of her very being when young.

Mary was deeply disturbed with what the passage of time had done, and our conversations did not help. During our talks, we had covered most everything in our lives from their time as little boys onwards, so there was little to talk about but reminisces, and they tended to sadden her. Melancholy had become Mary's constant companion, but gloom did not completely absorb her. As time went by, she seemed always able to gather some strength, some determination, especially when thinking of others, particularly her boys and their birthdays. She made jewelry items for gifts sent to family and friends, and we talked often about her getting into an internet jewelry business. For our boy's birthday, she wrote her thoughts and we compiled their essence into letters that I mounted to plaques for gifts, as follows:

Thoughts for your birthday, June 12th, 2019
Dear Squire,

You, our dear son, are a beautiful love story. The most beautiful people come from true love. You are truly loved from 1969 until always. I had a perfect pregnancy, not sick a minute, then 50 years ago today, the most handsome little boy was born into our lives. It was a long, hard journey, but contrary to what the doctor's said, we made it; after hard 52 hours.... Once out of coma some days later, I saw my beautiful baby for the first time and was told that I was unlikely to have a second pregnancy due to extensive internal damage.

Throughout the years we have watched you grow into a handsome, smart, and loving young man. We are so blessed to be called Mom & Pop. I know your father is proud to share his name with you.

So, Happy Birthday our wonderful son. We love you to the moon & back forever and always.
Happy Birthday William Alexander Gabbard, Esquire
From: Mom & Pop
Mary Alice Cheek Gabbard
William Alexander Gabbard, Sr.

Thoughts for your Birthday, April 24, 2020
Dear Wesley,

You and your brother are truly miracle babies. We had been married over four years, and doctors thought that we would never have children. Then, my first pregnancy was perfect, I was not sick a minute. Then... Long term care brought both of us to health.

Later, during 1972, while we lived in Cary, North Carolina, a medical exam revealed that I was four months pregnant. I had not missed my cycle and had no idea that another infant was within me. Beginning close medical care from then until another C-section at about eight months, you were born with no complications a little early, healthy, and beautiful. Both of my babies began their lives as

291

cotton-tops without a blemish and steadily grew from my breasts. I thank God for the gifts of two healthy sons who have been and will always be the miracles of our lives.

So, Happy Birthday our wonderful son. We love you dearly, with all our hearts.
Mom and Dad.
Mary Alice Cheek and William Alexander Gabbard

By April, 2020 we were deep into the most worrisome times of our lives with the most severe shift in outlooks that we had ever experienced; the Covid-19 pandemic. It was sweeping across America and the world in truly Biblical proportions with rapidly climbing numbers of deaths reported each day, and our boys were in the middle of it. With every phone call Mary caught her breath in fear; was this the message that one or both of our boys were its victims? Mary's worry meter stayed pegged, and she often came to me in tears, needing a hug. Without a word said, I knew what worried her.

During the previous Christmas, we had a lengthy holiday with Wesley and his family in their Florida home, a time of little activity by Mary who did not feel well enough to do much of anything. After arriving home early in January, she worsened into what appeared to be the beginnings of pneumonia. There were days during mid-month when she had a low grade fever and some difficulty breathing, needing the aid of breathalyzers from time to time.

Doctor visits and advice from our boys brought her through that month-long bout while she used it as a launch for reducing her weight. Along the way, I was also afflicted for a week or so with what I suspected to be a cold, then fully recovered with no lingering after effects.

By mid-February, she was feeling much better and was encouraged with her weight loss. By embarking on a reduced diet and frequent but short exercise routines on our equipment, during those weeks, she lost sufficient weight to get into some of her fashions that had languished in her closets. Her determination was showing desired results. Proud of herself, she was further encouraged with improved diagnostics of bodily functions reported to her by her primary care physician, a doctor who had attended med school with Squire. To celebrate both her achievement and Valentine's Day, we went out to lunch, exchanging cards, smiles, and kisses.

Good days during February were just the beginning of an encouraging spring; as time went by into March, then April, Mary continued feeling better. Our springtime brought another flourish of flowers in our yard, among them our azaleas, each one a gift to Mary during one of her surgeries. Her TV time, however, continued to be discouraging with pandemic reports. Also troubling was the shift of politics away from what both of us believed to be the proper path for America. Both topics dominated unrelenting daily news broadcasts.

I encouraged her not to watch the news saying that if it did not benefit her, that if she could do nothing about what she saw and heard, why watch the news? It was just aggravating. So, she began artistic works bought at a hobby store.

Our boys kept us informed of medical issues, advising to avoid contact with the virus, to remain reclusive, and to reassure us that they were being careful to avoid becoming infected. Further, admonishments that Mary's physical condition attacked by the virus would likely be devastating caused her more worry, but such advice was necessary for her to be cognizant of the risks of exposure, advice that drove her worry index even higher. There were no laugh wrinkles to be found among the state of affairs as she saw them.

May was a typically beautiful month, but being reclusive meant that Mary went nowhere other than medical appointments. I shopped for groceries. With a host of colorful blooms and bright sunlight attracting her out, she ventured onto our decks and to our flower beds that had been repeat photo locations during years past.

May 30 was a spectacular day. As usual, I was up early. And, as usual, Mary slept in, her normal rising time being 9:30 or after. I was so enthused by the gorgeous day that I decided to get one of our roadsters out for a spin, and wrote of it:

293

Saturday, May 30, 2020

The morning was perfect; cool, crisp, dry with blue overhead, another Albuquerque morning that I so enjoyed a half century ago(+), just right for a Tiger ride. I had not driven the car since the Chattanooga MotorFest - last October! Has it really been 7 months? Checked all the checkables; there was nothing left to do but turn the key. It's alive! 40 PSI oil pressure; suitably warmed; that rumpity-rump from its Crane Fireball cam spoke to me. Let's go! We did. Along the way, I reminisced about a day in early May, 1966 when Mary and I stood in our local Sunbeam dealership's showroom looking at a red Alpine and a white Tiger, the more I learned about Tigers, the more I wanted my very own hot rod Tiger. Acquired during the mid-1970s, the first of three Tigers, my old hot rod nearly went to the crusher because of extensive rust. That removed and the body back to solid steel was a long and costly undertaking that led to completing the restoration about ten years ago. Has it really been that long? Snatching gears; revving up; gearing down. What a blast! My very own hot rod Tiger!
Alex Gabbard

Once the Tiger was parked back in the garage, about the time I thought Mary would be rising, I went to her and said; "Good morning sweetie," and gave her our morning kiss. "It's a gorgeous day, really nice, like Albuquerque. If you'll get up and get dressed, I'll go get your Alpine and we'll go for a ride. Okay?"

She looked at me from her pillow; "I just don't feel like it," she said while extending her hand to take mine.

"That's okay. How about breakfast... what would you like?"

"Not now. I'm not hungry."

I kissed her hand as I had done countless times and helped her get to and from our bathroom. Back in bed, I said, "Well, I'll check on you about lunch time. Okay?"

She nodded confirmation, and I returned to the garage to another project. When lunch time arrived, I went back to Mary who was still not up. That was not particularly unusual because she had spent much of her time in recent years in bed. But I wondered. "Are you okay?" I asked.

She nodded.

"What would you like for lunch?"

"I'm still not hungry. I'll get up later and make a peanut butter sandwich," she said

I placed my hand on her cheek with more caresses and fondled her ear lobe, my love touch, and as usual, she pressed my hand with hers, then kissed the heal of my hand. We had done that exchange for decades. For me, just touching Mary was its own reward. "If I can do anything for you, let me know, okay?"

She looked at me, those beautiful eyes that had captured me so long ago, and with her little smile she said, "I love you."

"I love you, too, sweetie."

That exchange was also our normal.

Except for the spectacular weather conditions, this was another day in the repetition of aging that had become our lives together. Nothing about the day was unusual, so I continued with various projects interspersed with checking on Mary. About 4 o'clock, she was sleeping on her back, and I did not wake her. Another hour or so later I went to ask her request for dinner, already preparing orange chicken, her favorite. She was lying on her right side, right arm curled, her head on her small pillow on a larger pillow, and that one on her wedge pillow, in a position I had often seen. Asking what she would like for dinner, she did not respond. I tapped her covered arm, usually getting an instant response. Not this time. I shook her gently; still no response. I noticed that she was not breathing, and when I laid my hand on her exposed arm, she was cold. I knew then that death had taken my beautiful Mary.

My phone call to 9-1-1 brought authorities into our house within minutes. I could tell by their questions that they were determining if any foul play was involved. The medical examiner made his assessment and handed me her wedding rings. I was beyond crushed, stunned with disbelief, trying to suppress sobs. I was asked to step outside, and while I stood on our sidewalk, three men emerged from our front door with a bundle in a white sheet that they placed on a gurney, then wheeled it across our yard to a waiting hearse. I watched... this cannot be real... that cannot be my beautiful Mary... this is not happening.... Wake up! Wake up! Thoughts swirled through my head in an avalanche.

Then, they were gone.

Minutes passed before I could move.

The world around me was the strangest quiet. I had never felt so strange, an odd emptiness. More minutes passed as I stood there. I called Squire, "Really bad news. Your Mom..." and Wesley.

The sun dipping further westward shown brilliantly, the afternoon as magnificent as the morning had been. I went back into the house, and sat on our couch where Mary and I were sitting the evening before, holding hands, watching another old movie. We would never do that again.

Never... all those old rock 'n' roll songs about always, forever, never... those words from young love that we had known had an altogether different meaning now. My perspective of reality radically changed, a new period of adjustment was imposed that I did not want. The love of my life was no longer there.

What she began on a pretty Sunday afternoon during March, 1963, when I was three months into my 17th year, was no longer there. She had always been there with her flirty little smile, her cute, "Hi", her beautiful... her... I was thinking about... looking for... With every sound the house made I looked up expecting it to be Mary. The thought that she would never come to me again was beyond sobering. Never... I was... I don't know how to put in words what I was.

I walked here and there, then sat in the quiet and looked into the kitchen at the pan on the stove where I had started to make orange chicken for Mary. More than a half-century earlier, that pan was among the cookware purchased for her Hope Chest, a sixteenth birthday addition for that mysterious someone yet to come into her life. I was that mysterious someone, and we had prepared countless meals with each of the pieces. The entire set had lasted a lifetime, and I would never... never... never again prepare a meal for her. Never.... That word had taken on an entirely different meaning.

I had wanted to compile this book as a gift for Mary, our lives together, and I had no inkling that she was so near death. I believed that her steady improvement throughout the spring months of 2020 indicated more years to come, adding to our 55, including the possibility that by-pass surgery would give her a new lease on life. Discussions with Squire and Wesley resolved her likely cause of death to be her heart condition, her old nemesis, her last faint. In her final position, there was no sign of struggle, no sign of pain. She simply went to sleep and did not wake up... at home, at peace.

Wesley responded to my Tiger ride story that day:

What a great ride....
Wishing mother had done it one last time..... sigh.....
Love you Pop

Long time friend and author, Judy D. wrote of Mary's passing;

Alex, I am so sad to hear about your beloved Mary. She was a breath of fresh air and always so positive and friendly. I enjoyed visiting with her so much. May God bless you with good memories.

When looking through albums of photos of Mary, many my own capturing of the moment, my memories of her are this story, our story. Along the way, we had struggles and disagreements but never a fight; never a yelling match; never a quarrel; never going to bed mad, I believe, because we had a shared sense of what was important, being together. We lived the very thing that she wanted in her proposal to me; "Whatever happens, we'll do it together." We kissed each night and we often laid arm in arm and talked, her head on my chest, her touch indescribable. We hugged and kissed each morning, and when

297

looking back, I wish I had done more, much more. I wish... I wish... I ache to talk with my beautiful Mary, to hold her, to kiss her. I wish... I wish....

We came together a teenage girl and boy of the early 1960s, healthy, vibrant with instant affection for each other that matured with her butterfly moments years later, and that union, our union entwined together never changed. After living with Mary for more than a half-century and months compiling this story, I remain struck by the irony of ironies for a love story; her very last words spoken to me were, "I love you."